Acclaim for Jed Dian

"In a time of social angst, confusion, and ...   ]
is a refreshing and much needed voice or   a
is a timely and necessary resource for men and the women who love them."
                    —**Sarah Hunter Murray,** PhD, author, *Not Always in the Mood:*
                                    The New Science of Men, Sex, & Relationships.

"This is a wonderful book. Jed celebrates the evolutionary roots of maleness and offers guidance for men and their families. Just when there is ever growing conflict between left and
right, men and women, Jed's book brings us together and offers gems of practical inspiration
for restoring personal and relational wellbeing in challenging times."
                    —**Michael Dowd,** author, *Thank God for Evolution*, and host,
                                            The Future Is Calling Us to Greatness.

"There has never been a time more crucial than now for good men to shine. Jed offers solid
analysis and practical advice for men to become their best and for women to understand
what makes a good man."
                    —**Mo Gawdat,** former Chief Business Officer for Google [X] and
                                author of *Solve for Happy: Engineer Your Path to Joy.*

"Jed's book is unique in offering an in-depth understanding of why men are the way they
are and do the things they do. Based on his fifty years of experience working with men and
their families, he gives all of us the tools for living fully, loving deeply, and making a positive
difference in our lives. This is a wonderful book for both men and women and I highly recommend it to everyone who wants to know what it means to be a truly 'good man' in today's
world."
                    —**Kenneth R. Pelletier,** PhD, MD, Clinical Professor of Medicine,
                            UCSF School of Medicine, author, *Change Your Genes, Change Your Life.*

"Jed Diamond has discovered and expressed clearly, ways for each of us to reclaim our full
selves—in ways that can be easily practiced."
                    — **John Jeavons,** author, *How to Grow More Vegetables, Fruits, Nuts, Berries, Grains, and*
                            Other Crops, Than You Ever Thought Possible on Less Land with Less Water
                                    Than You Can Imagine, Director, Ecology Action.

"Men's work brought us together nearly 40 years ago and I know Jed as a deeply human and
brilliant man. I hold Jed as the teacher men can truly trust. This toolbox of a book has a big
gift for everyone."
                    —**Bill Kauth,** co-founder of The ManKind Project, Author of *A Circle of Men:*
                                    The Original Manual for Men's Support Groups.

"Jed Diamond has been a pioneer at the leading edge of men's evolution for five decades. His latest work on the *12 Rules for Good Men* reveals his depth of understanding, compassion, and skill in guiding both men and women into healthier, respectful, and compassionate relationships. In the midst of the highly politicized and often vitriolic dialogue in modern gender dynamics, Jed offers a wise and healthy approach to understanding, celebrating, and honoring differences."

— **Daniel Ellenberg**, PhD., APA President Elect of the Society for the Psychological Study of Men & Masculinities

"*12 Rules for Good Men* gets right to the core of how men have been trapped in the legacy of beliefs and behaviors that no longer serve them or the world today. Jed Diamond gives us a concise and profound guide for healing from the crippling effects of the Man Box. He embraces the gift of maleness so both men and women can discover the next step in our evolution of living more authentic, dynamic, and joyful lives."

— **Joseph Culp**, actor/writer/director of *Welcome to the Men's Group*, a film about the inner life of men.

"Dr. Diamond artfully articulates the path for men to find the essence of their maleness. Through the warm storytelling of his own journey, he brings the 12 Rules to life and demonstrates to us that he is a trustworthy guide for this journey."

— **Jackie Black**, Ph.D., author, *Love Like a Black Belt: Cracking the Code to Being a Happy Couple.*

"I consider *12 Rules for Good Men* to be the crown jewel on Jed's 50+ years as a counselor, educator, and author in the field of men's health. I highly recommend this book to anyone, male and female, younger and older, as a treatise on the most important principles of what it takes to be a good man in the world today."–

— **Stephen Johnson**, Ph.D., author of *The Sacred Path: The Way of the Spiritual Warrior, a Journey to Mindful Manhood.*

"Jed Diamond has dedicated his life to those willing to do the hard work of listening and reflection. What continues to impress me most about Diamond's work is the harmony he offers between the philosophical and practical, the inspiration of spiritual words and the commitment to necessary action."

— **Ken Goldstein**, Chairman, Good Men Media, Inc., bestselling author of *From Nothing* and *This Is Rage.*

"We look to be at sea as individuals, as citizens, as workers—in every possible way. Nowhere is this truer than when it comes to 'How to be a man.' In this time of confusion, displacement, and change, men need genuine guidance. Jed Diamond brilliantly offers that guidance in his new book, *12 Rules for Good Men.* Men know that they need 'something' but they hardly know what. This is what they need! Highly recommended."

— **Eric Maisel**, author, *Overcoming Your Difficult Family.*

"Jed's book is not an ego-boosting, thumping of the chest that too many mistakenly believe is needed to 'restore' the virility of men from bygone eras. This is a missive that helps men find the heart and soul of the person they were meant to be. He accomplishes this not by hardening the false narrative that has left men emotionally and physically diminished but by giving them the ability to explore what it truly means to be a man. It is an honest exploration of the qualities and vulnerabilities men should embrace and share."
        —**Michael Reitano**, MD, expert in sexual health, Physician in Residence for Roman.

"As the MeToo# Movement inspires all humans to honor and commit to the safety and well-being of women, men have a wonderful opportunity to develop their ability to be sensitive, kind and protective. Many women seek a deeper understanding of how to empower the noble manhood in their sons, brothers, and partners. Jed Diamond's book is packed with knowledge and insights, offering a clear path for a male at any age to do the conscious work to become a confident, wise, and loving man."
        —**Carista Luminare**, Ph.D., Founder of ConfusedaboutLove.com.

"I first met Jed more than ten years ago when he had the distinction of being the only male columnist writing for the National Association for Baby Boomer Women. With this latest book, Jed continues to examine the concept of maleness, beginning by tracking back millions of years to discuss theories of the evolution of male and female."
        —**Anne Holmes**, Boomer-in-Chief, National Association of Baby Boomer Women.

"Beyond the typical self-help book, Jed Diamond nails the subject of men's emotional struggles using a compelling mix of science, candor and compassion, then goes the extra mile and outlines timely and effective coping strategies. It tops my recommended reading list for my patients and friends, both men *and* women."
        —**Laura F. Dabney**, MD, psychiatrist and author, *Strong Men: Emotional Courage, Mental Weakness and the Power to Know the Difference.*

"We men like rules because they give us structure, something we can rely on. If we know the rules of a game, we can master it. Jed has mastered the game of life, and the game of love. Take advantage of his expert coaching by reading the book and following his advice."
        —**Lion Goodman**, PCC, author of *Creating on Purpose* and *Menlightenment.*

"12 Rules for Good Men are the result of Jed's lifetime of leadership in men's work, represents the power and wisdom of an elder of the men's movement. In a world of dramatic change, where men are seeking more compassionate meaning and purpose in our lives, Diamond provides a roadmap for healing and connection. *12 Rules for Good Men* is a powerful invitation for men to end our isolation and heal our deep wounds, and in doing so, help heal the wounds of the world."
        —**Mark Greene**, author, *The Little #MeToo Book for Men.*

"Helping men for the last forty years, I am so happy to recommend this important resource. Listen up men, Jed has very important things to say to you in his new book. Your life can be changed for the better."

—**Barry Vissell,** MD, co-author of *To Really Love a Woman* and *To Really Love a Man.*

"This timely and relevant book offers guidance for both men and women who want better relationships and a better world. Jed writes with intelligence and heart. A must read for women and men who are ready to experience better relationships and contribute to a more compassionate world. Brilliant and timely!"

—**Joy Taylor,** author of *Inspired: 7 Wisdoms of a Soul Inspired Life,*
Women's Leadership Trainer.

"Jed Diamond has hit the bullseye once again with this book. I was both moved and en-lightened by Jed's clear insights and wisdom regarding how men can show up in the world as open-hearted, authentic, healthy, mission-driven men. Jed's unabashed love of men and men's work shines through from the very first page. Read this book- it is profoundly life changing!"

—**Rick Broniec,** MEd., bestselling author of *The Seven Generations Story:*
An Incentive to Heal Yourself, Your Family and the Planet.

"As a psychotherapist for over 40 years, I consider Jed Diamond a friend and colleague who, for the past 50 years, has taught and written about men's issues. In his new book, *12 Rules for Good Men,* he shares a wealth of wisdom that covers a range of crucial areas such as accepting maleness and our warrior spirit, healing wounds, and creating a mission for life. While this book offers priceless insights and tools for men to live and love deeply, it also helps women understand men. The rules are simple; the wisdom profound."

—**Leonard Szymczak,** LCSW, bestselling author of
The Roadmap Home: Your GPS to Inner Peace.

"12 Rules for Good Men is for any man who seeks to challenge his potential to become happy, successful and connected. Jed Diamond is a true gift for men who want to better understand themselves and for women who want to understand men. Do yourself a favor, buy the book now and read it!"

—**John Schinnerer,** Ph.D., High Performance Coach and host of
The Evolved Caveman Podcast.

"In the face of radical feminism, gender neutrality, and cultural diminishment of the tradi-tional male archetype, Jed Diamond makes a compelling assertion: 'Men can't be fully alive to themselves, to the women they love, to their families and friends, unless they understand and embrace their maleness.' This book is a gift for all men who care about their impact on the world and want to become the most effective human beings for their spouses, families, communities, countries, and the planet as a whole."

—**Brent Green,** author, *Generation Reinvention* and *Questions of the Spirit*

"With many touchstones to salient quotes and useful references, and, especially, a chapter about the science of adverse childhood experiences — the foundation of understanding why we behave the way we do — Jed Diamond has done it again. The prolific writer and psychotherapist who specializes in helping men live full, authentic and loving lives, provides great guidance on how to do just that in *12 Rules for Good Men*."

—**Jane Stevens,** Founder, publisher ACEsConnection.com and ACEsTooHigh.com.

"Jed Diamond has dedicated his life to helping men be better men, helping them love themselves, understand their feelings, and embrace the complexity, strength and beauty of being a man. *12 Rules for Good Men* is the culmination of his wisdom, his extensive research, his years of practice, and his love for men and the women who love them. This is a book one can turn to again and again for inspiration and encouragement. I highly recommend it."

—**Jude Walsh, EdD,** author, *Post-Divorce Bliss: Ending Us and Finding Me.*

"Jed's breakthrough work is inspiring and enduring. I predict this book will reside on nightstands and in the hands of men's leaders and in the backpacks of truth-seekers around the world."

—**Steve Dailey,** Founder and Head Coach, AchievementBridge.

"Perhaps now more than any other time in history, men are asking, 'What does it mean to be a man?' In particular, they're wondering, 'What does it mean to be a *good* man?' Jed Diamond answers those questions in *12 Rules for Good Men* with a depth of understanding that goes far beyond the trivial answers we usually get. Assembled from his years of counseling men and his own personal journey, Jed shares his insights into what it takes to build a full and abundant life."

—**Michael Clark,** Founder, Ananias Foundation, author *From Villain to Hero.*

"*In 12 Rules for Good Men,* Dr. Jed Diamond has masterfully laid out a roadmap pointing men, and the women who love them, toward a path to more fulfilling relationships, a deeper understanding of how to recognize and transcend trauma and ultimately to embrace the 'Gift of Maleness.'"

—**Zander Keig,** LCSW, co-editor, Manning Up: Transsexual Men on Finding Brotherhood, Family, and Themselves.

Also by Jed Diamond

Inside Out: Becoming My Own Man

Looking for Love in All the Wrong Places: Overcoming Romantic and Sexual Addictions

The Warrior's Journey Home: Healing Men, Healing the Planet

Male Menopause

Surviving Male Menopause: A Guide for Men and Women

The Whole Man Program: Reinvigorating Your Body, Mind, and Spirit After 40

The Irritable Male Syndrome: Understanding the 4 Key Causes of Depression and Aggression

Mr. Mean: Saving Your Relationship from the Irritable Male Syndrome

Male vs. Female Depression: Why Men Act Out and Women Act In

MenAlive: Stop Killer Stress with Simple Energy Healing Tools

Composting Abbie: A Whale of a Book

Stress Relief for Men: How to Use the Revolutionary Tools of Energy Healing to Live Well

The Enlightened Marriage: The 5 Transformative Stages of Relationships and Why the Best is Still to Come

My Distant Dad: Healing the Family Father Wound

Healing the Family Father Wound: Your Playbook for Personal and Relationship Success

For Carlin, who challenged me to write a book about
the gift of maleness and forever inspires me with her wisdom,
brilliance, and charm. I could not ask for a better life partner.

12 Rules for Good Men

JED DIAMOND, PhD

Eric, Hope you enjoy this,

Best wishes

Jed

Waterside Productions Dec. 26. 2019

Printed in the United States of America

First Printing, 2020

ISBN-13: 978-1-941768-84-6 print edition
ISBN-13: 978-1-941768-90-7 POD edition
ISBN-13: 978-1-943625-24-6 ebook edition
ISBN-13: 978-1-943625-05-5 audio edition

Waterside Productions
2055 Oxford Ave
Cardiff, CA 92007
www.waterside.com

Every serious thinker must ask and answer three fundamental questions:

1. What is wrong with us? With men? Women? Society?
   What is the nature of our alienation? Our dis-ease?

2. What would we be like if we were whole? Healed?
   Actualized? If our potentiality was fulfilled?

3. How do we move from our condition of brokenness to wholeness?
   What are the means of healing?

—**Paul Tillich,** philosopher

Free Interactive Site With Resources for You

As I write this book, I realize that there is so much more I want to share with you. I can only put so much inside these covers, but I have additional information I'd like to share—ebooks, articles, and new resources that I found too late to include in the book.

If you'd like to learn more, I invite you to go to:

http://menalive.com/register-12-rules/

And register your copy. This will give you immediate access to much more material and will allow you to connect with me personally.

Contents

Foreword

By Iyanla Vanzant

Host of *Iyanla: Fix My Life* on the Oprah Winfrey Network, OWN,
and six-time *New York Times* best-selling author.

I first met Jed when he asked me to be on the faculty of a course he was offering to men and women to help improve their love lives. He had read my book, *The Spirit of a Man*, and asked me about my experiences at the Million Man March in Washington, DC, and what I had learned about men and women in my work since then.

I have often wondered what men talk about when they get together. I suspect they talk about sports. I'm sure they talk about work. I believe they talk about women—what they want from us, do to us, think about us. But, what do they talk about when there are a million of them who don't know each other?

I first began to learn about the deeper truths of men's lives at that historic march in 1995. I remember it like it was yesterday. My place was one of the safe houses men could come to when they arrived for the march. I don't think I'd ever been in the presence of that much testosterone. It was wonderful to see so many men coming from everywhere, all ages and sizes, races, and backgrounds. They came on busses and by foot. I had bikes in my yard and cars and vans in the driveway. People slept on the floor and we had breakfast together in the morning.

Looking out over the crowd, I saw my father there on that mall, although he had been dead for eleven years. I saw my former husband out there. He, too, has been on the other side for quite some time. My brother was there. My son was there. In fact, all the men in my life I have ever told, "Do something! Just do something!" were out there, whether or not they were physically present. I saw them making an effort, taking a step to do something for themselves. It made me proud. It made me humble. It scared me half to death!

For me, it was the birthing of what I call the *male heart opening*. That was when men first understood they could come together, they could share their pain and challenges, their issues, knowing there was a soft place for them to fall.

Men have fallen out of their hearts into their heads. Women have fallen over their hearts into their heads. We have both fallen out of the grace of spirit. We have been conditioned to honor a system of values built on contempt and disrespect for who we are as a community of people. This conditioning has taken us away from certain basic principles that are living memories in our DNA. These principles, that I believe are etched into our subconscious memory, are the keys to our basic nature. As a result of our fall, we are in conflict with both the value system of the society in which we live and our own basic nature.

Now when I think of some of the horrific, horrible thoughts that I've had about men, about my father, my exes, my children's father, I just have to drop to my knees and forgive myself. Not forgive *them,* but forgive myself.

For now, what I understand is that I would wish to be anything in the world other than a man. I'd be a rock in the park or a grape in the bunch. I think men have such a difficult time because of the expectations placed upon them, as well as the lack of training and guidance that they receive in order to live up to and execute the things expected of them.

But when I was raising my son, I really became aware of the lack of *manhood training* that is available. Today, in the 21st century, we really see it: with the number of men who are incarcerated, the number of men who are walking away from their children and families, the number of men who are experiencing hypertension, the number of men who are contracting prostate cancer.

I believe all of this is the result of the lack of manhood training. When men get the opportunity, through rites of passage, they can grow from being a boy into a man, and learn the things that are truly male. There's an African proverb, "If you don't initiate the young, they will burn down the village to feel the heat."

The brutality I have witnessed against men who do not know how to be men, who do not have the skill, who haven't learned, is stunning. The verbal brutality, the emotional brutality, and the psychological brutality is heartbreaking.

And I raise my hand and acknowledge I was one of the offenders—until I had my son, until I saw my grandson, until I buried my father, and my brother, I couldn't see it. My father who took his own life and my brother who died of a drug overdose on the eve of his 50th birthday, woke me up. I had to rework my entire consciousness about men in order to be able to give my son and grandsons what they needed.

But more importantly, I had to learn to be able to be the kind of woman that could share space with a man, because I was not that kind of a woman. Most women won't tell you that. I will tell you that when I saw all those men on the mall it scared me. Because, oh my God, if they wake up, if they really get it together, this is going to be a problem. I realized I had become the man. Yes, *I have become the man.* And when a male was in my presence, in my company, he had very little space to be a man. Because my expectations of him were so low. That's brutal to force a man to fit into the space where there is no room for him. I realized I was out of order.

I was out of order in my thinking, out of order in my expression, out of order in my behavior, out of order in my demands and requirements, out of order in my expectations, but I didn't know that for so many years. So, I had to forgive myself and learn.

The way I learned, you're going to laugh at me, was by studying nature. I learned how to be a woman on the History Channel. Here was the turning point for me. I was watching a program where they did a piece about birds. And they said that in 90% of the bird species, the male bird builds the nest. He gathers all the twigs and the sticks, he finds the place, and he builds what he hopes will attract a female. He does his mating dance until he attracts a little female chickadee and he brings her to the nest.

Before she accepts his offer, she tests the nest. This is going to be the place where she is going to lay her eggs and take care of her babies. Now if she didn't approve of the nest, she flew away, left him on the branch—and he got no nookie. If she did like the nest, she would snuggle up. And . . . the rest is history. So, I said to myself, I have never requested, required, or anticipated that a male would build my nest.

So, I built the nest myself. I made the rules. I did everything. Then, I invited him in to live under the auspices of my control. Because you always get what you expect. If you expect the man to disappoint you, he will. If you expect him to do very little, he will. If you expect him to fail or falter or build a poor nest, he will. Not because of him, but because of you. You always get what you expect.

Many women think they have a positive view of maleness, but they often have an underlying fear that he'll fail. It was then I began to raise my expectations of men in my life, and to do that I had to be in a different place with myself as a woman. And I went back to nature. What is this feminine energy and feminine power and what do I have to do? I really studied that, so I could be better within myself, to be a better partner, a better mother, a better grandmother, a better teacher, a better minister.

What is wonderful about Jed's book is that he recognizes the importance of finding the essence of our maleness and femaleness in the natural world. He offers a unique understanding of why men are the way they are and do the things they do. His twelve rules offer real guidance to men. They also help women understand the truth about men. He helps us all to heal old wounds and recognize that men and women are natural allies and must come together if we are going to create a world that is sustainable for our children, grandchildren, and future generations.

Introduction

"Man up."
"Be tough."
"Be the breadwinner."
"Open up."
"Be gentle."
"Be a better father."

Everyone seems to have an opinion on how men are supposed to be. There was a time when men were put forth as the standard for being human. Professor Henry Higgins, in *My Fair Lady,* lamented, "Why can't a woman be more like a man?" Today, things are changing.

After I finished writing my fifteenth book, *My Distant Dad,* I told my wife, Carlin, "I've been helping men and their families for fifty years now and I'd like to do more mentoring, teaching, and relaxing." Her reply surprised me. Although Carlin has always been supportive of my work and interested in my books, she's never gotten directly involved in what I wrote, until now.

"I think you've got at least one more book you need to write," she told me. "You've devoted your life to helping men and their families, but these are difficult times. Men and women need real guidance to better understand that males are a great gift to the world. They want to know what it means to be a good man in today's crazy world and who men really are underneath the armoring they are forced to wear in order to meet the demands of society." I took some time to reflect on her words and decided she was right. I wanted to write a book that would help men and women recognize that they are natural allies, but that men need guidance and support to recognize and appreciate their essential maleness.

When I pick up a book, I want to know how it will help me. But I also want to know about the person writing it. Who are they? What life events shaped their healing journey? This is more than a professional sharing of what I've learned. I'll also share my personal struggles and how I overcame them and the things I'm still working through in my life.

This is a confusing time to be man. Manhood today is maligned and misunderstood. Some believe maleness itself is inherently destructive and should be eliminated.

Others view males as superfluous. This idea is reflected in the witticism, "A woman needs a man like a fish needs a bicycle." Some view men as being unsuited for today's world. In her book, *The End of Men and The Rise of Women,* Hanna Rosin says, "The feminist revolution is here. Women are on the rise and men are on the decline." Finally, some believe that traditional masculinity itself should be eliminated and we'd be better off just seeing ourselves as human beings.

I have a different view. Evolutionary science tells us that the division of life into male and female began one billion years ago. This ancient lineage continues today. Men are not better than women, but there are important differences between males and females. Men can't be fully alive to themselves, to the women they love, to their families and friends, unless they understand and embrace their maleness.

Today, good men are needed more than ever. As my colleague Charles Eisenstein recognizes, it is time for men to come together to help bring about "the more beautiful world our hearts know is possible." We are living at a time when too many people break the rules of society. In fact, rules themselves are seen as suspect by many. We say we want to be free, but without rules we live in constant chaos that leads to continual conflict of one group against another.

I think rules can not only be helpful, but that also they are essential if we are to become the men we are meant to be. Some are afraid that we've lived too long with rules that favored men over women. I agree. These new rules that I'm proposing are ones that I feel will benefit men, women, children, society, and the planet we all share.

I'm not saying these are the only rules or the rules you *must* follow. These are the rules I have found most helpful in guiding my own life and the thousands of men and women I have worked with over the last fifty years. Although my professional experience has been working with individual men as well as men and women who are in heterosexual relationships, whatever your sexual orientation or background, if you are a male or someone who cares about men, this book will help you.

Many men are under extreme stress in their lives and too many have become anxious, angry, and depressed. Work/life balance has become increasingly difficult to achieve, with many men feeling overworked while others are unemployed or working at jobs that are unsatisfying. Family life is often strained, and many of us don't feel as loved or loving as we want to be. We have become disconnected from ourselves, from those we love, and from the earth we all share.

This book brings together what I know about restoring our lost connections. In my work as a therapist specializing in gender-specific health practices, I teach men to answer with an empathetic YES to three questions we must all address before we die:

1. Did I live a fully authentic life?
2. Did I love deeply and well?
3. Did I make a positive difference in the world?

As you move through the book, I'll be your guide all the way. Some of the rules may be new to you. Others may be familiar, and you may already be putting them into practice. Each one builds on the others and together they will help you know yourself as never before. You don't have to act upon rules in the order I give them here. You may go from rule 1 to 6 to 3 to 9 and so on. Trust your intuition, go where your heart leads you. At the end of each chapter, I include "bottom line" information that acts as a summary to help focus your actions. At the end of the book, there is a listing of resources for further exploration.

If you have questions or concerns, come visit me at www.MenAlive.com. I post articles every week, answer questions, and connect with those who are committed to living fully, loving deeply, and making a difference. We can't do it alone, but we can change the world if we work together.

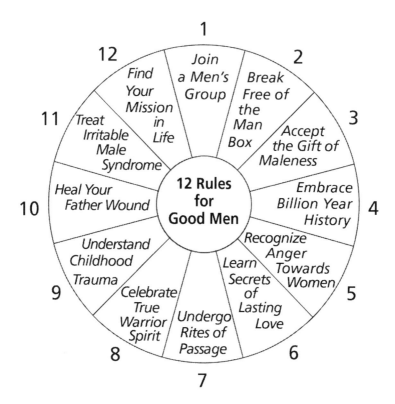

1 Join a Men's Group
2 Break Free of the Man Box
3 Accept the Gift of Maleness
4 Embrace Billion Year History
5 Recognize Anger Towards Women
6 Learn Secrets of Lasting Love
7 Undergo Rites of Passage
8 Celebrate True Warrior Spirit
9 Understand Childhood Trauma
10 Heal Your Father Wound
11 Treat Irritable Male Syndrome
12 Find Your Mission in Life

12 Rules for Good Men

Mentoring Men to Live Fully,
Love Deeply, and
Make a Positive Difference

Rule #1

Join a Men's Group

"The world needs a man's heart."

~Joseph Jastrab

Looking back on our heritage as men and our lives as hunter-gatherers over the last two million years, one of the things that stands out to me is that men spent considerable time in small groups with other men. This occurred naturally as men went away from the camp hunting for game to feed their families and the tribe.

One of the most significant aspects of my own life occurred in 1979 when I joined a men's group that has now been meeting regularly for nearly forty years. I'd like to share a little background on the events that led up to my joining this men's group, what I've learned, and why I believe that joining a men's group is one of the most important rules we need to follow in order for you to become your own man and be wildly successful at the game of life.

Like all beginnings there is no single moment I can name when I began my quest to find a men's group. But I know that the birth of my son, Jemal, on November 21, 1969 was a seminal (pardon the pun) moment.

When my first wife and I met and fell in love in college, we would sit on a little grassy knoll overlooking the ocean in Santa Barbara. We were students at the University of California and we enjoyed being together and thinking about our possible futures after we graduated and gotten married. We knew we wanted to have children and decided we would have one child, then adopt a second one.

We knew we wanted two children, but felt that with so many people in the world it didn't feel right to add to the world population which was already moving beyond what the environment could support. "Let's have a child and depending on if the child is a boy or a girl, we'll adopt a child of the other sex." It was a young person's dream, but after we graduated and got married, we began the first step of the journey.

After trying to get pregnant for two years, we finally got the good news that a baby had been conceived. One of my sperm had been chosen by my wife's egg and a new life was beginning. We wanted as natural a childbirth as possible and took classes based on the Lamaze method and practiced the breathing and relaxation techniques we hoped would be helpful.

When the time came to go to the hospital, we were ready. A bag was packed, contractions were getting closer together, and we were ready to go. We drove from our home in Pinole, which looked over the San Francisco Bay, and drove to Kaiser hospital in Vallejo. We checked in and began a long process of labor. When the time came for my wife to go into the delivery room, the nurse smiled and turned to me. "Okay, Mr. Diamond, you can head for the waiting room and someone will let you know as soon as your baby has arrived."

I knew the rules. I was disappointed, but also relieved. I had always been sensitive to pain—mine, and others. I passed out once when I had my teeth cleaned and another time when I had volunteered to give blood. I wanted to be there for the birth and support my wife, but I also didn't want to have to be carried out on a stretcher.

I kissed my wife and as she was wheeled toward the delivery room, I walked the other direction to the waiting room. But as I got ready to push through the doors, something stopped me. I heard the sound of my unborn child whispering in my ear. "I don't want a waiting-room father. Your place is here with us." I turned around and walked back down the hallway and pushed my way into the delivery room. There was no question of leaving if asked. My child called and I answered.

Shortly thereafter our son, Jemal, was born. Amid tears of joy and relief, he was handed to me. In that moment, I made a vow to him that I would be a different kind of father than my father was able to be for me, and I would do everything I could to bring about a world where fathers were connected to children and their families throughout their lives.

The connection I had with my son at the moment he came into the world was the first step on my path to becoming my own man. I took off time from work so I could be with my wife and son in the weeks following his birth. I did all the things an engaged, loving father did. I played with him, fed him, changed diapers, held him when he cried, and worked hard to make a good living to support him and my wife.

Once Jemal was born, we decided to adopt and in 1972, Angela came into our lives and our family was complete. My wife and I were both influenced by the Women's Movement. I believed from the beginning that liberating women from societal constraints would also allow men to free ourselves from the constraints that limited men. Our daughter, Angela, was African American, and named after the city where she was born, Los Angeles, and also the political activist, Angela Davis.

As the children grew and we moved further into the 1970s, my wife got more involved with the women's movement. There was a big event planned at the Asilomar conference center near Monterey and she was planning to go. The event flyer said that men were invited as well, and I thought it would be a great opportunity to meet interesting men and women. I had attended numerous conferences at Asilomar and it was one of my favorite places—rustic cabins, decent food, beautiful setting on the Monterrey coast, very relaxing.

It was a three-day event. I was overwhelmed to see 800-1000 women in attendance and perhaps 12 men. In addition to wanting to learn about what we all could do to break free from the societal restraints on what women (and men) could become, I thought it would be a great place to meet some kindred spirits. I was a bit jealous of all the camaraderie and support my wife was getting from other women and the "consciousness raising" groups she attended. I thought there might be opportunities to meet other guys and join a men's group.

The first evening we were asked to break into same sex groups of six and I was with five other guys. Our first instruction was to get to know each other, talk about why we were there, and how we felt. I was immediately disappointed to hear the guys talk about "guy stuff:" sports, sex, and jobs. I wanted to know how they felt, if they were as afraid as I was to be with so many women, some of whom were obviously hostile to our presence. We limped along through the introductions and my efforts to expand the conversation went nowhere.

By the last day of the conference, I despaired at meeting the kind of men I longed to connect with. I wanted to be liberated from restrictive sex roles and I wanted my own group. I voiced my feelings to a small group of women who seemed pleased that there were some men in attendance.

"Hey, don't give up," one woman told me. "We're glad you're here. We need men who are supportive and men who want to do their own work." The other women nodded in support. Later that day, I got talking to one of the other guys who was not in my original group. He was going to start a men's group and I was excited to join. But when I found out that he was from New York, my hope for a men's group for me in California, were dashed. "Start your own group," he told me. "Reach out to some guys."

My First Men's Group: Telling the Truth About Our Pain

Driving home after the conference, I vowed to get a men's group started. I talked to one of my close friends, Brad, who also wanted to get a group together. We got his brother involved and a few other guys. Brad, like me, was a social worker. One of the other guys was a plumber, one was a teacher, and Gary had just graduated from college and was looking for work. We met weekly for three years.

We talked about everything, not just sex, but our hopes, dreams, fears, and friendships. We talked about our children and the difficulties we were having at work. We discussed the frustrations and joys of being married. The single guys talked about what they wanted in a partner and the worries about attracting someone good.

One of the highlights was when two of the single guys became interested in the same woman. My experience had always been that when it came to sex and love, men were always in competition with each other. If you wanted the same woman, you fought it out verbally or sometimes with fists. But I was pleasantly surprised when one of the two said, "Listen, we've been friends now for three years. Our friendship is important to me. If you're really interested in dating Shirley, I don't want to get in the way." The other guy seemed as surprised as I was that someone would even consider making friendship more important than "getting the girl."

Another man recalled an experience with his father that moved us to tears. "My dad was a policeman and I loved him deeply. He worked long hours and I didn't see him often. We would play a game when he would come home. I was six or seven years old at the time. I would climb up on a chair and my dad would reach his arms out and I would jump into his arms.

"On the day my world changed," he went on. "I climbed on the chair and reached out with my arms wide and threw myself toward my father. I was laughing and waited to feel the comfort of his warm embrace. But just as I would have been caught, my father turned away and I fell through the empty space and hit the end of the coffee table. I screamed in pain as I hit the floor.

"My father picked me up and in a harsh, adult voice said, 'Son, this is a lesson you need to learn. It's a hard world out there and you have to know that you can't trust anyone, not even your own father.' He put a towel on my chin and took me to the emergency room of the local hospital, where I got six stitches. It felt like my life ended that day. If I couldn't trust my father, I couldn't trust anyone in my life."

As many of us shed tears of sympathy, I wondered what kind of a world must this father have grown up in that he felt he had to teach his son in such a hurtful and dramatic way? I wondered what his father was like and what kind of male values were being taught?

I talked about the fact that my marriage was failing. The stresses of work, trying to raise two children, and make a living all combined to cause us to become more distant from each other, with fights becoming more frequent. Women's liberation had also involved "sexual liberation" and both of us were drawn to sexual exploration and "open marriage." Whether it was the problems we were having at home that led us to become involved with others or whether our extramarital exploration stressed our marriage to the breaking point, we eventually went to see a marriage counselor, but it was too late to save the marriage. We ended up, like so many of our contemporaries, going our separate ways.

My Present Men's Group: A Commitment for Life

I had a rebound relationship that was sexually exciting and emotionally draining. I went with the "sexually exciting part" and we were quickly married. I became the part-time dad and saw my kids on weekends and continued the stressful relationship, now with my "ex." I got a new job and moved from Stockton to Mill Valley. I was depressed most of the time and was looking for the support of a new men's group. One day, I saw a flyer tacked up on a bulletin board.

"Men, come and share a day with other men and hear psychologist Herb Goldberg, author of *The Hazards of Being Male*. We will explore the complexities of men's roles today." It was sponsored by the Men's Growth Collective, a group of guys who had been meeting as a support group for some time.

We gathered for the "Herb Goldberg Day" on April 21, 1979 at 42 Miller Ave. in Mill Valley. There were twelve of us, plus organizers. What stood out to me at that first gathering was a recognition that men had many challenges that needed to be addressed. In the last years of my marriage, it felt like my wife got a great deal of support from women, but it seemed that many in the women's movement either viewed men as the cause of women's problems or felt the system favored men at the expense of women.

Although I believed that many aspects of the system were harmful to women, I also saw that many aspects of the system favored women. When we were dealing with issues of child custody and support, it became evident to me that the system favored my ex-wife in many ways. It was assumed that the mother would be the best parent for minor children. When I attempted to get custody of both my children or share custody, the system thwarted my efforts. Further, though some men benefitted from the system, many suffered severely from the demands of the system.

The speaker, Herb Goldberg, had said in his book, *The Hazards of Being Male,* "The male has paid a heavy price for his masculine 'privilege' and power. He is out of touch with his emotions and his body. He is playing by the rules of the male game plan and with lemming-like purpose he is destroying himself—emotionally, psychologically, and physically."

The day with Goldberg wasn't about gender politics or trying to figure out who was more harmed by the social system. It was about taking responsibility for our own wounds and supporting each other in healing. One of the exercises we did was to have each man reflect on the times we had felt dropped or betrayed by other males in our lives.

I talked about my father's anger and his leaving the family when I was 5 years old, something I had rarely discussed with anyone, and certainly not in front of a group of strangers. As other men talked about their own experiences, I realized I wasn't alone. Many men had experienced a father wound. But there were other hurts and betrayals.

One man talked about being the youngest in his family and having two older brothers who tormented him. Another talked about his hunger to have a child. He was willing to give up a relationship that was good in all other ways, except she didn't want children. I'd never heard a man talk so fervently about wanting to be a dad.

After the day had ended, we all had opened ourselves up to vulnerabilities and wounds we had never shared before. We felt like we had found soul brothers and wanted to continue the experience. Tom, one of the organizers, invited anyone inter-ested to meet the following Thursday at his home on Thalia Street in Mill Valley. Twelve of us showed up and we discussed the idea of meeting weekly for a men's group. After a few weeks, the group was reduced to eight and we began on a journey that continues now almost forty years later.

I remember feeling anxious initially. Even though we had all experienced the engagement and openness at the Herb Goldberg day, now we were in a small group, up close, without a designated leader, although Tom acted as the host to guide the initial meetings. We each "checked in" and told the other guys what was going on with each of us lately.

I was going through a major transition period in my life. My first marriage had ended. I was a part-time dad trying to navigate the conflicted feelings with my first wife and how best to work out child-support and visitation. My second marriage was now more stressful than sexy, yet I was hanging in there. My reason for staying had more to do with my addiction to pain and suffering, along with depression and guilt over the ending of my first marriage and estrangement from my children, than it did because of pleasure and joy.

I had gotten a temporary job at Howard Johnson's restaurant. I hadn't gone look-ing for a job that was more fitting. I couldn't see myself going back and working as a counselor when my own life was so out of balance. I felt I was dying emotionally and the men's group was my place of refuge, a safe harbor from the chaos of my life.

The other guys in the group had varied backgrounds. We were all white, mid-dle-class guys. All of us were in transition with our lives, and all of us to one degree or another were dealing with our own life wounds and our challenges with sex, love, and relationships. The format of the group was simple.

Eight of us met every Wednesday for about two hours. The first part of the eve-ning involved a check-in. After we each had a chance to share our feelings and be heard, anyone who had an issue they wanted to get into in more depth would have a chance to delve more deeply.

The after-group time together in Tom's hot tub became an integral part of the group. We weren't working anymore. We were enacting an ancient ritual of men sit-ting in a circle, telling our stories, looking at the stars, and being together.

Later when we all went to hear Robert Bly tell stories and recite poetry, we heard him talk about the importance of guys being together. "Men must come together," said Bly, "in order to hear the sound that male cells sing." What a wonderful recogni-tion that our very cells vibrate together to create a symphony of beautiful male music. The longer we've been meeting, the richer and more joyful our time together has become. Looking back over our forty years together I realize there were a number of stages the group has gone through, which I'd like to share with you. I will say that as we met together regularly, we never thought about these *stages*. We just enjoyed the experience of being together. Yet, looking back, these stages were evident.

The 7 Stages of Our Men's Group

Stage 1: Learning to Trust and Open Up

Most of us have grown up with an ethic that says, "Real men are successful. They don't have problems. If they do have a problem, they work them out themselves. Other men are potential competitors. Anything you let slip about your life will be used against you." I expressed some of these beliefs in my first book, *Inside Out: Becoming My Own Man*. I called them "The Commandments That Move Me."

1. Thou shalt not be weak.
2. Thou shalt not fail thyself, nor fail as thy father before thee.
3. Thou shalt not keep holy any day that denies thy work.
4. Thou shalt not express strong emotions, neither high nor low.
5. Thou shalt not cry, complain, or ask for help.
6. Thou shalt not be hostile or angry, especially towards loved ones.
7. Thou shalt not be uncertain or ambivalent.
8. Thou shalt not be dependent.
9. Thou shalt not acknowledge thy death or thy limitations.
10. Thou *shalt* do unto other men before they do unto you.

During the first few years of the group, we spent time testing the waters of this new world of guys to see if we could trust each other. We would share relatively safe things about ourselves and see how they were received. We spent a lot of time talking about our *love lives* and about the challenges we were having. We also talked a good deal about our *work lives*. After the group as we sat together in the hot tub, we just basked in the joy of being together.

In the summers my two children, Jemal and Angela, came to visit and I would often bring them to the group. Tom's little house was small and he had a bunk bed in the living room. I'd put the kids to bed, and they'd fall asleep listening to the sounds of guys talking about life, love, and work.

Years later, they both recalled the experience very positively. If, as Robert Bly suggested, children need to grow up hearing "the sound that male cells sing," Jemal and Angela got a lot of that as they listened to our voices and felt the deep vibrations of men being men.

We would also get together to watch football games on TV. It was during the time that the San Francisco 49ers were at the top of their game and we loved rooting for our local champions. At Superbowl time, we had a regular ritual where we'd get all our families together—men, women, and children—and we'd play a game of touch football. We all got wet and muddy and had a wonderful time. After we cleaned up, we'd watch the Superbowl together and cheer for our team.

Stage 2: Revealing Our True Selves, Fears, and Insecurities

It took time to develop trust before we were ready to go deeper in sharing more sensitive aspects of our lives. One of the guys opened up about past criminal activity. He talked about having been arrested for bringing drugs into the country, having spent time in jail, and how it had impacted his later life. Another guy talked about his sexuality, his past marriage, and his present interest in exploring a "gay lifestyle."

Each person's openness led to another person having the courage to reveal a previously hidden part of his life. We were pleased to see that the group was safe enough for us to share. We could trust that what we said would be held in confidence and not shared outside the group. We also learned that we would be accepted, no matter what we had done in our lives. It was a wonderful feeling to know that we were safe. It was something I never felt, even in my own family.

We talked about the families we grew up in and the positive things we had learned, as well as the wounding that occurred. I talked about my father's "nervous breakdown," his taking an overdose of pills, and being committed to the mental hospital. I shared my mother's fear that she would die before I grew up and that the world was dangerous and I might die without warning. There were a number of fears that seemed to be core features of my life:

- My feelings will destroy me if I let them.
- I'll go crazy like my father.
- I'll be a failure at work and lose my family's respect.
- There's something dangerous and violent in me waiting to destroy the people I love the most.
- Women will *love* me, but underneath the surface, they will feel *pity* and *contempt*.

During this period, we learned that the group could deal with serious conflict. One of the guys had been studying to become a marriage and family counselor and needed to demonstrate that he had spent a number of hours learning various skills. He needed to show that he had skills leading a group. Since there was no designated leader in the group, we each contributed leadership skills.

When it was time for him to submit his hours for his license, I agreed to sign off on his application and say that he had spent a certain number of hours as the group leader. One of the other guys in the group, Norman, who like me, was a licensed therapist, said that what I was doing was unethical and threatened to turn me in to my own licensing board if I went ahead and signed off on the hours of our fellow group member.

This conflict became a central focus of the group for nearly six months. There were heated discussions and angry feelings. I remained willing to sign off on the hours. Norman remained steadfast in his determination to turn me in if I did so. Most of the group sided with me, but I worked to find a solution so that we could resolve things within the group so that Norman wasn't seen as "the bad guy." We finally were able to work things out and the group was stronger as a result.

Stage 3: Baring Our Bodies and Souls

I learned in the men's group, as in life, often an emotional conflict and confrontation between men can deepen the trust level. There's often a sense that *now that I've felt your emotions and know what's going on inside you, I can know you better and trust you more.* Once we were able to deal with conflict in the group and learn that no one was driven out and the group was stronger as a result, we were able to continue connecting on deeper levels.

In one of the groups, Tom suggested we try something different. We had gotten pretty comfortable with each other talking. We had taken our clothes off and jumped in the hot tub together, though it was in the dark and we were exposed for only a brief moment. Tom suggested we take our clothes off one at a time and let ourselves be seen in all our naked glory.

"I think it would be empowering to have us tell each man what we liked and appreciated about his body," Tom said. There was some uncomfortable discussion about why he was suggesting such a thing and what we might learn. But the consensus was "what the hell, let's give it a try."

The only time most have us had been completely naked was when we were alone in the shower or in bed with our wives or sexual partners. On a few occasions a woman had told me what she liked about my body, but I'd never experienced hearing anything from a man. We had talked about our fears of being seen as "gay" and the kind of ridicule most of us had grown up with if we were suspected of doing anything "girly." But this was different.

Taking our clothes off in front of other guys brought up hidden fears. Growing up, I was ridiculed for being short. I was teased a lot and got in fights when I couldn't talk my way out of them. There were always gay jokes that often had violent overtones. I still remember being taunted in Junior High school by a group of older boys. One of them, pushed me. "Hey, punk, you look like you would like a blow job."

When I backed away, the boys pushed forward. "I'll give you a blow job," the biggest boy taunted. "I'll stick my dick in your mouth and blow out your brains." I turned and ran, amid laughter and name calling.

Now I was waiting my turn to take my clothes off in front of guys I knew I could trust. But how do you ever know for sure if you can trust someone? I realized I was sweating profusely as I took off my jeans, shirt, and undershorts and stood before these group of guys. I took a deep breath and waited. "Well, I like the pattern of chest hair you have," one guy said. There were some nods of agreement. Another guy said, "You really have strong legs." Another liked the shape of my shoulders.

I was amazed. The comments were all positive and I felt like I was awash in validation that I never knew I needed. What guys noticed and liked was very different from things that women noticed. Women seemed to like my blue eyes, long eyelashes, curly hair, and one woman said she absolutely loved my "popcorn butt." I never asked her what a popcorn butt was, but was glad she liked mine. What I got from the guys felt like being seen by a whole line of fathers, brothers, uncles—all appreciating the essence of who I was. It was a magical experience that I've never forgotten.

Stage 4: Having Fun Together

Our Superbowl football game was the first of the events we did that included families. We later had picnics, hikes, going to plays, fun dinners, and parties. We also did more things together as a men's group. We went Greek dancing a number of times and learned to do Contact Improvisation.

In the group, we often went out to dinner together. I was introduced to good food that was new experience for me. I grew up with a mother who worked long hours and dinner was often a thawed streak with canned peas and applesauce. Now I learned about Italian food, good wine, barbequed ribs, oysters, and seafood.

Leading up to our tenth anniversary, we decided we would have dinner at "the best restaurant in San Francisco." Of course, for the guys who actually knew something about fine dining, deciding on the best restaurant was a task to be taken seriously. It was debated for six months leading up to the event in April, 1999.

We decided on Masa's restaurant and even with what I had learned about good food, I couldn't add much to the debate. I did conduct some online research and learned the following:

"Masa's was opened in July 1983 by chef Masataka Kobayashi. The restaurant uses Masataka's nickname, Masa, for its title. Upon its opening, the restaurant had a six-month wait list. Masa was murdered in 1984 and sous chef Bill Galloway ran the kitchen following Masa's death."

Since this was our tenth anniversary, we decided to wear tuxedos, rent a limo, and have us delivered in style. We had the limo driver take pictures of us at sunset in front of the Golden Gate Bridge. When the seven of us walked into Masa's, heads turned. I was wearing my red hat with a long pheasant feather. We were all seated at our table and since Masa's was a small, exclusive restaurant, we were the center of attention.

We laughed and made up a story, which we whispered to our waiter, that we were a group of retired CIA agents who had come together for one last meal before we would all be forced to go into hiding because our last covert operation went sour.

The meal was memorable, the food superb, the wine and after-dinner drinks fit for kings, and the desserts so good, we ended up having seconds. The bill for us all was also grand, but it was worth it. Ten years was an accomplishment that was worth celebrating.

Stage 5: Revitalizing the Group

Our regular meetings became times of joy and appreciation. We were comfortable with each other. We laughed, played, and went deeper. These guys had become family. But like all families, we reached a point where we got too comfortable. "I feel like we've become an old married couple," one of the guys said. "Everything is nice and easy, but it's getting a bit boring. We need to find new things we can do."

I suggested we do the New Warrior weekend developed by the Mankind Project. My friend, Bill Kauth, was one of the founders. At the time, I didn't know too much about their "New Warrior Training Adventure," but I felt, intuitively, that it was what we needed. We learned that the next weekend would take place in San Diego in June, 2011, and we signed up, flew down to San Diego, rented a van to drive to the site, and joined fifty other guys in connecting with a large group of guys to get to the core of what it meant to be a man in today's world, what was keeping us from our greatness, and how to find and embrace our life's purpose.

I'll describe our experiences in more depth in the chapter on Rites of Passage. Here's how the organization describes the experience: *The New Warrior Training Adventure* is a singular type of life-affirming event, honoring the best in what men have to offer the planet. We are only able to recognize the powerful brilliance of men because we are willing to look at, and take full responsibility for the pain we are also capable of creating and suffering. This is the paradox of modern masculinity, a lesson we are dedicated to learning and teaching.

We returned from the experience transformed. We felt a deeper connection with our personal path in life and saw our group in a larger context of being part of a worldwide movement of men and women who were committed to healing our wounds and changing the social institutions that kept men locked in the "man box."

Another adventure began for us when one of our members, our elder, John Robinson, suggested we meet with another men's group. "I just attended a gathering of numerous men's groups and an all-Asian men's group said they might like to meet with an Anglo men's group to explore issues of racism, and the different ways men relate in a world that is multi-racial and multi-cultural."

We liked the idea, and though it took many months of discussions before we had our first meeting, we began to explore a host of issues. For the first time, we got to experience what minority men face in a culture that often restricts men in ways that we white guys never experience.

Our group took on whole new levels of meaning and engagement and we no longer felt like an "old married couple," but young adventurers again addressing new aspects of what it means to be a man.

Stage 6: Making a Lifetime Commitment

Although we had been meeting for a long time and developing skills that helped us improve our relationships with our partners, made us more effective at work, and made us better men, we still felt the group was a training ground for our lives. I finally voiced a need that had been rumbling around inside me for a long time but finally surfaced.

"You guys mean a lot to me," I began. I was nervous and not sure I could express what I was feeling. "You helped me get through the lowest time in my life when I was caught in a destructive marriage that was pulling me under. You've been real brothers to me and I don't want to lose you." I had to pause. My emotions were beginning to overwhelm me. "I don't want this group to end. I want us to make a commitment to stay together forever, until death do we part."

I was prepared for laughter or disbelief. I wasn't prepared for the silence that followed. We began to discuss what it would mean to make such a commitment. It would mean that we couldn't allow ourselves to get bored to the point where someone would want to leave the group. It meant that we had to continue being honest, but to deal with each other in a respectful and caring way so that we didn't allow anger to pull us apart. It also meant that we would have to change how we did the group in response to life changes of our members.

When we began, we all lived in Marin County, across the bay from San Francisco and met weekly. But over the years we moved farther apart and we met every other week. When Tony and his family moved to Washington state, he dropped out of the group. But since we had made a lifetime commitment to the group and each other, we changed the format again and began meeting for four days, three or four times a year.

When our elder, John Robinson, died suddenly, we had to confront the reality of death and dying and how we would work through those issues together.

Stage 7: Dealing with Disabilities, Death, and Dying

When the group began, we were a group of guys who were mostly in our thirties and forties. Now, we're a group of guys who are in our seventies and eighties. Death and disabilities have gradually become a real presence in our lives and, therefore, important issues to be shared in the group.

As we got older, we discussed the two Ps, the prostate and the penis. The former seemed to be enlarging in ways that were troubling and the latter seemed to often fail to enlarge when we wanted it too. At various times, we tried Viagra and other related medications that were supposed to address erectile dysfunction. Generally, the consensus was that they were helpful.

In our group, guys dealt with join replacement to various legs, arms, and hips. We've dealt with depression, cognitive decline, urinary tract infections, cancer, and kidney disease. One guy was in an auto accident with a driver who had run a red light. Dick's leg was badly injured and he required surgery and spent time in a rehabilitation hospital.

He shared a room with a man who was both physically debilitated and also in serious cognitive decline. When our men's group guy returned, he talked more about at what point might you decide to end your life if there was no real hope for recovery and your quality of life was compromised. As we've gotten older, we have spent more time dealing with life and death.

We continue to have discussions about these issues. At the last meeting I brought a book that my wife was reading. She has been trained as a hospice volunteer and has worked with many individuals and families as they face end-of-life issues. The book, *Advice for Future Corpses (and Those Who Love Them): A Practical Perspective on Death and Dying* by Sallie Tisdale, a fine author and an experienced nurse who has spent ten years with people going through this final stage of life.

The book is authoritative, yet witty. She says at the outset, "I never died, so this entire book is a fool's advice. Birth and death are the only human acts we cannot practice." She addresses issues that we've all found are scary but important to discuss, including:

What does it mean to die "a good death?"

Can there be more than one kind of good death?

What can I do to make my death, or the deaths of my loved ones, good?

What to say and not to say, what to ask, and when—from the dying, loved ones, and doctors?

Since we also decided not to add any new members, we are aware that there will come a time when the group itself will die. For me, writing this book helps me share the gift of the group with others who may want to join a men's group in the future. It's a way to celebrate the joy of being male.

Bringing Men's Groups to the World

I've often been asked what goes on inside a men's group. My wife, and many others, have said, "I'd like to be a fly on the wall, so I could see what really goes on." Of course, that's never possible, but there is a way everyone can get a feel of the power, passion, love, life, craziness, and hilarity that goes on inside a men's group.

My friend and colleague, Joseph Culp, is an actor and film director. He created a magnificent film, *Welcome to the Men's Group,* that offers people a glimpse into the inner life of a men's group. It's not a documentary, but a full-length, well-scripted, and well-acted feature film. My men's group has seen it and all agree it captures the complex essence of a men's group.

On their website, www.TheMensGroupMovie.com, Joseph describes the film this way: Joseph Culp and Scott Ben-Yashar bring you a film that explores what happens in a men's group when people are no longer willing to hide behind social conventions.

Welcome to the Men's Group is a comedy-drama that explores real-life issues that affect everyone (not just men). The modern male is under pressure like never before, and *Welcome to the Men's Group* explores how men deal, or don't deal, with these issues, and how it effects their lives and families."

Joseph says, "We hope this movie will inspire millions of men to start untangling their inner lives so that they may live happier, more fulfilling lives, resulting in a better world for everyone."

I've longed to see younger men step forward who see the value in reclaiming our ancient practice of men coming together in a group. I met Dan Doty when he asked to interview me for a podcast he was doing. I shared my experiences with men and we talked about family, fathering, and our children. We hit it off and I learned about the larger vision he has to create and support men's groups all over the world through a new program, appropriately called EVRYMAN (yes, this is the way they spell it and there's an interesting story that goes with it).

I asked him, "Why EVRYMAN?" and he told me, "It's what makes more sense to me than anything else. I used these tools to address my own needs, and then realized the world needed them even more. EVRYMAN is my opportunity to share with men and others all the amazing gifts I've received throughout my life."

Dan has partnered with a group of guys who want to bring this work to the world. "Since early 2017, EVRYMAN has grown rapidly across the globe," Dan says. "We've launched weekly EVRYMAN groups, run retreats, expeditions, and launched our Veteran Integration Initiative (assimilating civilians and veterans). But we're just getting started. We aspire to support one million men over the next five years through a community of men deeply committed to emotional wellness."

Bottom Line: Being in a Men's Group Combats Loneliness and Keeps You Alive and Well

As I've noted, there are a lot of good reasons to join a men's group. It offers friendship, camaraderie, a place to share our feelings, and to be heard and respected. But the bottom-line benefit is that it combats loneliness.

A 2018 study conducted by Cigna Health reported that loneliness is reaching epidemic proportions and it is seriously impacting our health. The survey of more than 20,000 U.S. adults ages 18 years and older revealed some alarming findings:

Nearly half of Americans report sometimes or always feeling alone (46 percent) or left out (47 percent).

One in four Americans (27 percent) rarely or never feel as though there are people who really understand them.

Only around half of Americans (53 percent) have meaningful in-person social interactions, such as having an extended conversation with a friend or spending quality time with family on a daily basis.

Loneliness is more than just a feeling of low mood. It has a significant impact on our health and well-being. A 2010 study by Brigham Young University found that loneliness shortens a person's life by fifteen years, about the same impact as being obese or smoking fifteen cigarettes a day.

Other studies have found connections between loneliness and a wide range of health problems, including increased risk for heart attacks, stroke, and cancer. Lonely people are more likely to suffer from sleep deprivation, depression, and drug abuse. They also are more likely to suffer from cognitive decline.

Men, I believe, are particularly vulnerable and the loneliness increases in men as we age. We often lose connections with friends and family and fail to make new connections. Joining a men's group may be the single most important thing we can do for our health.

Rule #2

Break Free From The Man Box

*"So, we 'man up,' hold it all in,
climb the ranks, compete
for more, take the brunt,
grunt, hide in the box where
we at least know the rules
and the roles, and rationalize
living in the cave of it because
our fathers and grandfathers
did the same."*

~ Cameron Conaway from *Man Box: Poems.*

first encountered the concept of the Man Box when I was a child, though I didn't call it that back then. I just insisted *I want the red ones.* Let me explain. When I was four years old, I announced that I was tired of my white baby shoes and I wanted "big boy shoes." My mother dutifully took me to a shoe store and I was entranced by the colors and variety available. It was like going from a world of black and white and discovering that there was color in the world. I wandered past all the shoes looking at each pair until my eyes lit up.

"Mommy, mommy, I want those." I was jumping up and down and pointing to the most beautiful shoes I had ever seen. They were red Keds.

I finally settled down enough for the salesman to sit me down, measure my little feet, and go in the back to find the right shoes. The wait seemed interminable. But finally, he emerged from the back with a number of boxes.

"I brought a couple of different sizes just to be sure," he told my mother. He smiled broadly and it seemed even better than Christmas when he opened the box and folded back the tissue paper covering the shoes. "Here you are," he proudly announced.

My smile collapsed when he took out the first shoe. It wasn't the shoe I had admired. It said "Keds" on the heel, but it was blue, not red. I was crestfallen.

"But I want the red Keds," I was finally able to say.

He smiled and patted me on the head. "Red is for girls," he told me and smiled at my mother. "Blue is for boys." That seemed to settle thing s in his mind. Blue was for boys and I was clearly a boy, so I must wear the blue shoes.

I thought about that for a second and a half. I had never heard of colors being assigned by sex. I had thought all shoes were white until recently. But even as a small child, I knew what I liked.

"I want the red Keds," I stubbornly told him, though I was beginning to feel a little shaky and tearful.

He turned to my mother for support. The truth was certainly clear to him. We didn't want to start out life on the wrong foot.

I looked at my mother and she looked at me. I held my breath waiting for her response. "Give the boy want he wants," she told him and her voice was firm. I had heard that tone in her voice when she had made a decision and there were to be no arguments. I felt triumphant, like I had won a great contest. I smirked to see the salesman shake his head, but go back to get the shoes I wanted.

He returned with my new red Keds, and I was overjoyed. I put my feet in the shoes and he laced them up. I was on cloud nine.

I learned early on that the Man Box was not just about restricting what males could do and be, but tied in with the economy that made more money selling us products that would make us feel more manly (certain color shoes, aftershave lotions and colognes, baseball caps, tight fitting Levis, etc.) or womanly (certain color shoes, perfumes, hats, tight fitting Levis, etc.).

My mother and I left the store hand in hand, though I quickly dropped her hand and ran up and down the sidewalk to get the feel of my red Keds. The shoes felt great, but it felt even greater to know that my mother had stood up for me and let me know that what I wanted counted for something.

The Man Box Decision That Nearly Killed Me

The next encounter I had with the Man Box was a life and death decision I made when I was five years old. I remember playing with my toys in the corner of our kitchen in our little house on Hesby Street in Sherman Oaks. My mother was having an animated discussion with two of her woman friends. I was engrossed with my toys and wasn't listening to the words, but like all children, I was picking up on the feelings and I was becoming increasingly uncomfortable.

They were all talking about their husbands. I don't remember all the details of what they said, but their tone of voice was seared into my brain and I still shudder recalling the discussion nearly seventy years later.

"My Bill can't seem to keep a job," one woman said. "He loses a job and I have to go out to work to support us, but then he finds a new job and he wants me to quit. I don't mind, I'd rather be home, but his jobs never last and we're back to square one."

Another woman chimed in with a big sigh and a similar story. "Glen has a job, but he doesn't make much money. We're always struggling and we end up fighting more. I don't like how it affects the children."

My mother began talking about my father and I listened to every word. "Muni…" she hesitated and choked up a bit. "Muni tries to work, but it's hard to find a job doing what he loves to do. He's a writer and has done some radio shows and is trying to break into television, but he just can't make it. He's sullen sometimes and angry at others. I just don't how what the future will bring."

Clearly, it was a man's job to be the "breadwinner," and if he failed at that primary job, he wasn't really a man.

What I remember most was the feelings—a mixture of sadness, anger, contempt, and pity. Sitting in the corner, I made a vow that I would never let women talk about me the way they were talking about their husbands. I would die first. I would find a job that paid good money and never be out of work. Like the women in our kitchen, I assumed that if a man was out of work it must be his own fault. He must not be trying hard enough or he wasn't willing to do what it takes to be successful.

My vow to never be out of work almost killed me. My working career started early. I had my first job when I was eight years old. It was a seasonal job selling Christmas cards. I had a big book with samples of cards that people could choose from, and I lugged it around the neighborhood. With my father out of the house, I felt it was my job to be the man of the house and I took my job seriously. I felt proud to be doing my part to keep our family together.

I got a paper route when I was nine and had to fight off bullies who tried to steal my money. I worked hard in school and ran a drug and alcohol treatment program as soon as I got my degree. I was never out of work until I hit my forties and was the clinical director at a private health clinic. Budgets were always tight, and for the first time in my life I was let go. I fell into a deep depression. Even though I knew I wasn't to blame, I couldn't shake the feeling that I had failed as a man. Luckily, I was able to get into therapy, but it took me two years to recover. I could still hear the words of the women talking about their men exploding like bombs inside my heart and soul.

Once in the Man Box, it takes a long time to get out, if you ever do. Breaking free isn't easy. For most of us, it's like the water a fish swims in. We're not even aware that we're in it. It's just the world we live in. In order to get free we have to understand what it really is and how deadly it can be.

The Man Box and Our Beliefs About Men

I first heard the term "man box" in Paul Kivel's 1992 book *Men's Work: How to Stop the Violence That Tears Our Lives Apart.* He called the set of demands that men must be and the feelings that go with them as constituting the "act like a man box."

A colleague of mine, psychologist Ann Neitlich, was the first person to make the connection between the demands of the Man Box and demands placed on women. In her book *Building Bridges: Men's and Women's Liberation,* she says, "It has long been clear that women are oppressed by society with men carrying out that oppression. What has not been as clear is the societal oppression of men, with devastating effects on the lives of men (and women)."

She goes on to say, "The societal oppression of men leaves most men feeling less than fully male, never quite able to live up to the standard of a 'real man;' emotionally and physically numb; unable to deeply give and deeply receive love, to nurture, to be tender, and to pay good attention to others... Women's and men's conditioning, while different, are opposite sides of the same coin." Neitlich says that the qualities men are taught they *must be* are the exact qualities women are taught they *must not* be, and vice versa.

Men *Must Be* and Women *Must Not Be:*

Economically powerful
Physically strong
Courageous
Cool and stoic
Responsible
Logical
Active
Aggressive
Hairy
Muscular
Outspoken
Rugged
Tough

Men *Must Not Be* and Women *Must Be:*

Gentle
Nurturing
Tender
Feeling
Domestic
Beautiful
Soft
Passive
Receptive
Sweet
Hairless

Quiet
Giving
Apologetic

She concludes that "one must fulfill these societally determined requirements or pay the price of not being considered a 'real' man or woman."

Tony Porter is an author, educator and activist working to advance social justice issues and Chief Executive Officer of A CALL TO MEN, which educates men all over the world on healthy, respectful manhood. His inspiring TED talk describes the Man Box and how it harms women and men. Tony is the one who originated the simple term *Man Box*. His book, *Breaking Out of the "Man Box": The Next Generation of Manhood*, guides men to free themselves and to become the great men they are meant to be.

The Deadly Demands of the Man Box

There are many ways that men are harmed by the strictures of the Man Box. It impacts our physical and emotional health, our self-esteem, our relationship with ourselves and those we love. Perhaps the most devastating impact is that it contributes to the disproportionate rate of suicide between males and females.

According to figures from the Centers for Disease Control, males end their lives by suicide at rates 4 times higher than females. But certain age groups are more vulnerable than others. The suicide rate for those ages 20-24 is 5.4 times higher for males than for females of the same age. In the older age groups, suicide is predominantly a male problem. After retirement, the suicide rate skyrockets for men, but not for women. Between the ages of 65-74, the rate is 6.3 times higher for males. Between the ages of 75-84, the suicide rate is 7 times higher. And for those over 85, it is nearly 18 times higher for men than it is for women.

The strictures of the Man Box also are related to external violence. "Humankind is in the throes of a savage epidemic," says writer Mark Greene. "It is a blight on every continent and is at the heart of every bloody war and every catastrophic environmental disaster. It reigns over the bodies of Trayvon Martin and Matthew Shepard alike." He goes on to say, "In America, we have many ways of isolating and attacking difference. For American men, the social mechanism many have come to call the Man Box is the dominant frame for performing masculinity."

Most guys I know grew up and had experiences where deviation from the dictates of the Man Box was punished by our male peers. I still remember being teased mercilessly at age nine when I came to school with new jeans that had elastic in the waistband and I wasn't wearing a belt. I was pushed around and called a sissy, and I had to fight physically in order to be left alone. When I got home, I threw the jeans away, much to my mother's surprise. "I thought they looked nice on you," she told me. I was too ashamed to tell her how the other boys reacted to my social gaffe.

But the Man Box is also reinforced by women. I remember as a teenager, there was a girl that I liked but was shy to approach. The local swimming pool was where we "played around." The guys would playfully grab the girls and thrown them up in the air. The girls would squeal with delight. Even back then, I didn't want to appear too aggressive, so I didn't play the games for fear the girl I liked would think I was "one of those kind of guys" who is just trying to get a girl to have sex with him.

I was surprised when she came up to me one day and asked why I wasn't attracted to her. I explained that I was attracted, but I didn't want to be too aggressive like the other guys. She explained that girls like guys who are aggressive. They want us to pursue them sexually, but to stop if they want us to stop, but to keep going if they are giving us the green light. "How do I know if you're giving the green light?" I asked. She smiled and dived under the water. I finally asked her out on a date, but never was sure what color lights she was flashing.

Man Box culture often demands that men be aggressive and violent. Ann Silvers is one of the few writers I've met who recognize that women can be abusive as well. In her book, *Abuse OF men BY women: It happens, it hurts, and it's time to get real about it,* she says, "Abuse of men by women is an everyday occurrence. The examples are all around us. If we aren't seeing them, we aren't looking for them."

In reaction to the violence inherent in the Man Box culture, many men feel ashamed of being abused by a woman and often remain silent. "Until I witnessed a male friend being abused by his wife," says Silvers, "I was among the hordes that don't appreciate the amount of abuse men are experiencing from their female partners or the devastation that it creates."

Mark Greene says, "Although the Man Box defines and enforces what is considered to be 'real manhood,' women are as culpable as men in the policing and the enforcing of its harsh rules. When American men attempt to express masculinity in more diverse ways, it can often be the women in their lives who force them back into the Box. This can be due to fears of economic and social isolation or out of a refusal by those women to engage in the kind of self-reflective emotional discourses that exiting the Man Box can trigger."

The Man Box is Recognized as a World-Wide Problem

Promundo, a global leader in promoting gender justice and preventing violence by engaging men and boys in partnership with women and girls, studied the Man Box culture in the US, UK, and Mexico.

The study says, "The Man Box refers to a set of beliefs, communicated by parents, families, the media, peers, and other members of society, that place pressure on men to be a certain way."

The study describes seven qualities that men must follow when they are trapped inside the Man Box, along with a number of messages that embody each quality.

Self-sufficiency

A man who talks a lot about his worries, fears, and problems shouldn't really get respect. Men should figure out their personal problems on their own without asking others for help.

Acting Tough

A guy who doesn't fight back when others push him around is weak. Guys should act strong even if they feel scared or nervous inside.

Physical Attractiveness

It is very hard for a man to be successful if he doesn't look good. However, women don't go for guys who fuss too much about their clothes, hair, and skin. A guy who spends a lot of time on his looks isn't very manly.

Rigid Masculine Gender Roles

It is not good for a boy to be taught how to cook, sew, clean the house, and take care of younger children. A husband shouldn't have to do household chores. Men should really be the ones to bring money home to provide for their families, not women.

Heterosexuality and Homophobia

A gay guy is not a "real man." Straight guys who are friends with gay guys are suspected of being gay themselves.

Hypersexuality

A "real man" should have as many sexual partners as he can. A "real man" would never say no to sex.

Aggression and Control

Men should use violence to get respect, if necessary. A man should always have the final say about decisions in his relationship or marriage. If a guy has a girlfriend or wife, he deserves to know where she is all the time.

The study points out that fitting in with the prescribed roles can help a man feel good about himself, but being locked in the Man Box can also be destructive, particularly to a man's mental health. Those who subscribe to the Man Box beliefs:

- Are 3-6 times more likely to make unwanted sexual comments to women.
- Are 3-7 times more likely to use physical violence.
- Are twice as likely to have had suicidal thoughts in the last two weeks.
- Are 2-4 times more likely to have refrained from doing something for fear of appearing "gay."

A follow-up study looked at the costs of the Man Box for society and found that "a minimum of $20.9 billion that could be saved by the US, UK, and Mexican economy if there were no Man Box."

Breaking Free From the Man Box

How do we break free from? The first step is knowing that there is a Man Box. We also have to realize that men who can't fit, like my father, suffer significant physical and emotional pain. Further, we have to recognize that even those who are adept at following the rules suffer as well. It's time for men to expand our understanding of what it means to be a man and what the benefits are of breaking free from the rigid requirements of the Man Box.

The old saying "caught between a rock and a hard place" is one that many men face. I'm sure my father didn't consciously decide the way out was to "break down," but a generation before the liberation movement that freed women from the role that limited her to being the "homemaker," both my mother and father felt trapped by the roles and restrictions that society believed were necessary for men and women to follow.

Temperamentally, my mother was much better at becoming the primary breadwinner. She had salable skills as an office manager and she liked being away from home. My father would have been a great stay-at-home dad if he could have seen that as a valid and important role. Instead, he tried to push himself to be the "manly breadwinner" and my mother pushed herself to be the "womanly nurturer." My father's breakdown had the effect of freeing him from the breadwinner role since he was no longer in the family, but in a hospital. My mother found a job and made a good living supporting herself and me.

Today, more and more people are recognizing that the old roles need to change. Breaking out of the constraints of an old system can free everyone.

The Women's Movement, The Men's Movement, and The #MeToo Movement

I was in college in 1963 when Betty Friedan's *The Feminine Mystique* was published. One of the courses I was taking was Anthropology. As a nineteen-year-old male undergraduate at UC Santa Barbara, I was very interested in better understanding that mysterious cultural group, college-age females.

I didn't have a lot of extra money for books, but I could afford the $.75 for the paper-back edition. I still have my copy with the title in red against a blue background, with the headline in red, "Over 1 million in print." Even before I opened the book, the bringing together of red and blue seemed a fortuitous sign. Plus, there was a cover quote from the famous anthropologist Ashley Montagu, "The book we have been waiting for...the wisest, sanest, soundest, most understanding and compassionate treatment of contemporary American women's greatest problem...a triumph."

I was hooked from the very first line: "Gradually, without seeing it clearly for quite a while, I came to realize that something is very wrong with the way American women are trying to live their lives today." Thinking back on my own family life, I thought of my mother trying to be a homemaker and my father trying to be the breadwinner when their talents were pulling them in other directions. Friedan called it "the problem that has no name" and focused her book on how the roles that limited women to being housewives needed to be changed.

My early experiences with "red Keds" had sensitized me to gender restrictions and my own family breakup demonstrated the consequences when we trap men and women inside boxes that ultimately disable them both. As the women's movement began to take off, I felt a part of it. I wanted women to be liberated because I loved women. I also knew liberated women made it possible for men as well to free themselves from the restrictive roles that harmed them.

When I heard about the First National Conference on Men and Masculinity sponsored by the National Organization for Men Against Sexism (NOMAS) to be held in Knoxville, Tennessee in 1975, I was excited. But like many men, the demands of my job took precedence and I couldn't go. However, I did go to the Second National Conference on Men and Masculinity the following year at Penn State University and still remember the joy I felt to be meeting with other guys to talk about issues of sexism and how men and women's liberation could be achieved.

Too often our ideologies can separate us, so I never put a label on myself and resist putting labels on others. Although many write about "the women's movement" and "the men's movement," I've never seen them as separate.

Two colleagues who recognize the importance of bridging the men's movement and the women's movement are Leonard Szymczak and Rick Broniec. In their book, *Wake Up, Grow Up, and Show Up: Calling Men into the 21st Century,* they provide a new model and roadmap to help men wake up from the coma of toxic masculinity, grow up into becoming healthy adults, and show up as leaders alongside women to serve the world.

When more and more women came out and told the truth about sexual violence, I felt a connection and supported their truth-telling. #MeToo wasn't just about women saying, "me too, it happened to me." For me, #MeToo is about all of us, because the same abusive structure and beliefs that harm women also harm men. Men and women are natural allies in our struggle to heal. We are at a critical time in human history and as Dylan reminds us, "The times they are a-changin.'"

Mark Greene offers a cogent, caring, and insightful analysis of these changes in his publication, *The Little #MeToo Book for Men*. "Ask most men, regardless of where they are on the political spectrum, and they'll tell you," says Greene. "Something feels off. Something is not right. Daily we feel it, a surging dislocation, a weary dissatisfaction, and a restless sense of growing anxiety. It's the kind of discomfort you feel as you slowly realize the game is totally rigged; the game you've been bullied and shamed into playing all your life."

Greene validates what I've been feeling and I know many other men have been feeling as well. "I'm here to confirm men have, in fact, been cheated," says Greene, "and they are starting to understand this in ever greater numbers. From some quarters, men's voices are angry and reactive. They say that men are not allowed to be men; that women are taking over. Others feel deeply uncertain, wondering how to engage, even support movements like #MeToo and Time's Up without getting caught up in the binary crossfire of our culture wars."

He recognizes that supporting movements like #MeToo and Time's Up aren't about blaming and shaming men. They are about breaking free of the Man Box, a box that is suffocating men and those we love.

Bottom Line: There Are 10 Steps for Breaking Free from the Man Box and Reclaiming Our True Selves

I've worked for many years helping people break free from drug addiction, and I've learned some things that can help us all break free from the Man Box. Anyone who has been addicted to cocaine, nicotine, alcohol, or any other drug knows how difficult it is. At first the drug provides relief from life's pain and suffering. Only later do we recognize that the drugs are causing more pain and suffering.

Here are the steps I've found helpful in breaking out of the Man Box.

1. We notice that we are feeling bad.

Our feelings are the first clue that something is wrong. At first, the feelings are subtle. Something isn't right, but we can't put our finger on what it is. As time goes on, the feelings become stronger and more insistent. Many of us become more irritable and angry. Others become anxious, depressed, and withdrawn.

2. We become aware of ways we try to escape from our pain.

Most of us lead busy lives, so it's easy at first to ignore the feelings. When they become more demanding, we use tried-and-true methods relieve the pain. Some of us escape into work. We work harder and longer. It's a socially acceptable way to escape. If our partners complain, we can tell them we're working for the family. Some escape into drugs—a drink at lunchtime, a cocktail in the evening. Some escape into sex and pornography. Some escape into food, films, phones, and computers.

3. We recognize that we are feeling lonely.

The more we try to escape our pain and suffering, the more cut off we become. First, we cut off from our feelings. We become numb, tired, withdrawn. We then become more disconnected from friends and family. We feel alone in our lives and it hurts. Recognizing our loneliness forces us to see that we are harming ourselves and those we care about.

4. We understand the ways we "act out" and "act in."

We see that our irritation and anger are causing problems in our family. We realize that we have become short-tempered and overly sensitive. We see that our behaviors have become hurtful to those we care most about. We also see that we are also turning our anger inward. We see that we are not only abusing others, but we are abusing ourselves. We see that our physical and emotional health is deteriorating and we make a decision to reach out for help.

5. We stop procrastinating and actually take action to get help.

For most of us, there is a time lag between seeing the ways we act out and act in and the time we actually reach out for help. One of the basic rules of the Man Box is that "We solve our problems ourselves. Real men don't ask for help." So, breaking the downward spiral we are in isn't easy. It took me a full year after I believed my wife when she told me my anger and depression were killing the relationship and when I finally agreed to go to a doctor and get checked out.

6. We go beyond the quick fix and deal with the real issues that are causing the pain and suffering.

There are plenty of people who are offering quick fixes. Doctors are quick to offer a drug (called medications if it comes from a "medical professional.") I'm not saying we shouldn't take drugs. I took antidepressants for a while and they helped. Take a vacation, go on a cruise, get a potion from the health food store. They may be helpful, but they are usually not enough to bring about the kind of change that is real and will last.

We often need a change in our belief system. We need to get out of our comfort zone and take a deep dive inside. We stop and ask, "Who am I? What do I really want in life?" It can be a real exploration of the meaning of our lives.

7. We see the truth about the "civilized" state.

Like most people, I grew up being taught that things got better and better through time. The history books taught that things were bad in our primitive past, that hunter-gatherers' lives were short and unpleasant. This view was expressed by the English Philosopher Thomas Hobbes in his 1651 book *Leviathan,* where he offered the view that those who lived before the agricultural revolution experienced a constant state of "war of every man against every man" and the lives of the people were "solitary, poor, nasty, brutish, and short."

But as we'll see in Chapter 4, our hunter-gatherer past was not idyllic, but there were many things about it that were better than our present way of being on planet Earth.

8. We accept that we have an unhealthy addiction to "civilization."

I've been putting civilization in quotes because I want to help us recognize that viewing our present world as being civilized blinds us to the reality that we are really on a sinking ship and there is something better we can look forward to if we get off.

My colleague, Chellis Glendinning, describes connection between personal healing and social transformation. In her book, *My Name is Chellis and I'm in Recovery from Western Civilization,* she says, "Everybody I know who is serious about personal healing, social change, and ecological rebalancing is in recovery: recovery from personal addiction, childhood abuse, childhood deprivation, the nuclear family, sexism, racism, urban alienation, trickle-down economics, combat service in the trenches of the gender wars, the threat of extinction, linear thinking, the mind/body split, technological progress, and the mechanistic worldview."

9. We get support for the long journey home.

It isn't enough to get out of the Man Box. If we don't get into something better, we'll slip right back. That's why joining a men's group is so important. We need the support of other men if we are to live more authentic and joyful lives. Women can also be supportive. Many recognize that the Man Box harms them as much as it does the men and they want to partner with men who care about themselves, the women in their lives, and the planet we all share.

10. We connect our personal healing with healing our relationship to the Earth.

We live at a time in human history where we've become disconnected from the Earth. When that happens, we become disconnected from ourselves, from each other, and from our communities. As a result, we increasingly feel lonely, angry, and fearful. Reconnecting to our roots in the earth will go a long way to helping us survive and thrive at this critical time in human history.

Getting out of the Man Box allows us to become more authentically ourselves, to be who we really are, and to embrace the gift of maleness, the topic of the next chapter.

Rule #3

Accept the Gift of Maleness

"Boys and girls really are different, and so are the men and women they become. It is not, for me, a cliché or a pleasantry to say that I think we are very fortunate as a species to be able to acknowledge that."

~Melvin Konner, MD, Professor of Anthropology, Emory University

I've been interested in maleness for as long as I can remember. My parents wanted a child, but after ten years of trying to conceive, they had nearly given up. They learned about an experimental procedure of injecting my father's sperm into my mother's womb. They were overjoyed when they learned my mother was finally pregnant. "I walked down Fifth Avenue in New York," my mother used to tell me. "I was overjoyed knowing we were finally going to have a baby. I walked gingerly trying to be sure I didn't lose you."

They were sure I was going to be a girl and had considered only girl's names. But when I came into the world with my little penis proudly displayed, they were surprised. "It's a healthy baby boy," the doctor announced and my parents had to rethink what to name me. My father decided I should be named Elliott Diamond. Following Jewish tradition, he had picked the name of his nephew who had recently died.

He hoped that in receiving the name Elliott I would carry some of the virtues of his sister's first child. Elliott was beloved in the family and before his untimely death at age nineteen, he had demonstrated his father's musical talents and had begun composing popular songs. But my mother didn't like the name and recalled, "I cried for three days in the hospital until your father agreed to pick another name for you." They settled on John Elliott Diamond. *John* was my mother's father's name who had died at age 30 when my mother was five years old.

So, early on in my life, I was also confronted with issues of male and female, mother's preference vs. father's preference in names. It wasn't until I went to college that I decided to change my name to *Jed*. I thought it sounded manlier than *Johnny* which is what I had been called my whole life up until then. Jed captured in my initials both my mother's and father's heritage, but was my own name, which I've carried ever since.

Resolving the Conflict Between Nature and Nurture

When I was in graduate school in the 1960s, there was a great debate about what was more important in understanding human beings: our biological heritage as controlled by our genes or what we learned from our environment.

Within the scientific community, that debate has ended. We now know we are products of both. Our genes provide the blueprint of who we can be, but the environment determines how that blueprint is read. There is a new field of science called epigenetics, which demonstrates that we can actually change the way our genes operate, and hence change our lives. In his book, *Change Your Genes, Change Your Life: Creating Optimal Health with the New Science of Epigenetics,* Dr. Kenneth R. Pelletier says, "Epigenetics is the study of the *chemical tags* that park themselves on the genome that literally controls the activities of our genes. In a sense, these markers appear 'above' the genes—and is thus signified by the Greek prefix 'epi,' which means 'above' or 'upon.'"

Similarly, there has been debate about what constitutes male and female. Are there essential differences between the sexes, or are male and female traits determined by our culture? Again, the answer is both. Yet, questions of male and female stir strong feelings in most people.

Michael Gurian is one of the world's leading experts on gender-specific education and health care. In his book, *What Could He Be Thinking? How a Man's Mind Really Works,* he says, "In the last twenty years, I have surveyed scientific literature from thirty cultures on all continents, and no matter the culture I study, I discover what early brain scientists already knew: Socialized differences between men and women exist, but there is a primal nature to 'man' and 'woman' on which culture has only minor effect. This nature holds keys to better life, work, parenting, and especially, the success of all intimate relationships, including marriage."

The Essence of Being Male: We Produce Millions of Small Gametes

We might think about the things that distinguish boys and girls, i.e. genitals (penis/vagina) or chromosomes (XY/XX). Biologists have a very simple and useful definition of what is male and what is female, whether we are fish, ferns, or human beings. An individual can either make many small gametes (sex cells) or fewer but larger gametes. **The individuals that produce smaller gametes are called "males" and the ones that produce larger gametes are called "females."**

The female strategy produces gametes that are large and have a high rate of survival and fertilization. The male strategy is to produce as many as possible, to increase the chances of finding a large one. About 400 eggs are ovulated in a woman's lifetime. A healthy male produces 500 million sperm per day.

An individual must either invest in a few large eggs or in millions of sperm. Thus, there will always be many times more sperm than there are eggs. Consequently, sperm must compete for access to those rare eggs. The egg is not passive in the process, but gives off a chemical substance that allows one sperm to enter and rejects the rest. Although these basic facts of life may be obvious, the importance and implications may not be.

In fact, this difference in the size of our sex cells makes a huge difference in how we act as males. As we will see, it helps explain why males compete with other males, take more risks than females, fight more, and die sooner. "The cellular imbalance is at the center of maleness," says geneticist Dr. Steve Jones. "It confers on males a simpler sex life than their partners, together with a host of incidental idiosyncrasies, from more suicide, cancer, and billionaires to rather less hair on the top of the head."

Jungian therapist Eugene Monick concludes that these biological realities of sperm competition can tell us a lot about male insecurity and fear of failure. "What the sperm experiences in its life struggle toward the ovum is the ground or archetypal pattern for a man's daily struggle for virility. Body awareness that but one sperm will succeed, two million will die, is the raw material of masculine psyche, the fuel for a male's terror of fate."

There Are Ten Trillion Cells in Your Body and Every One is Sex Specific

David C. Page, MD, is a professor of biology at the Massachusetts Institute of Technology (MIT) and director of the Whitehead Institute. He is one of the world's leading experts on the fundamental differences between males and females. "At the Institute," says Dr. Page, "we focus on understanding the biology and evolution of sex chromosomes (X and Y), the role that the X and Y chromosomes play in fundamental sex differences beyond the reproductive tract, and the origins and development of germ cells—the precursors of eggs and sperm."

Dr. Page and his colleagues have been studying the Y chromosome since the early 1990s and their findings can help us all better understand what it means to be male. "There are ten trillion cells in human body and every one of them is sex specific," says Dr. Page. "So, all your cells know on a molecular level whether they are XX or XY.

"It has been said that our genomes are 99.9% identical from one person to the next," Dr. Page continues. "It turns out that this assertion is correct, as long as the two individuals being compared are both men. It's also correct if the two individuals being compared are both women. However, if you compare the genome of a man with the genome of a woman, you'll find that they are only 98.5% identical. In other words, the genetic difference between a man and a woman is 15 times greater than the genetic difference between two men or between two women."

Males Differ Genetically From Females and The Differences Are Significant

If you think a 1.5% difference in genetic makeup isn't a lot, consider that the human genome and the chimpanzee genome differ by 1.5%. It helps explain a lot to me when I recognize that I am as different genetically from my wife as I am from a male chimpanzee.

Dr. Larry Cahill, a neuroscientist at the University of California, Irvine, admits that like many fellow scientists, he used to think men and women were fundamentally the same outside the obvious areas of reproduction and sex hormones. However, following research on the different ways males and females react to certain medications, he changed his mind. He says Ambien (known generically as zolpidem) is a case in point. "We now know that women metabolize Ambien differently than men," says Dr. Cahill. "Women reach maximum blood levels *45 percent higher* than those of men.

"That is a textbook example of what is wrong. How did it happen that for twenty-some years, women, millions of them, were essentially overdosing on Ambien?"

This may be true for many other drugs, but we don't know it. And the reverse may also be true. While women are getting too much of a medication, men may not be getting enough.

This focus on important gender differences is not just going on in laboratories headed by men. In 1992, cardiologist Marianne J. Legato, MD, published *The Female Heart: The Truth About Women and Heart Disease* and revealed that women's presenting symptoms of heart disease are taken less seriously than men—and when women undergo cardiac surgery, they are less likely than men to survive.

Legato founded the Partnership for Gender Specific Medicine in 1997 and says, "Everywhere we look, the two sexes are startlingly and unexpectedly different not only in their internal function but in the way they experience illness." Rather than pretend there are no differences or try to minimize the differences, we would do well to celebrate them. Sex and gender differences are central to our lives.

Like Every Other Part of Us, The Male Brain is Significantly Different From the Female Brain

Louann Brizendine, MD, is a professor of clinical psychiatry at the University of California, San Francisco and Co-director of the UCSF Program in Sexual Medicine. Dr. Brizendine graduated from UC Berkeley in neurobiology, Yale School of Medicine, and Harvard Medical School in psychiatry.

She says, "the brains of females and males are not the same. Male brains are larger by about nine percent, even after correcting for body size. Women and men, however, have the same number of brain cells. The cells are just packed densely in women—cinched corset-like into a smaller skull." In her book, *The Male Brain,* she says, "Simplifying the entire male brain to just the 'brain below the belt' is a good setup for jokes, but it hardly represents the totality of a man's brain."

Here are some of the significant differences in the brain structure and function:

1. The anterior cingulate cortex weighs options and makes decisions. It's the worrywart center, and it's larger in women and smaller in men.

2. The medial preoptic area is the area for sexual pursuit. It's 2.5 times larger in the male.

3. The temporoparietal junction is the solution seeker. It's more active in the male brain, comes online more quickly, and races toward a "fix-it-fast" solution.

4. The hippocampus is the center for emotional memory. "It's the elephant that never forgets a fight, a romantic encounter, or a tender moment—and won't let you forget it either," says Dr. Brizendine. She notes that it's larger and more active in women and one of the main reasons that, as Dr. Legato suggests in the title of one of her books, *Why Men Never Remember and Women Never Forget.*

Another research scientist in the field of sex and gender differences is Dr. Simon Baron-Cohen. He is a professor of developmental psychopathology at the University of Cambridge and has been researching sex differences for over thirty years. In his book, *The Essential Difference: The Truth About the Male and Female Brain,* he details the significant differences between male-type brains and female-type brains.

His conclusions are both startling and clear-cut. "The subject of essential sex differences in the mind is clearly very delicate," he cautions us. But the findings substantiate the fact that males and females are different in large measure because of the different ways our brains are structured. "The female brain is predominantly hard-wired for empathy," he tells us. "The male brain is predominantly hard-wired for understanding and building systems."

Empathizing, Baron-Cohen tell us, is the drive to identify another person's emotions and thoughts and to respond to these with an appropriate emotion. The empathizer intuitively figures out how people are feeling, and how to treat people with care and sensitivity.

Systemizing is the drive to analyze and explore a system, to extract underlying rules that govern the behavior of a system; and the drive to construct systems. "Systems can be as varied as a pond, a vehicle, a computer, a plant, a library catalogue, a musical instrument, a math equation, or even an army unit," says Baron-Cohen. "They all operate on inputs and deliver outputs, using rules." He points out that although most males are better with systematizing and females with empathizing, this isn't true in all cases.

At the end of his book, *The Essential Difference,* there are two questionnaires, one to determine your "systemizing quotient (SQ)" and one to determine your "empathy quotient (EQ)." I remember answering the questions for the first time and hoping I would score high on having a male-type brain, though I knew I had great empathy for people.

However, to my dismay, I scored very low on the SQ test. Not only did I score lower on the SQ test than most men, I actually scored lower than most women. But I made up for it on the EQ scale. I scored higher than most men *and* most women. Accepting myself has meant coming to peace with a brain that makes it easier for me to empathize and more difficult for me to systemize.

Just as our gene expression can be modified by our life experiences, so too can our brain function be modified. We can all learn to be more empathic and we can also learn to feel more comfortable with structures and rules.

Testosterone: The Holy Grail of Manhood

Larrian Gillespie, MD, calls it the "Holy Grail of Manhood." Testosterone is an androgen that is produced both in the adrenals and testes of men. Women produce this same steroid from their ovaries, but as is true in all aspects of life, quantity is important. "The average male pumps out 260-1000 nanograms of testosterone per deciliter of blood plasma, dwarfing the minuscule 15-70 nanograms a woman gets to play around with in her body." She also says men produce estrogens, but in much smaller quantities than do females (at least until women go through menopause and their estrogen levels drop precipitously).

In her book, *The Alchemy of Love and Lust,* Theresa L. Crenshaw, MD, said, "Men have about 20 to 40 times more testosterone than women, which is one reason why our sex drives are so different. This forceful hormone is responsible for the drive associated with sexual appetite and patterns of aggression."

In an interesting article, "I Lived Like a Man For a Couple of Weeks. It Helped Me Understand My Husband," (*The Washington Post,* June 30, 2015) writer Ann Mallen describes her experience when her doctor prescribed a "special cream" to boost her testosterone:

> *I wanted to do them all. Men—young and old, thin and heavy, coiffed and shaggy—walked past my gate in Hartsfield-Jackson as I waited for my connection to visit my sister in Connecticut. Not all rated attractive, but I found the idea of sex with each captivating.*

My doctor warned me of "odd symptoms," but she didn't mention this constant sexual distraction. Or the irrational anger. The day before, I dropped a fork in the kitchen and kicked it. It clattered into the base of the cabinet, but that wasn't enough. I picked it up and threw it into the sink with a force intended to harm.

Does this sound familiar? Did you ever think that a man's "excessive" sexual desire, irritability, and anger were because he was a (fill in the blank of some of the negative things we say and think about men)? It may be more related to his testosterone levels than because he's a son of a bitch.

Mallen shared how her experience helped broaden her view of men.

Living for a few weeks with extra testosterone gave me a new understanding of men, Now, when I notice my husband glancing at an attractive woman, I don't take offense. Testosterone turns your head and makes you look. Sometimes, I whisper, "Yep, she's beautiful." He jokes that I'm now one of the guys.

The Hierarchies of Male and Female: Are Men Really on Top?

Yuval Noah Harari has his finger on the pulse of history. He earned his PhD in history from the University of Oxford and has written three international best-selling books, including *Sapiens: A Brief History of Humankind.*

In *Sapiens,* which has thus far sold ten million copies and been translated into fifty languages, he addresses critical issues facing humanity including race, caste, and gender. He says, "All societies are based on imagined hierarchies, but not necessarily on the same hierarchies." He goes on to say that "traditional Indian society classifies people according to caste, Ottoman society according to religion, and American society according to race."

"One hierarchy, however, has been of supreme importance in all known human societies," says Harari, "the hierarchy of gender. People everywhere have divided themselves into men and women. And almost everywhere men have got the better deal, at least since the Agricultural Revolution."

Men, in our society—particularly rich, white men—exercise the most power. But the power isn't just over women. It is over men of color, poor men, even men in middle-America who are losing their jobs to automation. Why would we create hierarchies with men of power at the top? There are many theories, but the one that makes most sense to me is based on male competition.

If you think about males throughout history, we competed with other males to rise in the male hierarchy so that we might be chosen by an attractive female who would see us as the best and the brightest. "As men competed against each other for the opportunity to impregnate fertile women," says Harari, "an individual's chances of reproduction depended above all on his ability to outperform and defeat other men. As time went by, the masculine genes that made it to the next generation were those belonging to the most ambitious, aggressive, and competitive men."

However, there is a price to pay for being male. Even white men who have enjoyed a privileged status don't always have it so good. For instance, the high suicide rate for men is particularly high in white males. Psychologist Herb Goldberg, in his book *The Hazards of Being Male,* says, "The male has paid a heavy price for his masculine 'privilege' and power. He is out of touch with his emotions and his body. He is playing by the rules of the male game plan and with lemming-like purpose he is destroying himself—emotionally, psychologically, and physically."

The Most Unappreciated Fact About Men

Here's a thought experiment that will help us get to a key element of maleness. If our species were on the brink of extinction and we were desperate to repopulate the world, would we be better off having a hundred men and one woman or a hundred women and one man? Most of us would pick the latter choice. If we had a hundred men and one woman, the men would likely compete and battle each other. They might end up killing each other, and the lone woman would be out of luck mumbling to herself, "Damn, with survival on the line, all the men can think about is fighting each other, I'm left alone, and the human species dies." With one man, he has plenty of sperm to impregnate all one hundred women. The women would likely talk about the situation, empathize, and decide to share the man among themselves.

Think back to our male ancestors in the animal kingdom, competing with each other for access to females. Think about sperm competing to be the first one to the valuable egg. In the scheme of things, females are more valuable and males are more expendable. In his book, *Is There Anything Good About Men?*, social scientist Roy F. Baumeister describes things this way:

"Of all the people who ever reached adulthood, maybe 80% of the women but only 40% of the men reproduced." He goes on to say, "That's a stunning difference. Of all humans ever born, most women became mothers, but most men did not become fathers. You wouldn't realize this by walking through an American suburb today with its tidy couples." But it an important fact throughout our male history. "I consider it the single most underappreciated fact about the differences between men and women."

At the most basic level of life, males are likely to take great risks to be successful. We start new businesses. We risk crossing the ocean to the new world in search of riches. Most of us die young or fail at what nature considers the ultimate game of life, producing more offspring. In this game, females more often and easily succeed.

Females can also afford to play it safer in life. Their reproductive success is assured. Not only will women become mothers, but all mothers know the baby is hers. Males can never be as sure. *Was the baby mine or could she have had a secret tryst with the plumber?* Men can never rest easy as far as reproductive success. Hence the saying, "Mother's baby. Father's maybe."

The World of Males is Bipolar

Guys live in a bipolar world. I don't mean we all suffer from a mental illness, though some of us do. I mean that one of the corollaries of "most unappreciated fact about men" is that when we look at the highest rungs in our society—the President of the United States, those who represent us in Congress, Supreme Court Justices, heads of corporations, etc., we see mostly males.

Some feminists look at the fact that men occupy these positions of power and assume that the males are trying to keep the females from exercising their full potential. They feel men are the cause of women's inability to break through the glass ceiling.

But there is another reality that some men's activists tune into. They see mostly males at bottom rungs on the societal ladder, too. Boys drop out of school at higher rates than girls and get more Ds and Fs. Our prison population is mostly male. More males are violent and the victims of violence. More males than females are homeless. Males commit suicide at three to eighteen times the rate of females. Males suffer from nine of the top ten leading causes of death at rates higher than females. Males live sicker and die sooner.

Feminists look up and see men above them in the social hierarchy and assume men are keeping them down. Male activists look down and see men at the bottom and assume that it's women's fault. They think women now have it good and men are being kept down. It's a bipolar world of winners and losers, but why?

Why do males go to extremes? Why do we live in a bipolar world of winners and losers? Remember our earlier thought experiment about repopulating the world? We only need a few males, but lots of females. Baumeister concludes, "Nature plays the dice more with men than women."

One of the great gifts of maleness is that we have the potential to become wildly successful, but only if we're willing to risk falling on our face. Males are often the innovators, the creators, the builders of new systems. We risk becoming losers, but we all strive for greatness. One of the things I've learned about myself as a man is that we can learn a lot from our mistakes. Some of the most creative experiences of my life came when I'd hit bottom, when I wasn't sure I could go on living. I still remember the depression I went through when I lost my job at a health clinic. It took me a year to work through my anger, shame, and grief. I had to re-evaluate my life and what I was doing with it. The downtime led me to make a more serious commitment to writing and inspired my book, *Male vs. Female Depression: Why Men Act Out and Women Act In.*

The world is changing. Men don't face the same odds of reproductive failure as we did in the past. We can afford to play it safer, empathize more, care about ourselves, the women in our lives, and our children. The new challenge for many men is taking the risk to learn how to love deeply and well.

Learning to Love From the Heart is the New Male Frontier

Growing up, it was clear to me that the most important way that men expressed their love for their wives and families was by being a good breadwinner. My father had "a nervous breakdown" because he couldn't find work to support his family. He believed that a man's lovability would be judged solely by how successful he was in bringing home the bacon. This is the time when we need to expand our understanding of love.

Carista Luminare, PhD, has more than forty years' experience as a counselor, consultant, and educator to individuals, couples, and families. Along with her husband, Lion Goodman, she helps men and women learn about the nature of love based on secure attachment practices. She says, "It's important for men to consciously develop compassion and love as a personal power and ability."

Both Carista and Lion recognize that men need to learn to express love from our hearts, not just our heads. They quote the British politician, Andrew Bennett, who reminds us, "The longest journey you will ever take is the 18 inches from your head to your heart."

"Most women crave a man's empathy, tenderness, and ability to care, all three of which are heart virtues," she told me, "in order for them to feel safe and secure."

It took me a long time to make that journey from my head to my heart. For years, I knew in my head what it meant to love, but I had difficulty feeling it when I was with my wife. I often felt numb, cut off from my feelings.

It really wasn't until my first son, Jemal, was born that I broke through to my feelings of love. I realized, for the first time, that going out in the world and making a good living didn't replace the feelings of love and tenderness I felt holding my newborn child.

Opening up to my son enabled me to open up to my wife in ways that I had never experienced before. I came to see that making a good living wasn't enough. In fact, it was a secondary accomplishment to learning to listen, to look deeply into her eyes, to feel what she was feeling, and to share what was going on inside me.

I realized that I had never learned those skills as an adult because I had never learned them from my father when I was a child. In the first years following my birth, my father was often away looking for work. When he was home, he was anxious, worried, and often depressed about getting a job, which I'll describe more fully in Chapter 10.

When Carlin and I first talked about getting married, she told me, I can't always commit to *you,* but I'll always be committed to *us.* At the time I felt hurt and angry, although I didn't say anything. All I heard was that *I'm not committed to you.* If she's not committed to me, I thought she didn't love me. Maybe there was something the matter with me or maybe she wasn't the right partner if she couldn't commit her life to mine.

It took me years to realize that a commitment to us was a bigger and deeper commitment. It was a commitment to love, which we can learn to grow, even at times when our small selves are frightened and demanding. *Love me, love me, love me,* our small ego cries out to be heard. When we learn to love a child or are totally loved and embraced by a parent, we learn a deeper kind of love, one that heals our past and our present.

Relationship experts Harville Hendrix and his wife Helen LaKelly Hunt express this idea well in their book, *Making Marriage Simple: 10 Relationship-Saving Truths.* Truth #4 is called "Being Present for Each Other Heals the Past." They describe a new kind of love and a new kind of marriage:

"There is an old kind of marriage. In it, both people are elbowing each other, trying to get into the center. Each one expects the other to put the attention on *them* and *meet their needs.* This kind of marriage doesn't work. Today, a new kind of marriage is emerging: the Partnership Marriage. This marriage isn't about you...or even your partner. The Partnership Marriage is about something that is greater than either of you. It is about the two of you helping each other grow into full adulthood. And the healing of each other's childhood wounds as at the heart of this process."

Bottom Line: Being Ourselves Means Accepting the Gift of Maleness

One of the most well-meaning yet wrong-headed ideas is that the world would be better off if we just saw each other as *people,* not as *males and females.* In societies based on hierarchy where those at the top get more and those at the bottom get less, it's reasonable to want more equality.

The women's movement has been very positive in calling out the abuses of the system and pushing for more equal opportunities for women. But, the way to get there isn't by trying to convince us that gender differences don't exist, or if they do, that men should be more like women. The science is clear: there are significant differences between males and females, right down to the differences in our ten trillion cells.

Rather than denying our differences, let's celebrate them. Men and women are natural allies. Male and female, masculine and feminine, complement each other. The truth is that some men have been at the top of the hierarchy and have used their power to stay there. But, it's also true that men have been at the bottom of the hierarchy and have suffered as much at the hands of those on top as women have suffered.

Trying to eliminate our sex differences has as much chance of success as trying to eliminate gravity. But, like everything in nature, change occurs. Just as there are conditions in nature where gravitational forces exert more or less force, so too can the differences between male and female be modified. However, as we'll see in the next chapter, maleness and femaleness have a long history and are here to stay.

Rule #4

Embrace Your Billion Year History of Maleness

"The natural world is the largest sacred community to which we belong. To be alienated from this community is to become destitute in all that makes us human. To damage this community is to diminish our own existence."

~Thomas Berry

One of the first things I wondered as I began gathering information for this book was "when did 'maleness' begin?" In his book, *The Hidden Spirituality of Men: Ten Metaphors to Awaken the Sacred Masculine,* Matthew Fox says, "The universe invented sex and sexuality about one billion years ago." Our male lineage is ancient.

According to mathematical cosmologist Dr. Brian Swimme and historian Dr. Thomas Berry in their book, *The Universe Story,* life first evolved on Earth about four billion years ago. Prior to the evolution of sexual reproduction, cells divided into individual sister cells. Swimme and Berry call this living organism *Sappho.* But one billion years ago, a momentous change occurred. The first male organism—they call him *Tristan*—and the first female organism—they call her *Iseult*—were cast into the ancient oceans. Here's how Swimme and Berry poetically describe this first sexual adventure:

> *"These special cells were then released by Sappho into the currents of the enveloping ocean. They were cast into the marine adventure, with its traumas of starvation and of predation. Able to nourish themselves but no longer capable of dividing into daughter cells, such primal living beings made their way through life until an almost certain death ended their 3 billion-year lineage."*

But Tristan and Iseult possessed great fortitude and were willing to face adversity and danger in search of a potential lover, no matter the odds of failure.

> *"A slight, an ever so slight, chance existed that a Tristan cell would come upon a corresponding Iseult cell. They would brush against each other, a*

contact similar to so many trillions of other encounters in their oceanic adventure. But with this one, something new would awaken. Something unsuspected and powerful and intelligent, as if they had drunk a magical elixir, would enter the flow of electricity through each organism.

"Suddenly the very chemistry of their cell membranes would begin to change. Interactions evoked by newly functioning segments of her DNA would restructure the molecular web of Iseult's skin, so that an act she had never experienced or planned for would begin to take place—Tristan entering her cell wholly."

This billion-year-old story takes us back to the emergence of the first sperm, the beginning of maleness, and our first male ancestor. Think about the fortitude and courage it took for the first male to overcome the adversities of life in the primordial ocean to find a female who would allow him entry into her body. This is the first love story and the beginning act to a play that continues to unfold today. But as evolution continued, and the first multicellular animals appeared 700 million years ago, we started on the long journey to becoming the unique men we are today.

The triune brain of *Homo sapiens* shows our heritage from reptiles, mammals, and primates. Further, for more than 90% of our human history, we were hunter-gatherers and still carry those proclivities, skills, and sensibilities. Remembering our roots in the community of life is a powerful help in accepting ourselves as men.

Earl and Our Reptilian Heritage

Let's take a look at our reptilian heritage. Reptiles evolved 313 million years ago, according to Swimme and Berry. "The beings who created eggs were the first reptiles. They crowded out the amphibians to become the predominant terrestrial vertebrate." Modern-day reptiles include crocodiles, alligators, snakes, lizards, turtles, and tortoises.

According to Petset.com, the three most popular reptile names for male reptiles are *Apollo, Earl,* and *Bruce.* I like Earl as a male representative of our reptilian ancestors. There are three things that are most important to Earl. We can think of them as the 3 S's: *Safety, sustenance,* and *sex.*

Men often get a bad rap when we focus so much attention on eating barbeque ribs, fighting, or trying to get attractive women to have sex with us. But that's Earl for you. I'm not saying that we have no control over our desires. If that were true, we'd be constantly feeding our faces when we weren't fighting or f-cking or trying all three at the same time. I'm just saying Earl is part of our maleness and his desires have to be considered if we're going to understand ourselves and make good decisions about our lives and the lives of others.

Our reptilian brain isn't very social—no one tries to cuddle up with a snake, lizard, or crocodile. Though I think turtles are great, I wouldn't want to get in bed with one. Earl wants what he wants when he wants it, and he isn't much concerned about other's needs. Earl's mantra is "me, me, me, more, more, more."

We may not always embrace Earl's behavior, but he lives within all of us, and reptiles did pretty well for themselves. They're still going strong after 313 million years. Swimme and Berry say that our human lineage came on the scene a mere 2.6 million years ago. I hope we'll be around as long as the reptiles.

We Are Mammals: We Seek, We Rage, We Lust, We Care, We Panic, We Fear, and We Play

Scientists now believe that the earth was hit by a giant meteor and a series of massive volcanoes 65 million years ago. The dinosaurs and a great deal of other life was extinguished. This opened the world to an explosion of mammalian life including lemurs, tarsiers, monkeys, rodents, bats, whales, horses, and many more.

In their book, *The Archaeology of Mind: Neuroevolutionary Origins of Human Emotions,* Jaak Panksepp and Lucy Biven offer the following thoughts in their first chapter, "Ancestral Passion:" "This book takes us on an archaeological dig deep into the recesses of the mammalian brain, to the ancestral sources of our emotional minds."

Based on Jaak Panksepp's lifelong study of the neuroscience of emotion, he describes seven primary-process emotional systems that are part of our mammalian heritage. A stickler for language, he capitalized the systems so they wouldn't be confused with how we think about these words in common language: SEEKING, LUST, CARE, RAGE, FEAR, PANIC, and PLAY. Let's look more deeply at each.

SEEKING

The SEEKING system gets a mammal moving. It encourages foraging, exploring, investigating, curiosity, and expectancy. "Paradoxically," says Panksepp, "it operates independent of what it might actually find, 'a goad without a fixed goal.' It's like radar that never turns off, or a party guest who keeps scanning the room while holding a conversation, or a web surfer who finds a right-priced pair of Air Jordan 11 Retro shoes on Amazon, but keeps looking."

"When fully aroused, SEEKING fills the mind with interest and motivates organisms to effortlessly search for the things they need, crave, and desire. In humans, this system generates and sustains curiosity from the mundane to our highest intellectual pursuits," Panksepp concludes.

RAGE

When the SEEKING system is thwarted, RAGE is aroused. Anger is provoked by curtailing a mammal's freedom of action. We have come to see rage in negative terms and associate it with male violence, but it's a natural part of every mammal's behavior and has the positive purpose of keeping the animal alive and able to seek and find what he needs. It also helps animals defend themselves by arousing fear in their opponents.

"RAGE helps us defend our lives and our resources," says Panksepp. "RAGE is not only activated when we are attacked and need to defend ourselves, but also in situations of frustration, when access to expected reward is thwarted, including territorial conflicts." Certainly, our rage and anger need to be channeled so we can live well with others, but anger and rage are part of our mammalian heritage. Denying our anger and rage denies a huge part of who we are.

LUST

Lust is driven by the desire for sexual satisfaction. This system energizes us to want to "get it on." The evolutionary basis for LUST is based on our need to reproduce, a need shared among all living things. Through reproduction, organisms pass on their genes, and thus contribute to the perpetuation of their species. Both males and females lust for sex (otherwise we wouldn't be here), but different experiences, different hormones, and different brain neurochemistry create different patterns in males and females.

The hypothalamus of the brain plays an important role in the LUST system, stimulating the production of the sex hormones testosterone and estrogen from the testes and ovaries. While these chemicals are often stereotyped as being "male" and "female," respectively, both play a role in men and women. As it turns out, testosterone increases libido in just about everyone, but since males have a lot more testosterone than females, male lust is more demanding and less discriminating.

CARE

The CARE or nurturance system insures that babies are cared for. CARE is the basis for what later becomes love in human beings. Brain evolution has provided safeguards to assure that parents, usually the mother, take care of offspring. Some of the chemistries of sexuality, for instance oxytocin, have been evolutionarily redeployed to mediate maternal care, nurturance, and social bonding, suggesting there is an intimate evolutionary relationship between female sexual rewards and maternal motivations. Male mammals can nurture their children, but the drive isn't as strong as it is in females.

PANIC

Mammals need parental care in order to survive. When a mammal loses connection with the nurturing parent, they are in danger of losing their lives. The PANIC system energizes the mammal to do everything it can to reconnect with the parent. "Young socially dependent animals have powerful emotional systems to solicit nurturance," says Panksepp. "They exhibit intense crying when lost, alerting caretakers to attend to their offspring."

In humans, panic attacks can be triggered by any threat of losing a needed loved one. Even as adults we feel dependent on our mates for nurturing and support. In males, the jealousy and rage we often see is related to the panic a man feels at the possibility of losing his source of nurture and care.

FEAR

When we think of our human feelings, we often associate panic and fear. But in Panksepp's research on the mammalian brain, he has demonstrated that FEAR is a separate system. "The evolved FEAR circuit helps to unconditionally protect animals from pain and destruction," says Panksepp. "FEAR leads animals to flee, whereas much weaker stimulation elicits a freezing response. Humans stimulated in these same brain regions report being engulfed by an intense free-floating anxiety that appears to have no environmental cause."

PLAY

The PLAY system is present in all mammals. This is one of the key aspects of Panksepp's research. He worked with rats and showed not only that they play, but also found that it is consistently accompanied by positive, intense social joy, signaled in the rats by making abundant high frequency chirping sounds, resembling laughter.

When animals are deprived of play, they look normal and they eat normally, they're just not as socially sophisticated. "Animals deprived of play are more liable to get into a serious fight," says Panksepp. "Play teaches them what they can do to other animals and still remain within the zone of positive relationships." For males, rough and tumble play is part of our heritage. Male mammals love to run, chase, pounce, wrestle, and play fight. Human males are no exception. Boys who grow up without a father often have difficulty with play and are more likely to respond with anger and rage in social situations.

These seven systems work together to form the basis of our emotional lives that gear all mammals to survive and thrive. When I think of these seven systems, I'm reminded of Carl Sandburg's poem, *Wilderness,* which begins: "There is a wolf in me...fangs pointed for tearing gashes . . . a red tongue for raw meat . . . and the hot lapping of blood—I keep this wolf because the wilderness gave it to me and the wilderness will not let it go."

We often try to suppress these basic emotions. Men are often taught not to express fear, panic, or care. We are taught to put a lid on our lust and suppress our anger and rage. Even play is something that we are told we need to outgrow. Sandburg reminds us that we all carry the heritage of our mammalian ancestors. I find it liberating to recognize my connection to the wild and to my animal ancestors.

The Third Chimpanzee: Coming Home to Our Place in the Animal Kingdom

After hearing about Charles Darwin and his theory of evolution, there is a story of one person's response, which probably captures the view of many at the time and perhaps more than a few people today. On hearing, one June afternoon in 1860, the suggestion that mankind was descended from the apes, the wife of the Bishop of Worcester is said to have exclaimed, "My dear, descended from the apes! Let us hope it is not true, but if it is, let us pray that it will not become generally known."

Well, we are not descended from apes, though we do share a common ancestor. The idea that we are part of the animal kingdom was repugnant to those who saw humans as being made in the image of God and whose job on earth was to subjugate the plants and animals that in their view of reality were put here for the benefit of humans.

Like the Bishop's wife, there are those today to have a difficult time believing in evolution and the fact that we are part of the animal kingdom. Yet, reconnecting with our roots is part of the journey to reconnect with ourselves. What modern science tells us is that we are very close in evolutionary history to the chimpanzees, and depending on how you classify different species, we could see ourselves as "the third chimpanzee."

Jared Diamond's book *The Third Chimpanzee: The Evolution and Future of the Human Animal,* he concludes, "A zoologist from outer space would immediately classify us as just a third species of chimpanzee, along with the pygmy chimp of Zaire [also known as bonobos] and the common chimp of the rest of tropical Africa."

Seeing ourselves as separate from the animal kingdom may help us feel special, but the price we pay is that we are cut off from our heritage. We become a rogue species, more like a cancer than one member in the community of life. Priest and cultural historian Thomas Berry warns us about our future should we continue on our present path. *"We never knew enough. Nor were we sufficiently intimate with all our cousins in the great family of the earth. Nor could we listen to the various creatures of the earth, each one telling its own story. The time has now come, however, when we will listen or we will die.* (emphasis added)"

The Hunting-Gathering Lifestyle is the Original Affluent Partnership Society

Hunting and gathering was likely the subsistence strategy employed by human societies beginning some 1.9 million years ago by *Homo erectus,* and carried on by *Homo sapiens* 300,000 years ago. We still have tribes of men and women practicing the hunting-gathering lifestyle today.

In 1966, I was in graduate school at UC Berkeley and heard about a symposium at the University of Chicago called "Man the Hunter" that was organized by anthropologists Richard Lee and Irven DeVore. It brought together for the first time, experts who had studied our hunter-gatherer heritage and a book was produced from the conference presentations two years later.

We generally refer to our early ancestors as hunter-gatherers, or gatherer-hunters, since it was the gathering activities of the women that brought in the majority of food. Yet, a broader, more comprehensive name might be "affluent partnership societies" since equality, cooperation, and abundant leisure are such key elements of hunter-gatherer societies.

Riane Eisler, author of *The Chalice and the Blade,* contrasts two models which describe societies. "The first, which I call the dominator model, is what is popularly termed either patriarchy or matriarchy—the ranking of one half of humanity over the other. The second, in which social relations are primarily based on the principle of linking rather than ranking, may best be described as the partnership model. In this model—beginning with the most fundamental difference in our species, between male and female—diversity is not equated with either inferiority or superiority.

"In the domination system, somebody has to be on top and somebody has to be on the bottom. People learn, starting in early childhood, to obey orders without question. They learn to carry a harsh voice in their heads telling them they're no good, they don't deserve love, they need to be punished."

By contrast, "the partnership system supports mutually respectful and caring relations," says Eisler. "Because there is no need to maintain rigid rankings of control, there is also no built-in need for abuse and violence. Partnership relations free our innate capacity to feel joy, to play. They enable us to grow mentally, emotionally, and spiritually." She also points out that the partnership system was prevalent through most of human history until relatively recently, around seven thousand years ago.

Eisler argues that cultures based on domination arose somewhat spontaneously, probably during a period of relative chaos. This period may have been caused by rising populations, scarcity of resources, natural disasters, or a number of other possibilities. Partnership societies, unprepared in terms of both attitude and technology, were naturally conquered, destroyed, and suppressed by dominator peoples/societies.

The Agricultural Revolution and the March to "Civilization:" History's Biggest Fraud?

Since the symposium in 1966, our modern world has continued to produce more and more "stuff." Many believe that we have created a world out of balance and we are in danger of collapse. One person who questioned our modern view of "civilization" was the biologist Jared Diamond. I was much influenced by his 1987 article, "The Worst Mistake in the History of the Human Race."

"To science we owe dramatic changes in our smug self-image. Astronomy taught us that our earth isn't the center of the universe but merely one of billions of heavenly bodies. From biology we learned that we weren't specially created by God but evolved along with millions of other species. Now archaeology is demolishing another sacred belief: that human history over the past million years has been a long tale of progress."

The modern view is that hunger-gatherers were *primitive,* leading lives that were "solitary, poor, nasty, brutish, and short," as the philosopher, Thomas Hobbes, described those who lived outside the bounds of "civilized society." Civilization, by contrast, was the crowning achievement of human progress.

"Recent discoveries suggest that the adoption of agriculture, supposedly our most decisive step toward a better life," says Diamond, "was in many ways a catastrophe from which we have never recovered. With agriculture came gross social and sexual inequality, the disease and despotism that curse our existence."

Historian Yuval Noah Harari, author of international best-seller, *Sapiens: A Brief History of Humankind,* agrees with Diamond's assessment. "Rather than heralding a new era of easy living, the Agricultural Revolution left farmers with lives generally more difficult and less satisfying than those of foragers. Hunter-gatherers spent their time in more stimulating and varied ways, and were less in danger of starvation and disease."

Dr. Harari goes on to say, "The Agricultural Revolution certainly enlarged the sum total of food at the disposal of humankind, but the extra food did not translate into a better diet or more leisure. Rather, it translated into population explosions and pampered elites. The average farmer worked harder than the average forager and got a worse diet in return."

Harari concludes, "The Agricultural Revolution was history's biggest fraud."

For most of our evolutionary history, we saw ourselves as an integral part of nature, intimately connected within the web of life. In his seminal and iconoclastic book, *Ishmael,* Daniel Quinn described two cultural stories that have been competing with each other. The old story was that all life was connected and there was no need for one species to dominate another. Quinn called those who live by this story in harmony with nature *Leavers.* With the advent of large-scale agriculture, 6,000 to 10,000 years ago, a new story was enacted by people who saw themselves as separate from nature. They imagined it was their job to dominate and control the earth for the benefit of mankind. These people Quinn called *Takers.*

The Taker story makes as much sense as one in which the brain decided it was the dominant organ in the human body and its job was to take whatever it needed from the other organs. "Hey, I'm top dog here and you other organs must serve me and only me." Of course, no real brain would ever do that, but if it did, the kidneys would fail, the lungs would become diseased, the rest of the organ systems would shut down and the organism would die.

The Taker-story is now in danger of creating lonely, disconnected, people who may bring about the end of the human race.

Males have been part of the Leaver story since the first male, single-celled, animals evolved one billion years ago, continuing through our reptilian history, and early mammals, chimpanzees, ancient humans, and our hunter-gatherer ancestors.

We are at time in human history when we need to remember our evolutionary roots as equal members in the choir of life on planet Earth. We must give up our belief that we are separate from the rest of life and the masters of the universe. It's a kind of arrogance that will kill us if we don't humble ourselves and get reconnected with the community once again.

A Vision of Our Future

I was given a vision of our future in 1993 during a sweat lodge ceremony at a men's conference. The sweat lodge is an ancient ceremony present in cultures throughout the world and is often used as a time for cleansing, prayer, and for asking for guidance or visions about the future. In the fourth round of the sweat lodge ceremony, the lodge became so hot that many of the men were forced to crawl out. I was sitting at the very back in the hottest spot. I wasn't aware of the heat because I was transported by a vision:

> We are all on a huge ocean liner. It is the Ship of Civilization. Everything that we know and have ever known is on the Ship. People are born and die. Goods and services are created, wars are fought, and elections are held. Species come into being and face extinction. The Ship steams on and on and there is no doubt that it will continue on its present course forever.
>
> There are many decks on the Ship, starting way down in the boiler room where the poorest and grimiest toil to keep the Ship going. As you ascend the decks, things get lighter and easier. The people who run the Ship have suites on the very top deck. Their job, as they see it, is to keep the Ship going and keep those on the lower decks in their proper places. Since they are at the top, they are sure that they deserve to have the best that the Ship has to offer.
>
> Everyone on the lower decks aspires to get up to the next deck and hungers to get to the very top. That's the way it is. That's the way it has always been. That's the way it will always be.
>
> However, there are a few people who realize that something very strange is happening: the Ship of Civilization is sinking. They try to warn the people, but no one believes them. The Ship cannot be sinking, and anyone who thinks so must be out of their mind. When they persist in trying to warn the people of what they are facing, those in charge of the Ship silence them and lock them up. The Ship's media keep grinding out news stories describing how wonderful the future will be.

The captains of the Ship smile and wave and promise prosperity for all. But water is beginning to seep in from below. The higher the water rises, the more frightened the people become and the more frantically they scramble to get to the upper decks. Some believe it is the end of the world and actually welcome the prospect of the destruction of life as we know it. They believe it is the fulfillment of religious prophecies. Others become more and more irritable, angry, and depressed and use alcohol, drugs, and other forms of self-medication to escape the pain.

But as the water rises, those who have been issuing the warnings can no longer be silenced. More and more escape confinement and lead the people toward the lifeboats. Though there are boats enough for all, many people are reluctant to leave the Ship of Civilization. "Things may look bad now, but surely they will get better soon," they say to each other.

Nevertheless, the Ship is sinking. Many people go over the side and are lowered down to the boats. As they descend, they are puzzled to see lettering on the side of the ship, T-I-T-A-N-I-C. When they reach the lifeboats, many are frightened and look for someone who looks like they know what to do. They'd like to ride with those people.

However, they find that each person must get in their own boat and row away from the Ship in their own direction. Though each person must row their own boat, they must stay connected to others. When everyone, each in their own boats rowing in their own direction, reaches a certain spot, a new kind of network will emerge . . . It will be the basis for a new way of life that will replace the life that was lived on the old, sinking Ship of Civilization.

Since those in charge of the Ship of Civilization do not want to have people off the ship claiming a better way of life, they do their best to silence them. They do their best to discredit dissenters. Those who seem to be attracting too many followers are killed. It is clear that those who get off the Ship must communicate in ways that don't draw attention to themselves.

I slowly came back to the present and found myself alone at the back of the Sweat Lodge. I wasn't quite sure what had happened, but the vision was clear in my mind and has remained so ever since. As a scientist, I don't usually put much store in "visions." Yet, over the years, I have come to trust the intuitive glimpses into the future that many people see. In the years since the vision, a number of people from different backgrounds have validated the essentials of what I experienced.

Daniel Quinn talks about the way forward as we move beyond civilization. In his book, *Beyond Civilization: Humanity's Next Great Adventure,* Quinn begins with a fable that describes our past and lays the foundation for our future:

"Once upon a time life evolved on a certain planet, bringing forth many different social organizations—packs, pods, flocks, troops, herds, and so on. One species whose members were unusually intelligent developed a unique social organization called a tribe: Tribalism worked well for them for millions of years, but there came a time when they decided to experiment with a new social organization (called civilization) that was hierarchal rather than tribal. Before long those at the top of the hierarchy were living in great luxury, enjoying perfect leisure and having the best of everything.

"A larger class of people below them lived very well and had nothing to complain about. But the masses living at the bottom of the hierarchy didn't like it at all. They worked and lived like pack animals, struggling just to stay alive.

"'This isn't working,' the masses said. 'The tribal way was better. We should return to that way.' But the ruler of the hierarchy told them, 'We've put that primitive life behind us forever. We can't go back to it.'

"'If we can't go back,' the masses said, 'then let's go forward—on to something different.'

"'That can't be done,' the ruler said, 'because nothing different is possible. Nothing can be *beyond* civilization. Civilization is a final, unsurpassable invention.'

"'But no invention is ever unsurpassable. The steam engine was surpassed by the gas engine. The radio was surpassed by the television. The calculator was surpassed by the computer. Why should civilization be different?'

"'I don't know *why* it's different,' the ruler said. 'It just *is*.'

"But the masses didn't believe this—and neither do I."

Bottom Line: Embracing Our Connections to Our Ancestral Past is the Hope for Our Future

One of the great myths of modern life is that evolution always moves in a positive direction and things get better and better over time. The truth is that species can and do become extinct. Civilizations also come and go. Many insist that everything is fine in our modern world, or even if not fine now, that our civilized way of life is the best that has ever been. The truth is that we are out of balance with nature and if we continue on our present path, humans will become one of the shortest-lived species that has ever lived on our planet.

We know that the deadliest aspect of modern life is our disconnection from ourselves, each other, and the natural world. We see the manifest of our disconnection with the continuing increase in anxiety, depression, and suicide, particularly among men.

In his book, *Lost Connections: Uncovering the Real Causes of Depression—and the Unexpected Solutions,* Johann Hari describes nine causes of depression including our disconnection from meaningful work, from meaningful values, from other people, and from the natural world.

Reconnecting with our billion-year history of maleness and accepting our place in the natural world is essential for our survival. As it became clear to me in the sweat-lodge vision, there is an alternative to going down with the Ship of Civilization. We can get into our lifeboats, connect with others, and form the new society that we can create beyond civilization.

Throughout human history, males have always been the explorers, the ones who left the safety of the camp to look for a better life. In these modern times, males have a unique role to play in leading our people to a new promised land, one that recognizes our deep affiliation with nature. But to do that, we must address our anger and fear of women, the subject of the next chapter.

Rule #5

Recognize Your Anger and Fear Toward Women

"If a person continues to see only giants, it means he is still looking at the world through the eyes of a child. I have a feeling that man's fear of woman comes from having first seen her as the mother, creator of men."

~Anais Nin

Growing up, I was a nice, well-behaved little boy. I was my parents' pride and joy. For years they had tried unsuccessfully to conceive. They finally went to a fertility specialist and agreed to a procedure, experimental at the time, to inject my father's sperm into my mother's womb, and it worked. But things changed when I was five years old; my father had a "nervous breakdown" and was hospitalized. My mother was forced to go outside the home to work and I was put in "nursery school" while she was away.

I became more withdrawn, but did my best to put on a "happy face" for my mother. Yet inside I was seething with anger. Periodically I would explode in rage and usually take it out on my dog, Spotty. I would choke him until I would realize what I was doing and stop. I would feel terribly guilty and tell my doggie I loved him and would never hurt him again. I'd keep my promise, until the next time.

As I got older, I began to feel increased anger towards my mother, though I rarely expressed it directly. I was always afraid my anger might cause her to leave and then I'd be all alone. When I grew up and got married, I had similar feelings towards my wife. I was loving and nice most of the time, but periodically I'd blow up. We'd fight, make up, and then fight again. Eventually, the marriage fell apart. I remarried, and the cycle started over again.

After a second divorce, I decided I would try to figure out where my anger was coming from. By then I was a successful author and psychotherapist, and I saw a lot of my clients whose male anger was undermining their relationships. I wondered if I was just picking the wrong women. Maybe my anger was justified. It usually seemed to me that the women in my life were always doing things that justified my anger.

My first wife was forever late. No matter what time she said she would meet me, she would always be late. My second wife was critical. It seemed I was always doing things that displeased her and she was cutting in her criticisms. Falling asleep after a particularly satisfying bout of lovemaking, I was awakened by her pounding my chest. "How dare you fall asleep on me," she screamed.

There were always reasons to be angry, but I also noticed that I would get angry at women for no reason at all. It just seemed there was something about women, generally, that rubbed me the wrong way. Yet, there was an equal and opposite feeling that women were wonderful and I would look up to them, lavish them with love and affection, and put them up on a pedestal. I was very confused.

My professional background is in biology and psychology. I've learned that most of the issues we face as humans are multidimensional and cross the lines of many professional disciplines. I've long believed that if we are going to understand and solve the problems we face, we need to seek out experts in many fields. That's how I came to meet David Gilmore.

I was attending an international men's conference and David was one of the speakers. I liked his topic "Manhood in the Making: Cultural Concepts of Masculinity" and bought his book of the same title. He had studied cultures all over the world and though he looked like a traditional academic with tweed jacket and short hair, he had exciting new things to say about why men are the way they are.

I reconnected with him when his book, *Misogyny: The Male Malady,* was published. I thought if anyone could give me insights into male anger toward women, David was the one. The dictionary defines misogyny as "the dislike of, contempt for, or ingrained prejudice against women." Gilmore offers a broader definition in his book:

He describes misogyny as "an unreasonable fear or hatred of women." He goes on to say that "this feeling finds social expression in the concrete behavior—in cultural institutions, in writings, in rituals, or in other observable activity."

His research is impeccable and his discoveries surprising. Gilmore explores cultures from Western Europe to the Middle East, from the jungles of South America to the remote uplands of New Guinea, from preliterate tribal peoples to modern Americans. He looks at ancient and modern cultures and all those in between. **He finds that in all places around the world, there has been a tendency for men to fear and hate women.**

I'm always interested in the personal perspective when looking at issues. We rarely get them in books written by professional scientists, and I was glad David shared some of his personal story about his interest in the topic.

He says, "Since I am a man writing a book about man's inhumanity toward woman, I feel I should explain my motives, if only by way of exculpation. Like most baby-boom males, I consider myself a tolerant and enlightened man, and I harbor sincere fondness for women as friends, lovers, colleagues, workmates, and of course, paragons of physical beauty."

That sounds like me and most men I know. He goes on to say, "However, I do recognize occasional negative stirrings in myself, feelings that certainly exist in most of my male friends whether they will admit it or not: these include impatience, peevishness, a tendency to scapegoat females, ancient, uncontrolled impulses (usually erotic), frustrations in trying to communicate, and anger over inherent differences."

These, too, resonated with my own experiences. But I was surprised and dismayed at the near universal findings of misogyny in men from cultures throughout the world and through time. Even the males in surviving hunter-gatherer cultures seem to exhibit this disturbing trait of misogyny. A quick summary of his findings, reported in his well-documented book, include the following:

- One of the last-surviving hunter-gatherer tribes live in the highlands of New Guinea in the South Pacific. "These men believe not only that women are inferior to men, but that women are also polluting to men, sexually dangerous to men's health. The men declare that women's monthly menstrual flow in particular is the most powerful and deadly poison on earth; one drop is absolutely lethal to men, boys, and male animals."

- The ancient Greeks often displayed a fierce misogyny, putting woman in the category of the God-given ills. Poets charged that women were the original source of *kakó*, or evil, in the world, which was created by the gods to torture men. The ancients populated their cosmos with she-demons and sorceresses such as Pandora, who brought all trouble into the world, and the sinister island-dwelling Circe, a witch who turned men into pigs.

- Gentle Yurok Indians of northwestern California, like the Greeks, speak of "a woman's inside," the vagina and uterus, as the doorway through which sin and social disorder entered the world.

- The Christian Bible, the Muslim Qur'an, the Hebrew Torah, and Buddhist and Hindu scriptures condemn woman, not only for her spiritual defects, but also for her body, which they deride in the crudest terms. All these great religions blame woman for the lust, licentiousness, and depravity that men are prone to, and for committing the original sin or its theological equivalent. Weak and gullible, it is Eve, like Pandora, who introduces sin and sorrow into the world.

Lest we think that misogyny is merely an unfortunate part of our past, we need only listen to the women who have come forward under the banner of the #MeToo movement to recognize that sexual violence continues to pervade the US as well as countries throughout the world.

As I report these findings, I realize I have resistance to believing them, even though the research is solidly based and facts are clear. I want to believe men are better than this. Humans are better than this. I am better than this. Clearly not all men engage in these practices, just as all men growing up in the slave-holding south were racist. But the facts do show that there is a part of the male experience throughout the world that is both fearful and angry towards women.

The Other Side of the Coin: Gynophilia and Men's Worship of Women

No men I know want to feel that they "hate women." And most of us don't. When I wrote my book, *Mr. Mean: Saving Your Relationship from the Irritable Male Syndrome,* a number of my colleagues in the men's movement wrote me off. "You're demeaning men," they told me. "It's unfair, reverse sexism." But I felt that getting at the truth is not demeaning. It can be difficult, but in the long run it helps us all.

I've learned that denying the truth just causes additional pain and suffering. Whether you are male or female reading these words, notice how you are feeling inside. What do the examples of misogyny bring up in you? Do you want to dismiss them or embrace them? Do you want to run away or go deeper?

Jamie Buckingham said, "The truth will set you free, but first it will make you miserable." Gloria Steinem voiced a similar thought when she said, "The truth will set you free, but first it will piss you off." I've often said, "The truth will set you free, but first it will kick your ass."

There's another truth that I think we need to understand and recognize. Just as there are societies, and men within societies, who both fear and denigrate women, there are also groups and individuals who view women in a very positive light. They almost worship women, feeling they are goddesses and can do no wrong. I've seen that tendency in many male clients I've seen over the years.

I was surprised to learn that David Gilmore's research was clear. The same societies that denigrate and put women down also worship and elevate them. Gilmore has a whole chapter in his book describing the opposite of misogyny which he calls "gynophilia." He says, "Like so much having to do with men and women, misogyny is only one piece of the puzzle. To be sure, many men hate and fear women, but just as many love and revere them. It is obvious that two edges of this mental sword are related in some labile fashion and share origins in the ancient touchstone of the primitive male cerebellum."

He suggests that both ends of the spectrum, hate & fear/love & reverence, drive us up and down, back and forth. They frustrate and confuse us. I would add that they can drive us crazy. Gilmore describes our human dilemma this way:

"*Woman* has the uncanny power to frustrate man's noble (but unrealistic) ideals, to subvert his lofty (hollow) ends, and to sully his (deluded) quest for spiritual perfection; but she also, and not coincidentally, provides him with the greatest pleasures of his earthly life. These pleasures are not just sexual release, but also other life-sustaining comforts that only a woman can provide (based on the organization of most societies): food, tenderness, nurturing, and heirs. It is not surprising that the men who most deplore and distrust women are the same ones who most admire, want, and need them; the most histrionic and poignant rituals of woman-adulation occur in the same societies responsible for the most egregious and sordid examples of woman-bashing."

He concludes by saying, "Like misogyny, gynophilia is a kind of male neurosis, for it stems from the same unresolved conflicts and it has both a carnal and spiritual manifestation with the usual repetitive rituals and inventive folklore."

Male Ambivalence and Our Love/Hate Obsession with Woman

One of the things I've learned over the last seventy-five years is that life is tough and a primary reason is that relationships are tough. As I've said, I was married twice and divorced twice before I met my present wife, Carlin. We've been married, now, for nearly forty years. It hasn't always been easy, even with all I have learned about how to have a great relationship.

There was a time when I wasn't sure we were going to make it. I sought out a psychotherapist and did sessions individually and together as a couple. After one of the early sessions, in a letter to the doctor, she described the roller-coaster of ups and downs that were undermining our marriage:

Dear Dr. Lacy,

The thing that is most difficult for me is Jed's rapid mood changes. He gets angry, accusing, argumentative and blaming one moment, and the next he is buying me flowers, cards and sends me loving notes with smiles and enthusiasm. He gets irritable, angry, and red in the face, demands that we talk; then he cuts me off when he judges I have said something offensive to him.

I feel like I'm living with Dr. Jekyll and Mr. Hyde. Everything seems nice and he shows me how much he loves me. Then it can change in an instant and it's like I'm living with a monster. I get frozen, feeling that no matter what I do or say, it will be "wrong" for him. At this point, he becomes competitive and I feel that he needs to win something. His intensity and the coldness in his eyes scare me at these times. I usually shut down and try to protect myself and it takes a lot of time for me to return to being loving and open with him.

When we began counseling, I acknowledged my anger, but I felt justified. In my mind, she was going out of her way to provoke me. "Who wouldn't get angry when someone hits you in the head with a two-by-four," I would scream. Carlin would look at me in surprise. "I've been nothing but loving towards you until your anger blows up on me and then I withdraw to protect myself."

But even after our successful therapy and getting our relationship back on track I observed a strange phenomenon going on inside me. At times I felt Carlin was wonderful, everything I could ever want in a partner. But then it was like a dark cloud would come over me and she seemed to change. One minute I was in bed with my friend and lover. But then, in a blink of an eye, I found myself in bed with a stranger who wanted to harm me.

It was crazy-making. I knew nothing had changed. We hadn't had a fight. She hadn't withdrawn, but it was as though a switch was thrown in my brain and instead of a goddess, I was in bed with a wicked witch. I couldn't understand what was happening. It was like those perceptual illusions I learned about in my college psychology class.

From one perspective, we see a pretty woman with a red neckband looking away from us. Then the picture "flips" and we see an old hag with red lips and a big nose. That's how it felt when my mind would flip from seeing my wife change from Ms. Wonderful to the Wicked Witch of the West.

I saw a similar pattern in many of my clients.

Here are a few of the letters I received from men and women who recognized this "love/hate" pattern in men:

Dear Dr. Diamond,
My husband and I have been married for twenty-two years and for the most part it has been wonderful. But all of a sudden, he's become mean towards me. It's like all the love is gone and he hates me. He's become more sullen, angry, and moody. Nothing I do is right. My husband used to be the most positive, upbeat, funny person I knew. Now it's like living with an angry brick! I'm totally confused. What is going on? LT

Dear Dr. Diamond,
I am forty-eight and have been married for twenty-six years. I'm noticing that I am unusually cross and nasty with my wife who I love very much. It just comes out unexpectedly before I realize it. Then it is too late. I feel like apologizing but, somehow, I never do. I can see the hurt in her eyes and I feel terribly guilty. I don't understand why I do this. Can you help me? BT

Dear Dr. Diamond,

Our marriage is in trouble. Recently, my husband has become dissatisfied with our relationship. He tells me, "I love you, but I'm not in love with you anymore." What's worse, he's became angry and blaming. He calls me names, yells at me, looks at me with such hatred, I want to disappear. He's never hit me, but I'm afraid of him. When he gets mad, he calls me a bitch and a lot worse. I love my husband with all my heart and I want to get him the help he needs. I know that he must be suffering. If he would just acknowledge the problem, I'm sure we could work things out. Can you help me get through to him? LM

Dear Dr. Diamond,

I have noticed that my relationship with my wife has begun to deteriorate. In the past, there were open displays of affection and frequent verbal affirmations. Now, I seem to be irritable all the time. My attitude seems to be "Don't come near me; don't talk to me; I had a hard day: I want the entire world to piss off." She now rarely tries to hug me, never initiates sex, and talks to me probably about half as much as she used to. It's gotten to the point where I find out what's going on in her life from my mother or sisters. We're both miserable. Can you help me? JT

Dr. Gilmore concludes that the studies show that everywhere in the world, "men's feelings toward women are contradictory, labile, bifurcated, and ambivalent." The key to understanding men's love/hate relationship with women is to better understand the nature of this primal, male ambivalence.

Gilmore recognizes that men who hate and hurt women also hate and hurt themselves. "One must also point out the tendency toward masochism in misogyny, the pain men inflict upon themselves. Rather than only hurting women, misogyny also rebounds bitterly upon its perpetrators, a common enough psychological outcome when a powerful ambivalence leads to self-doubt and self-hatred."

Getting to the Root Cause of Men's Love/Hate Ambivalence Towards Women

Whenever we see a pattern that is pervasive through time and present in cultures throughout the world, we must turn to biology and evolution to enable us to understand what is going on. The thesis of this whole book is that we can't understand why men are the way they are or how to be successful in today's world without understanding our evolutionary history of being male.

So, let's see what we can learn about the nature of maleness that can help us understand our anger and fear towards women.

1. Our billion-year male heritage evolved from females.

In Chapter 4, I talked about our billion-year old male heritage. According to Dr. Brian Swimme and Dr. Thomas Berry in their book, *The Universe Story,* prior to the evolution of sexual reproduction, cells divided into two sister cells. A billion years ago, the first male and female cells evolved. In our very origins there is, I suspect, a male fear that females can get along fine without us, that males are not really needed.

Of course, I realize that I'm writing here as though a single cell has consciousness and can make choices. I know this is a controversial way to look at things, but I do believe that there is cellular wisdom that goes way beyond what we may think of as human consciousness.

2. The essence of maleness is small.

As I described in Chapter 2, the Man Box demands that men must be big and strong. Yet, biologically, the essence of maleness is *small.* In humans, for example, the female egg is microscopic, yet it is large enough that it could contain 250,000 sperm.

How would you feel if you had to go after someone who was 250,000 times bigger than you were? I suspect there might be some fear involved.

3. Sperm compete with other sperm for access to a single egg.

Sperm counts vary from about 20 million to 100 million sperm cells per milliliter of ejaculate. Healthy guys produce from 1.5 ml to 5 ml of semen each time they ejaculate. That means there are 20 million to 100 million sperm competing with each other to merge with that single egg.

I can imagine after swimming like crazy and fighting off the competition, I want to be the first one to the egg so I can enter and claim my prize. Scientists originally thought the egg was passive and it was only the sperm that were active. However, recent research indicates the egg may be picking the sperm it allows to merge with her. Joe Nadeau, principal scientist at the Pacific Northwest Research Institute, says, "It's the gamete equivalent of choosing a partner."

So, even after competing and fending off the competition, it's the female egg that makes the final choice of which sperm is allowed to enter. In an article in *Quanta Magazine* reporting the research, staff writer Carrie Arnold says Nadeau's hypothesis is "that the egg could woo sperm with specific genes." She goes on to report that this "is part of a growing realization in biology that the egg is not the submissive, docile cell that scientists long thought it was. Instead, researchers now see the egg as an equal and active player in reproduction, adding layers of evolutionary control and selection to one of the most important processes in life."

If I were a sperm and bested millions of other competitors, I might be a little pissed off if some other sperm was chosen over me.

4. Without the influence of hormones following conception, you would stay on the path to becoming a female.

It is often said that the default setting for all mammals, including humans, is female. According to Richard Bribiescas, PhD, primary investigator in the Yale Reproductive Ecology Laboratory, "We all start as a generic embryo. You have a set of male or female sex chromosomes, but the distinction doesn't kick in until your hormones enter the picture. Without hormones like testosterone, you would stay on the path to womanhood."

All guys carry that female influence in their bodies.

Once again, our male bodies are under the influence of feminine forces. It takes a secure man to embrace all that feminine energy within us and if we fail to do so, we will be forever in conflict with ourselves and the women in our lives.

5. Males compete with other males and females choose the one they want.

Just as sperm compete with other sperm to get chosen by the magical egg, so too do males compete with other males to win the female of our dreams. Even gay males are in competition for the person they desire. But for the majority of us who are heterosexual, males are dependent on females to be chosen. We can try to be big and strong, good-looking and successful, smart and charming. Yet, the woman can still slam the door on our desires just by saying "no."

True, there are always males who won't take "no" for an answer. Females can be coerced into having sex and even raped. But there are consequences. Husbands, fathers, brothers, sons, and other relatives have always taken a dim view of a male who coerces a female into having sex. The #MeToo Movement has brought the power of a united female voice to say "no" to coerced sex.

6. Males feel engulfed by WOMAN.

Sam Keen is a philosopher and author of numerous books including *Fire in the Belly: On Being a Man*. I've known Sam for many years and believe he offers insights into why men are the way they are that can help us better understand men's hunger for women, along with our anger and fear.

"It was slow in dawning on me that WOMAN had an overwhelming influence on my life and on the lives of all the men I knew," Keen says. "I'm not talking about women, the actual flesh-and-blood creatures, but about WOMAN, those larger-than-life shadowy female figures who inhabit our imaginations, inform our emotions, and indirectly give shape to many of our actions."

If you knew Sam, who is tall, good-looking, and successful, you might be as surprised as I was when he shared the deeper truth about his life. "From all outward appearances, I was a successfully individuated man. I had set my career course early, doggedly stuck to the discipline of graduate school through many years and degrees, and by my mid-thirties was vigorously pursuing the life of a professor and writer. Like most men, I was devoting most of my energy and attention to work and profession."

I could definitely identify with Keen's early experience. My own life trajectory was similar as was "the rest of the story." Keen continues saying, "But if the text of my life was 'successful independent man,' the subtext was 'engulfed by WOMAN.' All the while I was advancing in my profession, I was engaged in an endless struggle to find the 'right' woman, to make my relationship 'work,' to create a good marriage. I agonized over sex—was I good enough? Did she 'come'? Why wasn't I always potent? What should I do about my desires for other women? The more troubled my marriage became, the harder I tried to get it right. I worked at communication, sex, and everything else until I became self-obsessed. Divorce finally broke the symbiotic mother-son, father-daughter pattern of my first marriage."

Sam's story is like my own and that of millions of men. When we are engulfed by WOMAN, we are out of touch with our true selves. We project all our hopes for a life of passion, joy, and meaning on to this or that woman, but it never works out because we are really longing for the mythical WOMAN of our dreams. Yet, we continually deny the reality and the power that this mythical female figure exerts in our lives.

"I would guess," says Keen, "that a majority of men never break free, never define manhood by weighing and testing their own experience. And the single largest reason is that we never acknowledge the primal power WOMAN wields over us. The average man spends a lifetime denying, defending against, trying to control, and reacting to the power of WOMAN. He is committed to remaining unconscious and out of touch with his own deepest feelings and experience."

It took a long time for me to understand my anger and fear of women and to begin the journey of becoming my own man. Sam's experiences and his words have helped me. "We begin to learn the mysteries unique to maleness only when we separate from WOMAN's world," says Keen. "But before we can take our leave, we must first become conscious of the ways in which we are enmeshed, incorporated, inwombed, and defined by WOMAN. Otherwise we will be controlled by what we haven't remembered."

As long as we are controlled by what we haven't remembered we will continue to hate and love women, to hunger for them and also be afraid of them, to touch them tenderly and also want to hurt them.

I took my first step in remembering in a workshop for men and women. In one of the exercises all the women sat on the floor in a big circle and the men sat in a large circle around the outside of the women's circle. The men listened while the women talked about their lives, their desire for love, and also their fears. I was amazed at the depth of the women's sharing when they were just talking to other women.

When the women had finished, they were instructed to move out and let the men create the inner circle. As the women moved to the outside the woman in front of me patted the spot on the rug where she had been sitting. It was a caring gesture, a non-verbal invitation: *Welcome, come have a seat here and share your story.* I smiled and sat where she had invited me. Immediately I moved aside. It was as though I had sat on a hotplate. She looked surprised and patted the spot again, again with no word, but the intent was clear: *It's okay, have a seat. You're safe here.* Once again, I sat where she had offered and again felt like I couldn't sit there, moved to another spot, and burst into tears.

All this happened during the thirty seconds it took for the women to move to the outer circle and the men to move to the inner circle. "Nothing" had happened. Yet, here was a guy sitting in a circle with thirty other men weeping. The leader finally noticed that "something" had happened. "So, what's going on for you?" he asked.

It took me awhile to gather my thoughts. I described the woman's kind gesture of offering me the seat she had vacated, then continued. "By sitting on the spot she had offered, I realized that I was doing something I had done all my life. I felt I was always trying to plug into the energy of a woman. I always acted strong and independent, but deep inside, I felt I didn't have any independent energy of my own. But in this instance, I knew I couldn't sit there and I moved. It was terrifying to be in a new spot, to be unplugged from the force field of the woman. I was afraid I would die. When she offered the spot again, I immediately sat there, but just couldn't do it.

"The final move to my own spot was a recognition that I have to separate myself from the force field of the woman, even if it kills me. I'm not sure if I have what it takes to be my own man, but I've got to find out. My tears are about the fear and terror I feel being all alone with myself and also tears of joy for finally making the break."

I soon realized I was not alone and that telling my truth in the company of other men was the first step toward manhood. When I looked up and saw that many of the women had tears running down their cheeks, I knew that this journey to becoming my own man was one that women were coming to understand, love, and support.

7. Throughout human history, most men lost out in the competition to be chosen.

As I pointed point in Chapter 3, men had to compete for access to females. Females choose who they want to mate with and go for the most successful males. As a result, some men win, but most men lose. Most men who ever lived did not have descendants who are alive today. Their lines were dead ends.

"The difference in reproductive success is crucially important," says social psychologist Roy Baumeister. "It provides a powerful basis for understanding why men and women act differently. For a woman, the path to success seems to have been fairly straight. There was little reason to take chances or strike out on her own. There was no reason to try to separate herself from what everyone else was doing. Play it safe, be like everyone else, and there would be sufficient chances to become pregnant. She just had to choose a good offer, such as a man who could and would provide for her and the children.

"In contrast, the average man was destined for reproductive oblivion. The option of playing it safe would have been a foolish one," says Baumeister. Most of the men would fail to reproduce, and if you failed to pass on your genes, you were a loser in the evolutionary game of life. We're descended from the guys who were successful, but we live with the fear that if we don't keep proving ourselves, we will end up on the scrap heap of oblivion.

Sneaky Fuckers, Crazy Bastards, and Incels

We know that humans aren't the only species where some males get more than 50% of the available females and many don't reproduce at all. Think of elephant seals, gorillas, and wild stallions where a few males dominate the other males and have sexual access to many females. If you're not the alpha male, you run the risk of having no sex at all. What's a male to do?

The term "sneaky fuckers" was coined by evolutionary biologist John Maynard Smith to describe subordinate males who take advantage of the opportunity to mate with females while dominant males are otherwise occupied. Recently, a team of anthropologists at UCLA led by Dan Fessler coined the term "Crazy Bastards" to describe males who engage in risky, daredevil behavior that may even put their lives at risk.

Until recently, I had never heard the term "incel." Incel stands for "involuntary celibate," a man who cannot have sex with anyone because nobody will have sex with him. The world of incels has come out of the shadows recently. Dr. Tim Squirrell is a researcher studying social interaction in online communities. "Incels have been on my radar for a while," he says, "Misogyny is easy to find on the internet, and there's no shortage of men willing to tell women that they have it worse. But while misogyny is inherently violent, the ideology incels subscribe to is almost unique in the way it makes violence seem like the only solution."

The rise of the incel culture is a good example how certain aspects of human nature can either be modified or enhanced. In recent years, we have become more aware of the large number of men, often white men in power, who feel entitled to sexually harass or abuse women. The #MeToo movement has brought these aspects of misogyny out of the closet and more and more people are saying, "No! No more rape, no more sexual harassment, no more domination and abuse."

Squirrell says incels believe that "women are hard-wired to seek out men who happen to be genetically blessed and they will never consider men who do not conform to societal standards of masculinity." Because they believe this will never change, that the birth lottery has condemned them never to be loved, many of them are extremely depressed and resigned to a life of solitude and self-loathing.

They are also extremely angry at women and in online groups they voice their rage. "In their more explicit posts," says Squirrell, "some incels dream of enslaving women and forcing them to have sex with them, and murdering the other males who have been on top for far too long. There have been a number of mass murders by men who identify with incel. Elliot Rodger, a 22-year-old from California who carried out the 2014 Isla Vista massacre, was supposedly part of the incel movement. In April, 2018, Alek Minassian was charged with ten counts of murder and fourteen counts of attempted murder after driving a van into pedestrians in Toronto. According to police, the dead and wounded were predominantly women. Minassian's Facebook post praised Elliott Rodger.

Males who are involuntary celibates have been around forever. Whether you are a low-ranking stallion, elephant seal, gorilla, or man, you run the risk of not being able to find a female who will want you. Females ultimately choose the males they want. For many males, the pain and suffering that results from feeling like a loser in the mating game can cause them to become self-loathing and hateful toward women.

Fortunately, modern humans are more monogamous than our ancestors. Most males today can find a female who will want to have sex with him. But incels remind us that there are still men who feel left out, who don't feel there are any females who will want them, who feel ashamed, immobilized, depressed, and angry. It's unlikely that there will be a movement of females who are angry because they are involuntarily celibate. Though there certainly are females who can't find a sexual partner, most females who want sex can find a willing partner.

Internet and Virtual-Reality Sex Are Keeping Males From Having Real Live Sex

One of the unexpected consequences of online pornography and virtual-reality sex is that many males are becoming increasingly unable to have real sex with a real partner. I see this increasingly with clients. Many young men, as well as older men, start off using online pornography as a temporary way to have sex, but find themselves increasingly hooked and addicted.

In the real world, finding a woman who will want to love, have sex with, and create a life together with a man takes time and energy. Even in our sexually permissive world, women are choosy and a guy has to woo a partner if he's going to be successful. But in the virtual sex world, we can have any partner we want and they will be ready, willing, and able to have sex with us 24/7. Further, the object of our desire will do anything we want, assume whatever position we want, always smile, always be nice, and never say "no."

Gary Wilson is a former anatomy and physiology teacher and an expert in the neurochemistry of addiction, mating, and bonding. In his book, *Your Brain on Porn: Internet Pornography and the Emerging Science of Addiction,* he says, "Overstimulated men report growing numb to life's subtler pleasures, such as the charms of real partners. At the same time, they can be hypersensitive to the sexual stimuli their brains associated with 'relief.' For many, the pursuit of more stimulating materials becomes mandatory to relieve the misery of feeling as if some key ingredient of their happiness is missing—and it is. Brain changes have temporarily dimmed their capacity for enjoyment."

In his famous TEDx talk, "The Great Porn Experiment," seen by more than 11 million viewers, Wilson says: "The widespread consumption of internet porn is one of the fastest-moving global experiments ever conducted." On his website, YourBrainOnPorn.com, he offers factual information to help males understand the impact of virtual-reality sex on their lives.

For the first time in human history, we are seeing widespread erectile dysfunction in young men. This has never happened before. If we understood the nature of addiction and how use of pornography can rewire the brain, we would be very concerned for our young men. And let's be honest, pornography addiction is not just a problem for young males; it impacts men of all ages.

Bottom Line: Understanding the Accepting the Truth About Our Anger and Fear Can Free Us

One of the most difficult lessons I had to learn was to accept that there was a deep-seated anger and fear of women at the center of my being. Even more difficult was to realize it was linked with an equally strong desire to place women on a pedestal and worship them. As a result, my relationships often went up and down like a roller-coaster.

I would fall head-over-heels in love, lavish the woman of my dreams with everything she could ever want, and then a rage would explode like lava from a volcano. I would do my best to hold it in, but eventually it would explode.

Getting to the root cause of this ambivalence has enabled me, and thousands of men I've worked with, to heal my own feelings of fear and rage, to get comfortable interacting with a woman, and to be able to embrace the other rules, including the next one on learning the secrets of real, lasting love.

Rule #6

Learn The Secrets of Real Lasting Love

*"Why will the work on your marriage be challenging? Not only is
the person you're married to like your parents, but the two of you are
also incompatible. It's as if there is a universal design and, mysteriously,
our incompatibility seems to be a key piece of the plan. Incompatibility
plays a crucial role in preparing you and your partner to
meet each other's needs."*

~Harville Hendrix, PhD

For a good deal of my life, I thought of love as something that was really women's business. My part of the love story was to find the right woman, fall in love, and try to convince her I was loveable in spite of being short, large-eared, big-nosed, and feeling awkward and inept around women. I thought nature would just take its course. Once I found the right partner, my one and only, my dream lover, my soul partner, I looked forward to living happily ever after.

But things didn't work out that way. After two failed marriages, I was confused and depressed and had questions that I hoped could be answered:

1. How can things start out good in a marriage and then turn bad?
2. If our first models for love are inadequate, is it really possible to have a good relationship as an adult?
3. If we're meant to find our one true love, what happens when we think we've found them and it doesn't work out?
4. How do you find the courage to try again when you've failed before?
5. What if all this "love and marriage" stuff just doesn't work in today's world? Should I just settle for finding a "friend with benefits?"
6. Is there really such thing as *real lasting love*?
7. What's getting in the way of finding my soul partner?

It's more than embarrassing to be a successful marriage and family counselor who can help others but seems to be making a mess of his own love life. After much resistance, I finally went into therapy myself, and being a reader, I went through every book I could find that might help me find some answers. It took some time, but I finally found what I was looking for and Carlin and I have been together now for nearly forty years.

Here are some of the important things steps we took on our journey that can help you:

1. Get clear about what you really want and what you won't tolerate.
I assumed that when the right person came along, I'd know it and I just had to wait for Ms. Right to appear in my life. Like in the old songs I grew up with, I'd find her *on some enchanted evening.*

I had to let go of my romantic-movie approach to love and get real. I sat down and wrote out all the things I wanted in a partner and all the things I knew I could tolerate. The list was many pages long and I won't bore you with the details, but getting clear was the first step to finding my perfect partner.

2. Make your relationship a priority.
I had a good job and loved to work. It fulfilled me and gave me my purpose in life. But I realized I had to make my relationship a priority if I was going to have one. I had to make "finding my dream partner" as important as "finding my dream job." In our stressed-out, hustle-bustle world, we often long for a relationship, but never put the time and effort into finding one or keeping it alive and well once we've found one.

3. Surface your negativity.
Before meeting Carlin, I would have said, "I want to have a partner to share my life with," but I realized I had a lot of negative baggage that got in the way of having the relationship I truly wanted. I spent time looking deeply and surfacing the negative messages I was telling myself:

- I don't want to get burned again.
- I don't have time for all this dating crap.
- The woman I want doesn't exist.
- Even if I found her, she wouldn't want me.
- I can't imagine committing to having sex with only one woman for the rest of my life.
- Marriage just doesn't work for me.
- And three more pages I won't bore you with here.

But it's important to get the negativity out where you can see it. Otherwise it stays hidden and undermines everything you do.

4. Recognize that there are many perfect partners waiting for you.

Most of us grew up with the romantic notion that there is a "one and only" just for us. It's nice to think there is a perfect soul partner just waiting for you. However, the notion has unforeseen drawbacks. It creates an underlying fear that we'll never find the right person, that needle in the haystack, who is waiting for us, but like the mythical unicorn, doesn't really exist.

It also creates a tendency to move on to someone else rather than getting to know someone well. Even when we find someone, we second guess ourselves. Maybe this isn't *the one*. I better keep looking.

The truth is, there are many potential soul mates. Don't get hung up thinking there is only one. That thinking works in romantic movies, but is deadly for finding your soul mate in real life.

5. Become aware of your distorted love filter.

Although I had a list of the qualities I wanted in a partner, I realized I also had a subconscious filter that drew me toward certain kinds of women who weren't right for me and away from others who were. I realized I was drawn to fiery women who were risk takers but were disasters to live with. My ex-wife was like that. Shortly after we met, I found that she slept with a loaded gun under her pillow. I should have run like hell. Instead, we had a passionate, crazy year together and got married even though we nearly killed each other with our fights. I also excluded women who were nice and loving, but seemed a bit boring when I first met them.

Cleaning up our filter so that we aren't subconsciously excluding partners who might be right for us and getting hooked on those who are disasters can keep you on the right track.

6. Reflect on and heal your past relationships.

We all have issues from the past that keep us from finding and holding on to our soul mate. Many of us have been married before or had serious relationships that didn't last. We all grew up in families, most of which were less than good models for soul-mate love. All our previous relationships can cause distortions that keep us from finding and keeping our soul-mates. Yet, understanding and healing our past relationships helps us find the person we're destined to be with now.

In fact, one of the hidden reasons we pick the partner we pick is to heal the wounds from the past. However, if we don't recognize how the issues from our previous relationships impacted us, including how we were influenced by our mother's and father's relationship with us and with each other, we will find ourselves looking for love in all the wrong places.

7. Recognize the evolutionary magnets that draw you to some and away from others.

Even though Carlin had all the qualities I wanted, the "chemistry" just didn't feel right. When we met, she seemed nice, but there wasn't the pizzazz I was used to having. Well, it turns out pizzazz is another name for the evolutionary-based magnets that are built into our brains to perpetuate the species, not help us find our soul mates.

First, she was five years older than I was. No big deal, my conscious mind thought, but evolution pulls us toward youth and beauty. Second, she was slightly taller than I am. Again, she scored 20 out of 20 on my list of *wants* and 0 for 10 on the *can't tolerate* list. But something just didn't feel right when we were together.

Yet, we hung in there with each other, talked about our discomforts, and soon sparks were flying and we both knew "we were the one." Both of us nearly walked away from a relationship that continues to get better through time. Don't miss out on the perfect mate because the chemistry isn't there at first.

Finding Real, Lasting Love

We all live in a world where everything is moving fast. People make quick decisions about whether someone is right for them. One of my clients, forty-six-year-old Josh, told me. "I met Cynthia at a party. We really hit it off and things went really fast. We went on a few dates and it seemed we were meant to be together. We got married a month later. But once we began living together, things started to go downhill. There were things about her that I didn't know. She had been abused as a child but had never dealt with the trauma and it totally messed up our sex life. She wouldn't go to therapy and we eventually broke up."

If Josh had gone slower, followed my seven-step approach, he would have likely found out more about Cynthia before getting married. He could have helped her get the help she needed or recognized that she wasn't the one.

These seven steps also can help a couple who are already together. I suggested them to Robert and Sue after they had been together for eighteen years and wanted to revitalize their relationship. "It really worked," Robert told me. "At first I thought your suggestion of going back to earlier stages and imagining that we were meeting for the first time was crazy. But you were right, it actually helped us get back in touch with the romance that we had lost touch with over the years."

I've found these seven practices helpful for those just starting out with a new relationship as well as those who have been together and want to revitalize a long-term marriage.

Practice 1: Acquaintanceship

The practice of *acquaintanceship* allows us to recognize that each person we meet is a gift from the universe. We see each person as a jewel to be appreciated without thought of whether they would be useful to us, or if they are marriage material, or might be good in bed. Instead of screening out everyone except those few we think have "potential," we enjoy each person we meet simply because they are a fellow human being.

I had a friend in college named Jeannie. She had the capacity to see everyone she met as a wonder. When you were in Jeannie's presence, you felt like you were special and Jeannie was overjoyed to be with you. Everyone she encountered felt bathed in the light of her attention. I still have memories of that gift of true acquaintanceship and try to practice it in my life.

Practice 2: Companionship

Companionship is about doing what you love to do in the presence of another person. Clients often tell me they go to places to meet people. Yet when I ask them if they enjoy the places they go and things they do, they acknowledge that they don't. "I hate going to bars," one woman told me, "but that's where I have to go to meet people." I suggest people do things they love and meet people there. It might be a book club, bird watching, or motorcycle racing. As long as you really enjoy it and there are other people there, you can begin practicing companionship.

If you want to see someone who truly understands companionship, watch a three-year-old playing in the sandbox with other children. The child is ecstatic to be alive, to be playing in the sand, and to be with other children having fun together. Take one child out and replace him with another and that's fine.

When we fully engage companionship, we are fully present in the moment, enjoying doing what we love surrounded by others who are doing the same. Companionship allows us the joy of playful connection.

Companionship, like the other steps in the process, offers a double benefit. We get to enjoy each step for itself. If things don't progress further, we still have the joy of having had fun with other people doing something we love to do. Second, we get to know people before we open bodies, hearts, and souls.

Enjoying each practice before jumping ahead gives us time to reflect and see if it's a person we want to go to the next stage with. Some people just enjoy having a companion, without having to go further in the relationship. Those in a long-term relationship can get back to the simple joy of finding fun things to do together.

Practice 3: Friendship

The practice of *friendship* combines being and doing. It is an interaction between two people who want to practice being themselves by doing things together with a partner. Where companionship can be done with a number of partners, the stage of friendship comes in pairs. It taps into the "power of two."

Friendship develops as we learn more about the other person and find out what we have in common. We get to know them. We learn what they like, what books they have read, what's important in their lives, and who are the people that are important to them.

We often think of friendship as a process of doing for the other person or having them do for us. It is really a process of getting to know another person and caring about what they are feeling. In friendship, we draw each other out. We care about who they are and how they are feeling and share more and more about who we are and what emotions are present in us.

Practice 4: Intimate Friendship

The practice of *intimate friendship* involves exploring the underworld. We begin to recognize in the other person things about ourselves we don't see or don't like. We may be drawn to another's warmth and ease, thinking we are more stiff and awkward. In truth we often see in the other person qualities that are there in us, but haven't been developed. We also begin to see things about the other person we don't like, which are often qualities that we don't like in ourselves.

The practice of intimate friendship allows us to reclaim lost parts of ourselves—to re-own our rage, terror, guilt, shame, and also to reclaim our ability to appreciate, accept, nurture, and love ourselves. Intimate friendship is about learning to love, heal, and accept the parts of ourselves that we have rejected.

This can be a time of deep connection. It can also feel very uncomfortable. Many people bail out at this stage. I encourage people to hang in there and go deeper. The stage of intimate friendship holds up a mirror to each other showing us what has been hidden and forbidden.

Practice 5: Sensual Friendship

The practice of *sensual friendship* involves touching. Most of us are touch deprived. We never got enough touching as infants, children, adolescents, and adults. Many of us rush into sex looking for the skin contact we never got.

Sensual friendship does not have to become a prelude to sex. It can be its own dance. In it, we relearn to hold hands and rekindle the heat of touching someone we have gotten to know. We return to the innocence of young love, where a touch of fingers or caress on the cheek could send us into paroxysms of pleasure.

To learn sensual friendship, we have to practice touching ourselves. Most of us rarely touch ourselves except when we are being sexual or when we are checking out our flaws.

In the stage of sensual friendship, we touch ourselves and our partner simply for the pleasure that we receive and give. Like all the practices, sensual friendship can lead to the next stage, but don't be in a hurry. Like a wonderful meal, savor the delights of each course. Many of us grew up in homes where there wasn't enough caring hugs and embraces. We need to learn to become more comfortable touching and being touched.

Practice 6: Sexual-Creative Love

The practice of *sexual-creative love* recognizes that the purpose of sex is pleasure, creation, and bonding. As we have done with so much else in modern society, we have reduced the process of sexuality down to the momentary pleasure we experience in the orgasm.

For two million years of human history, we sought out sexual partners not just for pleasure, but also to create children and develop the bond necessary to nurture and raise the children.

Those needs have not changed. Though we may not wish to create children each time we make love, the practice of becoming sexual-creative lovers recognizes that creation is always involved in lovemaking. Each act of love creates a bond with our partner and has the potential to create new life—whether the life is child, a poem, a dance, or an affirmation of the rebirth of the spirit.

Practice 7: Spiritual Life Partners

The practice of *spiritual life partners* recognizes that we cannot truly commit to be with a partner for the rest of our lives until we have gone through the other stages. It knows that the goal of spiritual life partnership is not only pleasure and happiness, but the spiritual development of both partners in the relationship, and the growth of the partnership itself.

In this practice we develop the security of knowing that the partnership is being held in the embrace of a spiritual essence. There may be many people we could be joyfully partnered with, but once we commit to this person, we are committed to being partners in bringing out the best in our mate, helping them heal and grow.

We also accept that the idea of making a lifelong commitment to someone is not always realistic. The world is changing rapidly, and so are we. The person we were when we first married is a different person than who we are ten or fifteen years later.

Carlin and I recognized early on that we would change through time, and vows we had made when we first married wouldn't necessarily be appropriate for the people we have become. As a result, we review our marriage every fifteen years. We decide anew whether we want to continue. So, far, we've been married three times (to each other). We're due for our next remarriage in 2025. We'll keep you posted.

Understanding the Reality of the Male-Female Dynamic in Creating Real Lasting Love

In our first remarriage ceremony, Carlin and I were in a workshop with the anthropologist Angeles Arrien and Native American elder Brooke Medicine Eagle. They created a wonderful ceremony, including a celebration of the male and female principles. Arrien described two universal organizing principles: The Dynamic and the Magnetic.

The Dynamic, she said, has to do with the capacity to initiate, expand, and move out. In Jungian psychology, it is associated with the Animus, in Asian philosophy with Yang, in Shamanic cultures with the energy of the Sun. It expresses the "seeker" part of ourselves.

Magnetic energy has to do with drawing in, receiving, opening, and deepening. In Jungian psychology it is associated with the Anima, in Asian philosophy with Yin, and in shamanic cultures, magnetism is associated with the energy of the Moon. Like the ocean waves that alternately crash on the shore and are drawn back out to sea, the dynamic and magnetic are two forces that continually interplay in our lives.

There are four universal dynamic functions and four universal magnetic functions that both men and women must develop. According to Arrien, 95% of cultures around the world agree on the following functions.

The four dynamic functions are:

1. Words, language, and logic.
2. Systems, deeds, productivity, and bringing into form.
3. Leadership and power.
4. Exploring the meaning of life.

The four magnetic functions are:

1. Vision, intuition, and perception.
2. Beauty, nurture, care, and healing.
3. Honoring the sacred through ritual and ceremony.
4. Incubating, reflecting, and exploring the meaning of relationships.

As Angeles Arrien reminded us, we all have a mixture of Dynamic and Magnetic functions and we can develop those aspects we may lack. Still, there are limits to how much we can change. Men and women are different, but not always in the simplistic ways a sexist society would have us believe.

90% of men express more Dynamic than Magnetic qualities and most women express predominantly Magnetic qualities. For most men, the Dynamic is Core. For most women, the Magnetic is Core. Here's how it works. If you have a male-type brain, the foundation of your manhood must rest on the dynamic, you feel at home in the world of structure and logic. You are drawn toward systems, understanding them and leading them. Developing your Dynamic functions is soul work for you.

Once you feel solid in owning and appreciating your Dynamic functions you can develop the Magnetic. You will be drawn to expressing your intuition more, expressing beauty in the world, honoring the sacred, and so on. This shift often happens at mid-life, as our testosterone drops.

I think of my friend John, who was the elder in our men's group, before he died.

Through most of his life he had been highly effective in developing his Dynamic functions. As a young man, he served as a Navy officer on a submarine. After the war, he went back to school in Chicago and was involved in local politics. He later moved to California and served for twelve years at CORO Foundation, teaching leadership skills.

At the height of his career, he became Director of Community Relations at The Rossmoor Retirement Community in Walnut Creek for nineteen years. I remember visiting at Rossmoor where he was so well known by the 10,000 residents, it was like walking with the mayor of the city.

But when John retired, he actively developed his Magnetic side. He became very interested in art and bought beautiful paintings, but also created his own original collage art. He became a mentor to younger men and would often meet them at local coffee houses and listen to their troubles and hear the stories of their lives. As he got older in the group, he would spend more time reflecting, meditating, and enjoying the camaraderie and relationships in the group.

Men and women have mixture of Dynamic and Magnetic brain functions. "The male and female brains occur on a gender continuum," says Michael Gurian, author of *Saving Our Sons: A New Path for Raising Healthy and Resilient Boys.* "Some males and females are more 'extreme male' or 'extreme female' and some male/female brains, when scanned, look somewhat more like the other gender's brain—I call these 'bridge brains' because they bridge the genders."

I have a bridge brain. Guys like us have brains that are more similar to the typical female brain. We empathize easily. We are intuitive, receptive, and nurturing. Many of us go into the healing arts. Until I reached a point in my own personal development where I could accept the Magnetic side of my life, I always felt unmanly. As a young man, I tried to become strong, powerful, dynamic, and driving, But I never seemed to be able to pull it off.

It was only when I accepted the Magnetic qualities as my soul work that I began to thrive. But as I approached midlife, I realized I needed to embrace more of the Dynamic side. I began travelling more and speaking at conferences all over the world. I developed new theories and practices in gender medicine and men's health. I went back to school and got a PhD in International Health. I spent more time with guys and played football with my children and grandchildren.

I found my relationship with my wife improved greatly when we each balanced our Dynamic and Magnetic sides, the Yang and the Yin, the Sun and the Moon. The sacred marriage of Dynamic and Magnetic must occur within each person. Our soul work comes first as we embrace either the Dynamic or Magnetic sides of our personality. For 90% of men, the Dynamic is our soul work. For the 10% who are like me, the Magnetic becomes our soul work.

We need both the Dynamic and Magnetic functions to be fully ourselves. We often seek the qualities of the other in a partner. Whether we are gay or hetero, we tend to look for the other quality in our partner. I'm very Yin, my wife is very Yang. I know many gay and lesbian couples. It's usually pretty clear which of the pair is predominantly Dynamic or predominantly Magnetic.

The Five Stages of Love and Why Too Many Relationships End at Stage Three

Joseph Campbell said this about the Hero's Journey: "You enter the forest at the darkest point, where there is no path. Where there is a way or path, it is someone else's path. You are not on your own path." If you follow someone else's way, you are not going to realize your potential. The journey toward real, lasting love is unique to each person. We can be guided, but ultimately the path is ours alone.

Currently our culture focuses a great deal of attention on finding the right partner. There are hundreds of websites that will help you find Mr. or Ms. Right. But there's much less focus on our internal love map. If our map is wrong, we're not likely to find a partner. Further, as difficult as it is to find a good mate, that turns out to be the easy part. Much more difficult is to make a good marriage that lasts and enhances the well-being of the couple.

Sharing the 5 stages of love and marriage and some of what I have learned will help you find your own, unique path to joy. Here are the stages:

Stage 1: Falling in Love
Stage 2: Becoming a Couple
Stage 3: Disillusionment
Stage 4: Creating Real, Lasting Love
Stage 5: Finding Your Calling as a Couple

Stage 1: Falling in Love is Nature's Trick to Get Us Paired Up

We all remember falling in love, that topsy-turvy feeling of total focus on another. We think about them all the time. We are bereft when they are out of our sight. We are happy for no reason when we are together. We want them body and soul. But what causes us to fall in love?

Here's a thought experiment that can teach us a lot. Imagine the implication of this simple truth: None of your direct ancestors died childless. We know your parents had at least one child. We also know your grandparents had at least one child. You can trace your ancestry back and back and back. You may or may not have children, and you certainly know people who will never have children. But all your ancestors did.

How did they do that? Well, they *fell in love* or at least they *fell in lust*, which often accompanies falling in love. It feels so good because all those hormones are triggered: testosterone, estrogen, dopamine, and many others.

Falling in love also feels so great because we project all our hopes and dreams on our lover. We imagine that they will fulfill our desires, give us all the things we didn't get as children, deliver on all the promises our earlier relationships failed to fulfill. We are sure we will remain *in love* forever. And because we are besotted with "love hormones," we're not aware of any of this.

Helen Fisher, PhD, is a world-renowned scientist who has researched the reasons we fall in love and why we fall in love with that special person. She is a biological anthropologist, a Senior Research Fellow at The Kinsey Institute, and Chief Scientific Advisor to the internet dating site Chemistry.com. She says that falling in love is much more than a feeling. "Romantic love," she says, "is a mammalian brain system for mate choice." It's nature's trick to get us paired up. It involves two brain/hormonal systems: lust and attraction.

Lust is a strong desire to have sexual intercourse and is driven, in both men and women, by the hormones testosterone and estrogen. When we are attracted, we lock into that special person and are truly love-struck and can think of little else. Scientists think that three main neurotransmitters are involved in this stage: adrenaline, dopamine, and serotonin.

Falling in love activates our stress response, increasing our blood levels of adrenalin and cortisol. This causes our hearts to race, our mouths to go dry, and we sweat when we are in the presence of our loved one. When Fisher scanned the brains of the "love-struck" couples, she found high levels of the neurotransmitter dopamine. This chemical stimulates "desire and reward" by triggering intense rushes of pleasure. It has a similar effect to taking cocaine. Serotonin is responsive for the lovely preoccupation and focus we have on our partner.

But here's something few people know. Although that wonderful feeling of "falling in love" doesn't go on continually forever, it does not fade away, never to return. Dr. Fisher told me, **"Romantic love is like a sleeping cat. It can be re-awakened at any time."** It may get lost, but it can return again in Stage 4. That's certainly what Carlin and I found.

It's understandable that we all have strongly positive memories of this stage of our relationship. But too many of us want to stay in this phase and feel we've lost something when the hormonally driven feelings of lust and attraction begin to wane. Further, as we hit Stage 3, "Disillusionment," many couples break apart and feel there is something wrong with their marriage. "I love you, but I'm not *in love* with you anymore," becomes a constant refrain. As a result, too many men and women leave the relationship before reaching Stages 4 and 5.

Stage 2: Becoming a Couple and Building a Family

This is the stage where the power of two becomes apparent. This is a time when we may have children and raise them. If don't have children, it's the time when our couple-bond deepens and develops. It's a time of togetherness and joy. We learn what the other person likes and we expand our individual lives to begin developing a life of "the two of us."

Once again, our hormonal and brain functions work together to enable us to connect more deeply with each other. Oxytocin, also known as "the cuddle hormone" and "the moral molecule," deepens the feeling of attachment and contributes to that loving feeling that we desire so strongly. Oxytocin is released by men and women during orgasm and also when they snuggle, touch, and look deeply into each other's eyes. The original purpose of oxytocin was likely to bond the mother to the baby, but like all hormones it has multiple effects in the body. The same loving feeling that bonds a mother and father to their baby girl or boy is present when we bond to our mate.

Another, hormone, vasopressin, also contributes to the attachment and bonding process. The power of this important hormone was recognized by biologists studying a small rodent called a vole. Prairie voles engage in far more sex than is strictly necessary for reproductive purposes. Like humans, they also form fairly stable pair-bonds. However, when male prairie voles were given a drug that blocks the effect of vasopressin, the bond with their partner deteriorated and they lost their devotion to their partner.

During this phase, we experience less of the falling head-over heels "in love" feelings. There is more of the feeling of deep affection for our partner. We feel warm and cuddly. The sex may not be as wild, but it's deeply bonding. We feel safe, cared for, cherished, and appreciated. We feel close and protected. We often think this is the ultimate level of love and we expect it to go on forever. We are often blind-sided by the turn-around that happens at Stage 3.

Stage 3: Disillusionment: The Stage We Never Saw Coming

No one told us about Stage 3 in understanding love and marriage. Stage 3 is where my first two marriages collapsed. For too many relationships, this is the beginning of the end. We all recognize Stage 1 when we first fall in love, and most of us are familiar with Stage 2 when we start a family or settle into a warm, loving, committed relationship. We think that this is all there is to a good marriage.

I knew marriage had its ups and downs, but I thought that once I found the right partner, it would be pretty easy to solve problems. I pictured us working together to figure out how to decorate our home, decide on a diaper service, split up parental duties as the children got older. I imagined that all the problems would be "out there" in the world.

It never dawned on me until we were deeply embroiled in conflict with each other that the most difficult problems seemed to be with my spouse, not with the outside world. Little by little, things changed at home. Our once happy household gradually filled with tension. We made love less often, but justified it because we were stressed trying to make a living while taking care of small children. We become more irritable with each other.

Most of us accept the reality that a marriage will have its ups and down, but few of us understand that there is an actual stage in marriage where we will feel disconnected and estranged from each other, where we will feel we're living with a stranger and wonder who stole the loving partner we thought we had married. Since we're not aware of this stage or the stage beyond it, we believe that these bad times must mean that the marriage is not working. Too many people give up at this stage. They either leave the marriage or come to believe that this is the best they can hope for and accept a marriage of convenience rather than one of passion, joy, and continual growth.

The Deeper Purpose of Stage 3

I finally took stock of my life and decided I had to figure out this love thing. By the time I met my present wife, Carlin, we both had been married twice before and we both had done a lot of work figuring out the true nature of love.

Carlin and I went through the wonderful times of falling in love, merging our families, and building a life together. But when we started to have problems and became disillusioned, we were more prepared to deal with it. We hit Stage 3 after we were together for ten years. We hung in there and went deeper.

The first purpose of Stage 3, Disillusionment, is to recognize and let go of our illusions of who the other person is and how they are supposed to act. Most of us have a fairy-tale view of love and marriage. Stage 3's job is to strip away the veil of illusion so we can see ourselves and our partner as human beings, not cut-out projections. It forces us to recognize the expectations that we have of ourselves and our partner and forces us to come home to the messy reality of living with a real person who has his or her own needs, hopes, hang-ups, and hurts.

Here are some of our illusions which we became aware of and released:

- If you are with the right person, marriage should be easy.
- If there are unresolved conflicts, something must be wrong with the marriage.
- If there is conflict in the marriage, someone must be to blame.
- A good marriage means that our love is constant and unwavering.
- If you really loved me, you should _____.

We each had our own set of fill-in-blank *shoulds*:

- You should never have fantasies of being with another.
- You should always know what I need.

- You should always be kind and gentle.
- You should never be involved with other things that may conflict with the time I believe should be for me.

The second purpose of Stage 3 is to help us uncover and heal our childhood wounds. Most of the conflict we experience during this stage that we attribute to our partner is actually linked to childhood wounding. We often have forgotten the trauma from childhood and don't recognize the connection with our adult conflicts. Stage 3 forces us to address our early family history.

Marriage experts Harville Hendrix and his wife Helen LaKelly Hunt say, "Since partnership is designed to resurface feelings from childhood, it means that most of the upset that gets triggered in us during our relationship is from our past." After working with couples for more than forty years Hendrix and Hunt have concluded, "About 90% of the frustrations your partner has with you are really about *their* issues from childhood. That means only 10% or so is about each of you right now."

Understanding that our present conflict will help us recognize what we need to heal from the past and our past traumas will help us know what we have to deal with in our present relationship. Even so, going through Stage 3 is always difficult. Sometimes it feels like we are going through hell. It helps to remember this bit of wisdom attributed to Winston Churchill: **"If you're going through hell, keep going."**

Of course, part of the hell is feeling we've been cheated. It isn't supposed to be like this. This is one of the illusions we need to release. It *is* supposed to be like this. To have a real relationship, we have to deal with the realities of the other person and come to peace with who they really are. It took a long time to realize that the feelings of stress, conflict, and disappointment did not mean we had chosen the wrong partner, but in fact, meant that we had chosen just the right person with whom we could deepen our experience of love.

I remember meeting the legendary psychologist and therapist, Carl Rogers, when he gave a talk about love and marriage. He was in his eighties then, and he and his wife had been married more than sixty years. My first wife and I had been together for less than a year and were anxious to hear the great man's wisdom about love and life.

At one point in his talk he turned to his wife, Helen. "Remember that stretch when things were so bad in our relationship?" She smiled and nodded her head. I was amazed to hear that my idol had problems in his relationship. But I was dumbfounded to hear what came next. "There was that bad patch of nine or ten years when things were awful." Helen smiled and shook her head as she too remembered. "But we hung in there and worked things out."

You must be kidding, I thought, Nine or ten years of things being awful? I couldn't imagine things ever being awful for me and my wife and if they ever were, I sure couldn't imagine staying in a *state of awful* for nine or ten years.

Now, having been married to Carlin for thirty-nine years, I understand that there

pull over

can be some pretty difficult times that can last a long time. But getting through those times together is how we learn about real, lasting love. The key to getting through to the other side is understand the twin purposes of Stage 3.

Once we recognize that the conflicts of Stage 3 don't mean we've chosen the wrong person or that we've grown apart but that we're ready to go deeper, our attitude changes. We understand that Stage 3 helps us begin to accept ourselves and our partner as real beings, not projections of all our childhood hopes and dreams. We also learn that we must heal our childhood wounds in order to come to peace with our parents and other members of our family as well as to move on to the next stage of love and marriage.

Stage 4: Real Lasting Love

The gift of Stage 4 is that we can quit trying so hard to live up to the expectations of society and of our partner. We can begin to relax and be ourselves. We all want to be loved for who we are, but until we recognize that we have been trying to please others rather than accepting ourselves fully, we remain uneasy. The longer we're in a relationship, the more we have to lose and the more we feel we have to keep up the façade.

Until we hit Stage 3, we're often not even aware we are wearing a mask. We become so invested in trying to be what we think our partner wants us to be, we lose ourselves. Stage 3 gives us the opportunity to come home to ourselves.

When Carlin and I got through Stage 3 and moved into Sage 4, everything changed. She accepted that she had been depressed for many years and got help. After gentle pressure from her, I went to see a doctor and got evaluated. My anger and mood swings were diagnosed as bipolar disorder and I took medications and worked with a psychiatrist to heal the wounds from my childhood.

We began to laugh and have more fun. We did something I thought was impossible. We fell in love again. I had thought that the "falling in love" phase only happened at the beginning and couldn't last. I learned I was wrong. Well, in a way I was right. Falling in love occurs at the beginning of a new relationship. Entering Stage 4, for us, was a new beginning. Many other couples learn the same thing.

Stage 5: Finding Your Calling as a Couple

I always thought that finding my calling was a personal pursuit. It never occurred to me that couples could have their own calling in life. This came to me when my wife challenged me to write this book and offered direct support for the process. She recognized that my life-calling has to do with helping men, but that I was reluctant to fully engage that calling because I didn't want to displease women.

I worried that if I focused on helping men, women would feel left out. Carlin helped me see that the best thing I can do to help women is to help the men in their

pull 2 ll over

lives, since men often need extra support and guidance from caring male elders.

I believe that couples are stronger when they have a shared passion outside of their personal careers and raising their families. It doesn't have to be a passion that they both share equally. Carlin recognizes that my work has been with men. Supporting me to help others has become our joint calling. I also have helped support her in her calling to reach out in our community. She organized community events and townhall meetings to address the myriad of issues a community faces. I helped in a supportive role.

We're at a time in human history where conflict is tearing us apart. Countries fight other countries, political parties fight their counterparts. The left and the right do battle for the hearts and minds of the citizens. Men and women fight each other and end up frightened and frustrated. Going through all five stages and learning to heal our love relationships can be a model of how we can heal and address all our major problems, from global climate change and depletion of resources, to drug addiction and violence.

I call the 5 Stages of Love a graduate program in the most important subject we will ever learn—how to love. The full journey is a rite of passage. We all need rites of passage to help us make important transitions in our lives.

Bottom Line: The Journey Finding Real Lasting Love is Not For the Faint of Heart

Too often we view our past relationships as failures. Yet, they force us to ask questions that are important for us to answer in order to move ahead with our lives. They can give us a framework to guide our further journeys to finding the love we long to have. The seven practices take us from Acquaintanceship to Spiritual Life Partnership and are helpful when exploring a new relationship or revitalizing an existing one.

Balancing the Dynamic and Magnetic functions in our lives helps us to fully embrace our unique male spirit and understanding the five stages of love shows us how to understand how Stage 3, Disillusionment is the critically important bridge between Stages 1 and 2, Falling in Love and Becoming a Couple, and Stages 3 and 4, Creating Real, Lasting Love and Finding Your Calling as a Couple.

Rule #7

Undergo Meaningful Rites of Passage
From Youth to Adulthood and
From Adulthood to Super Adulthood

*"If you don't initiate the young, they will burn down
the village to feel the heat."*

~African Proverb

Like me, millions of males have grown up in a home where our fathers were distant, absent, rejecting, or dominating. We also live in a culture where there is little guidance for males about what it means to be a man. Through most of human history, there were *rites of passage* created by the elders in the community that would guide us through the major transitions in our lives. But increasingly, meaningful rites of passage are missing from modern society.

A rite of passage is a ceremony and marks the transition from one phase of life to another. Although it is often used to describe the transition from adolescence to adulthood, it applies to any of life's transitions such as marriage, birth, beginnings, endings, and eventually, death.

Anthropologist and folklorist Arnold van Gennep first coined the phrase "rites of passage" in 1909. Interestingly, van Gennep grew up without a father in the home. All of us hunger for the guidance that comes going through meaningful rituals as we move through important stages of our lives.

Filmmaker Frederick Marx has spent his professional career exploring and documenting rites of passage. His most well-known film, *Hoop Dreams,* documented the story of two African-American high school students in Chicago and their dream of becoming professional basketball players. His new film, *Rites of Passage,* tells an inspirational story showing people exactly why ritually guided rites of passage and mentorship are necessary for all young people.

Marx says, "An estimated $500 billion is spent yearly on teen dysfunctions in the US: drug and alcohol abuse, teen pregnancy and STDs, school dropouts and expulsions, gang and property crimes, traffic accidents, ADD, ADHD, depression and violence."

Robert Bly wrote about the need for male initiation and mentoring in his book, *Iron John: A Book About Men*. "There is male initiation, female initiation, and human initiation. I'm talking here about male initiation," says Bly. "The grief in men has been increasing steadily since the start of the Industrial Revolution and the grief has reached a depth now that cannot be ignored."

Traditionally, rites of passage that helped young males transition from boyhood to manhood were initiated by the fathers and other male elders. Yet, increasingly we are living in a society with absent fathers. A number of organizations have come forward recently to provide ritual initiations for males.

The ManKind Project: A Modern-Day Male Initiation and Support Network

Bill Kauth is the co-founder of the ManKind Project. It offers one of the most powerful rites of passage programs I've ever experienced. I first met Bill Kauth in 1980 at a conference that had emerged from the consciousness of the women's movement. I immediately felt I was with a kindred spirit. We were both impressed with the positive energy of women coming together to break out of the old restrictions that society had placed on them. It felt good to support women, but we also recognized that men needed to find their own support and break free from their own restrictions.

As we talked, we realized we had a lot in common. We both had been trained as psychotherapists. We were both born the same year (1943) and both had complex relationships with our fathers. In similar ways, our "father issues" set us on a path to follow our own calling, which drew us to working with men. I talked about what I was learning in my men's group that had started in 1979 and he talked about his desire to create a way for men to come together to support each other in combining spirit and soul work and to find their own path to authentic manhood.

I still remember my own introduction to the New Warrior weekend. It was 1991, twelve years after my men's group began. We joked that we felt like "an old married couple." We knew each other well, felt safe and comfortable, enjoyed ourselves immensely, but were growing a bit bored with our time together. We decided to attend the New Warrior Weekend. Although it's impossible to describe any kind of ritual initiation because the real value is in the experience, here are some of the things I learned:

1. Being with other men in this well-crafted weekend experience was transformative. I felt a host of feelings: Anxiety, confusion, exhilaration, joy, and

true brotherly love. By the end, I felt more myself, more deeply connected to others, and with tools that I could use to be more successful in life.

2. I broke through my "Mr. Nice Guy" image to share a lot of my woundedness and anger. I found that my anger didn't destroy people. In fact, it was appreciated, and there was a group of supportive men to help me guide my anger and who taught me ways of expressing it that would help, rather than harm, myself and others.

3. Most of my life I felt like the Lone Ranger figuring things out on my own, doing what needed to be done by myself, solving my own problems. I thought being stoic, independent, and self-sufficient was what it meant to be a man. During the weekend, I learned to be part of a team, to work together in support of shared goals, and found that success was sweeter and more lasting when achieved together.

4. I got in touch with one of the primal emotional wounds I experienced in childhood that had never been dealt with, talked about, or healed. When I was seven or eight years old, I had a best friend named Woodrow. Everyone called him Woody and he lived a few houses down from mine. There was a stream three blocks away where we played in the summer. In the winter it became a raging river. Woody and three friends wanted me to come play by the river one day when it was still at its peak of wildness. I couldn't go and they went without me. Later that day I learned that Woody had fallen in and drowned. I was heartbroken and felt guilty that I hadn't been there. Maybe I could have saved him, I thought. It colored my whole life. I forever felt guilty, afraid to let myself get close to others, for fear they would die.

During the weekend, I confronted my loss for the first time and was helped to let go of my guilt and let down the barriers I had erected to protect me from the pain of his loss.

5. Although I had been doing men's work for some time, had counseled thousands of men and their families, and had been in a men's group, I had never before gotten in touch with my life purpose. During the weekend, I was able to do so and I still have the handwritten affirmation I had written. "My life purpose is to awaken the masculine soul to help men and the women who love them."

6. A weekend experience, no matter how powerful, is never enough to lay the foundation for real change once we are back in the real world—back to the stresses of life, the commitments we have to family and friends, the bills

that must be paid, the anxieties, fears, and worries we must handle, the decisions that must be made. After the weekend ended, we all joined a six-week "Integration Group" where we could learn specific techniques and practices to keep what we'd learned alive.

The Sterling Institute of Relationship: What It Means to Be Male and Female in Today's World

I first heard about the "Sterling Men's Weekend" from Howard LaGarde, a man I met at the wedding of a mutual friend. I had already experienced the ManKind Project's men's weekend and didn't think I needed another men's experience. However, I hit it off with Howard and wanted to learn more.

The Institute was started by A. Justin Sterling in 1979, but its origins go back further to his work with professional women. "I had a professional relationship with a director of a women's organization that counseled women about how to be successful in their career," said Sterling. "We began to see a correlation between women's ability to be successful in their careers and their inability to be successful in their personal relationships."

The organization referred women to Sterling, and he was successful helping them improve their love lives. He began doing seminars for women that focused helping women embrace the core of their female power and recognizing that there were real differences between men and women that needed to be accepted.

After offering Women's Weekends for some time, he found that the women wanted something for the men, and Sterling developed a Men's Weekend to complement the Women's Weekend.

Sterling's programs drew large groups of women and men to their weekends, but they were controversial at the time. Back in 1979, the popular view in the culture was that looking at male/female differences was just another way to "keep women in their place" and another way in which the patriarchy attempts to keep women down.

It has only been in recent years that sex differences have been recognized and accepted. We now recognize that males and females can be different without one sex dominating the other. We're now willing to address the anger so many men experience towards women, and to take an honest look at how we may have harmed the women in our lives.

I found Sterling's Men's Weekend quite different from my ManKind experience, but also found it powerful and helpful. Here are some of the things I learned:

Men have a lot of hostility toward women, some of it overt, but much of it hidden.

I thought I was one of the enlightened males who loved women, knew they were the equal of men, and believed that I had resolved all my "issues" with my mother, my first wife, my second wife, and my current wife. During the weekend I got in touch with a lot of the hidden anger I still carried and was able to express it and heal it in an atmosphere of support.

I could appreciate the gift of maleness.

When I celebrated the gifts of maleness in a group of 250 men, I felt joyful and powerful. Not the kind of power that wants to prove I'm better than someone else, but the kind of power that says, "I'm fine just the way I am, and men are wonderful beings, as glorious and worthy of love and support as women."

Like Robert Bly, I found Justin Sterling to be a charismatic leader who wasn't afraid to speak his mind.

In a world where it seems like men are always apologizing for being men, it was refreshing to be with a man who wasn't afraid to express his maleness and revel in the company of other men. When he offered tips on how to be more effective in our relationships with women, I found many of them to be quite helpful.

Like many strong men's leaders, Justin Sterling can be rigid and dogmatic.

Although I resonated with Sterling's view that there are significant differences between men and women in the way we express emotions, the ways our brains function, and our unique contributions to relationships, I found he had rather rigid views of how men and women were supposed to be that seemed more tied to the old sexist attitudes we were trying to get away from.

The importance of having a man who brings you to the weekend and brings you home.

In the ManKind weekends, many people provide leadership and many participate and support a man's getting to the weekend. With Sterling, there is a much more personal one-on-one connection between the man who helps you make a decision to go to the weekend and the man attending. In my case, Howard not only helped get me registered, but he drove with me to Los Angeles from San Francisco, saw that I got to the site, and returned to get me at the end.

One of the most powerful experiences for the weekend was at the end. We were all in a circle, more than 200 men, and I heard my name called. "Jed Diamond, it's Howard LaGarde. I've come back for you."

Most of us have had experiences of abandonment when an important man in our lives, often our fathers, left us physically or emotionally. Having a man take us to the weekend and come back for us heals a deep wound that most men feel.

Joining a group and putting what we learned into practice.

Following the weekend, we each were assigned to a small group led by two men who were experienced and had been through the weekend. We learned to talk with other guys, deepen our relationships, and practice what we'd learned and the commitments we had made during the weekend.

Remembering the joy of the outdoors and learning to play together.

Most of the follow-up groups were held outside in nature. Even in cities, we would find a park or go out to the beach. Meeting in nature is itself healing and reminds us of our roots as hunter-gatherers. We also played games like we did when we were kids. They were often competitive, which is part of the male experience. But rather than being "cutthroat," with winners and losers, all the games were engaging, fun, and no one ever felt like a loser. We just enjoyed the camaraderie of friendly male competition and fun.

We would often meet early in the morning or late at night so we could be in nature without other people. It felt like a return to our ancient roots and showed that we all have a primal connection to nature, even when we've become cut off and "civilized."

EVRYMAN: Bringing Men Together to Exercise Their Emotions.

I first met Dan Doty, one of the founders of EVRYMAN, when he contacted me for an interview. "I love your work," he told me. "You are one of my role models, and I hope be able to do the kinds of things you've done with men." EVRYMAN has a simple mission, Dan told me. "We bring men together to exercise their emotions so they can lead more successful, fulfilling lives." Along with co-founders Lucas Krump and Owen Marcus, they have struck a nerve with men all over the country. A recent article in *The New York Times* reported that "EVRYMAN started in 2016 and now has grown to over 800 men in around 85 groups across 50 cities."

Doty, Krump, and Marcus say, "At EVRYMAN we have two guiding questions: What do you feel? and What do you want? We've long denigrated feelings in men, and asking for what we want has come to be seen as self-centered and selfish, but EVRYMAN sees these simple questions as vitally important. They are magical questions, because when you unequivocally know the answers to these two questions, you will put people at ease, create safety, and have an opportunity for deeper connection."

In a recent interview in *The New York Times*, Lucas Krump offered an exercise metaphor for what they do. "We're CrossFit for your emotions."

A number of men were interviewed for the *Times* article:

Ebenezer Bond, 42, the founder of a marketing agency, said that until getting involved with EVRYMAN, he hadn't had a cathartic drag-it-out cry since he was sixteen. The retreat he attended in late 2016 opened the floodgates. "I was skeptical at first—I even deleted an initial email with the invitation to the weekend," Bond said. "But it was the single most transformational experience I've had as an adult male. I was able to express emotions in front of other men, something I'd never done before."

Simon Isaacs, who was invited by Bond to a later retreat, said he "panicked" when he learned, five minutes before he arrived at Race Brook Lodge in Sheffield, MA, that there would be no consumption of alcohol and minimal cellphone use. "I thought, 'What am I supposed to do: express myself?'" he said. Now Isaacs, 38, a founder of the millennial parenting site *Fatherly*, attends a weekly EVRYMAN group and calls it part of his "emotional retraining."

The Good Men Project: The Conversation No One Else Is Having

I was first introduced to the Good Men Project in 2009 by a men's health colleague, Stephen B. Siegel, MD. He had recently read the book, *The Good Men Project: Real Stories from the Front Lines of Modern Manhood* by Tom Matlack. In a review, he offered the following comments:

"As a urologist, I thought that I knew all there was to know about men. Thanks to the authors of this book, I have learned so much more. It's rare that men get together and talk about these type of issues—most of us run out of things to say after we talk about our favorite sports team and the car we want to buy. It is so important as individuals and, especially at times like these, that we define for ourselves and for our children what it really takes to be a *good man*. This book breaks down our roles as Fathers, Husbands, Workers, etc. and tells amazing stories of people that either are good men or figured out how to become one. We need these examples. We need to see that it is possible to fail initially, but succeed in the end. We need to show ourselves and our children that we get it."

To help promote the book, Matlack brought on an advertising consultant and social media expert, Lisa Hickey. Following the book launch, an online program, *Good Men Media,* was born with Lisa Hickey as CEO. She describes the program as "a multi-media, cross-platform content site and conversation asking the question 'What does it mean to be a good man in the twenty-first century?'"

I was impressed with the idea of the program and the potential dialogue that could occur around the simple, yet profound, question, "What does it mean to be a good man in the twenty-first century?"

As someone who has been doing "men's work" for fifty years now, I can attest to the fact that the Good Men Project (GMP) is having the conversation that no one else is having and the conversations are just the beginning.

- GMP is changing the conversation about men with a deeply engaged, passionate, articulate, and vibrant community.
- GMP has built a vast library of original, evergreen content written by more than 6,500 contributors—with new authors joining the conversation every day.
- GMP looks at the way men's roles are evolving in society.

The thing that is absolutely unique about GMP is that they are a "participatory media company." I've written literally thousands of articles for large web-based programs, including *The Huffington Post, Third Age, Scribd,* and many others. GMP is the only media company where the CEO meets every Friday with writers and readers. Everyone is invited to hear the latest updates from Lisa Hickey and invited to discuss ideas about important issues going on in the world.

"You already know GMP has been engaged in the conversation no one else is having," she told us at one of the Friday discussions. "Well, that conversation has been getting better and deeper and even more connected to actual social change. We have been rolling out 'Social Interest Groups'—groups of people who are coming together to discuss specific areas of interest. Each group has a weekly phone call and then participants can stay in touch during the week in the Premium Member Facebook community and our Facebook Groups."

Currently, there are twelve weekly Social Interest Groups:

- Sex, Love, and Relationships
- Stop Racism
- The Disposability of Men
- Human Rights
- Environmental Activism
- Masculinity Detox
- Political Activism
- Mental Health and Wellness
- Call With The Publisher
- Columnist and Editor Training
- Consciousness Intersectionality
- Writing and Publishing

I put GMP in this chapter because I believe they are creating true Rites of Passage in the world of the Internet. Most of us are "online" a good deal of the time and interact with online media. Most of us have lots of "friends" on Facebook and many of us interact on YouTube, Instagram, Twitter, LinkedIn, and many others. But GMP is evolving into a real community where there is dialogue, not just one-way communication.

Further, GMP recognizes that women's issues and men's issues are opposite sides of the same coin. Women's liberation and men's liberation will be achieved together or not at all. GMP is unique in having a very clear gender focus on men, but with a CEO who is a woman. The senior editors of GMP are both male and female, and the writers are also equally represented by men and women.

Meaningful Initiation: Guiding the Next Generations

I've always been amazed at how creative humans are in finding what may be missing in their lives. If the society doesn't offer meaningful rites of passage, we often try to create our own. Yet, I found I also benefited from being part of organized programs like ManKind, Sterling, EVRYMAN, and the Good Men Project. I wanted my children to have more guidance than I had growing up.

I was talking to my seventeen-year-old son, Aaron, following my New Warrior Weekend sponsored by the ManKind Project. "I've never heard you so excited a men's program in a long time. Could I go a weekend like that?"

"I don't know," I told him. "I'm not sure you're old enough, but I'll ask. It's a powerful initiation and I can't think of a better experience for a young man to help him make the transition from boyhood to manhood."

"What kind of initiation is it?" he wanted to know.

I read him a passage I had gotten on the ManKind website:

"In almost every global culture, rites of passage taught boys how to be men and become productive members of the 'tribe'. Often these experiences were harrowing and physically painful. These days, that old kind of initiation is no longer appropriate, safe, or useful. (Though dangerous initiations are still occurring in gangs, fraternities and adolescent acts of rebellion).

"MKP has created a modern initiation for men. The modern initiation is safe, non-shaming, and focused on the problems that face men in the twenty-first century. We conduct an initiation because we believe it is absolutely necessary for a man to learn in an unequivocal way what he is capable of, why he is here, and how to engage fully in his life."

"I definitely want to do it," Aaron told me.

I talked to my friend, Bill Kauth, one of the founders and learned that the weekend was focused on adult males, eighteen years old or older. "But he sounds like a mature young man," said Bill. "Have him call me and I'll see if I think he's ready for this kind of initiation."

Aaron's participation was approved. We learned that there was a new Center opening up near his home in Portland, Oregon and he would be attending the first weekend they were offering. I also found out that in each weekend there fifteen to forty participants and twenty-five to fifty men who help staff the weekend. I thought it would be a great experience for me to be on staff for a weekend initiation where my son was present.

I applied to be on staff and was accepted. I flew up from California to Portland. On the flight up, I thought a lot about Aaron. He had come into my life when I met his mother, Carlin, when he was three years old. When Carlin and I fell in love and got together, she moved to California with Aaron. Her two older sons were living with their father.

Aaron and I soon became close, but I was always sensitive to the fact that I wasn't his biological father. I was careful not to try and take over the parental responsibilities from his mother or to try and replace his father. Being a parent isn't easy. And being a stepparent has its own challenges. Carlin came to see that directly when my daughter, Angela, came to live with us when she was eight years old.

The site for the New Warrior Training Adventure was at a Boy Scout camp in a beautiful area outside of Portland. While Aaron settled in with the other initiates, I met with the other men who were staffing the weekend. Some, like me, were staffing for the first time. Others had staffed many previous weekends. We each were given various jobs to do during the weekend.

Like the initiates, we didn't sleep much during the weekend. I was awakened early one morning by one of the senior staff members. "You may want to get down to the gathering area," he told me. "Aaron is doing some significant personal work."

When I got there, I saw he was talking very personally about his father. I was keen to hear what he had to say and worried that he would feel I had not respected his connection with his biological father, but I was shocked to hear what was really bothering him.

"Since we've all been together, I've come to love Jed," he said. "But I feel he's always held back from me. He talks about not wanting to replace my father, that he's my 'stepfather,' not my 'father.' I don't understand why I can't have two fathers. I'm not confused about who they are and one can't replace the other."

I listened closely. I felt inspired by Aaron's wisdom. Why, indeed, couldn't a boy have two fathers? God knows, we need all the fathering we can get.

As if on cue, the man leading this part of the weekend saw me and brought me into the circle where Aaron was sharing his feelings. We embraced and I felt the love flowing. I told him I was sorry I had held back and after hearing him, I realize I don't need to do that. I can be fully present. We were both weeping with joy at that point.

Then someone came forward carrying a huge blanket. It was spread out and eight men held it, and Aaron and I were bundled together inside. He laughed and cried as we were thrown in the air together and caught and thrown up again. We tumbled and turned and finally came to rest together and were wrapped in the blanket while the whole group cheered us. It was one of the most joyful experiences of my life.

Ten years later, Aaron and I returned to meet with all those who had attended that weekend. The men were amazed to see Aaron, now grown into a fine, twenty-seven-year old young man who was out on his own. We both reflected on the importance of initiations for young men, and Aaron thanked the other men for allowing him to be part of the experience. They thanked him for his willingness to risk a new adventure at a young age. And they thanked me for trusting my son to the wisdom of the ManKind community.

Initiation for My Grandson, Deon

I met my first wife when we were in college. After we had fallen in love and it looked like we were headed toward marriage, we talked about children. We both wanted kids, but also felt that there were too many people in the world. We decided that after we got married, we'd have one child and then adopt a child.

Angela was the child we adopted. She is African-American and now has four children of her own. When her oldest son, Deon, was twelve years old, he said he wanted a "bar mitzvah." I was surprised to hear that. Both his mother and father are African-American, and though I'm Jewish, I've never been religious and I didn't go through the religious initiation ceremony when I was thirteen, as was the case with other Jewish boys I knew.

I talked more to Deon over the next year to get an idea of what he really wanted. It soon became clear that he wasn't interested in a Jewish ceremony where he'd learn Hebrew, but really a Rite of Passage that would prepare him for manhood. I wanted to offer him the kind of support Aaron had gotten in his ManKind Project weekend, but knew that Deon needed a different kind of experience. As a young, Black man, he faced different challenges than Caucasian youths, and I wanted a life-changing experience that would speak to his unique background and needs.

I've long believed that mentoring is critical to the well-being of our children and grandchildren, particularly the young men. It's also critical to the well-being of our communities. Many years ago, I attended a mentoring workshop with ritual elder Malidoma Somé. He said, "Elders and mentors have an irreplaceable function in the life of any community. Without them, the young are lost—their overflowing energies wasted in useless pursuits."

He went on to remind us that "old must live in the young like a grounding force that tames the tendency toward bold but senseless actions and shows them the path of wisdom. In the absence of elders, the impetuosity of youth becomes the slow death of the community."

Psychologist Robert Moore offers a chilling recognition of what happens when young men are not mentored or given initiations into manhood. He says we move *from healthy masculinity to monster-boy masculinity.*

It took another year to find the right program, but I was able to do so when I reconnected with my friend Stephen Johnson who was the founder and director of the Men's Center of Los Angeles (MCLA). I'd known Stephen for more than thirty years and had been impressed with the programs he's created over the years at the MCLA. In addition to their adult retreats, they had begun offering retreats for young, inner-city minority males between the ages of twelve and twenty. I thought that would be ideal for my grandson Deon.

I drove down from my home in Willits, picked Deon up at his home in Bakersfield, and headed for Los Angeles. Deon didn't say much driving down. He's a quiet kid. But he told me he wanted to do the retreat.

We needed a rest stop, so I pulled off the freeway in Encino and stopped at a small park. This little park had special meaning to me. I had remembered it from my childhood. It was a place my father had taken me numerous times before I was five years old. I thought we might get inspiration from being there, but was not prepared for what my grandson had to say as we sat in the grass. "You said you were interested in some kind of rite of passage from boyhood to manhood. What is it you're wanting to get from the experience?" I asked him.

I expected the usual shrug of a fifteen-year-old teenager and a short, "I don't know." But what he said was amazingly clear and concise. "I want three things," he told me. "I need *guidance.* I also want more *confidence.* And I want *respect.*" I told him I thought with that kind of clarity and desire he would get what he wanted.

I also asked him what he thought the qualities of a good man were for him. Again, I was surprised by his insights and vision. He seemed to be tapping into some deep well of longing and a clear vision of what he wanted. He certainly had found his voice and he offered these seven qualities he felt were important for becoming a good man:

1. A good man takes care of himself and his family.
2. A good man is a working man and has a job.
3. A good man knows what's right and what's wrong.
4. If he's right, a good man stands up for himself, but doesn't make the other person wrong.
5. A good man apologizes when he's wrong.
6. A good man helps people when they need help.
7. A good man always has a backup plan.

When we arrived at the site for the retreat, I was knocked out by the peace, serenity, and beauty of the place. It's located on a bluff 800 feet above Camp Hess Kramer and the Pacific coast and boasts spectacular views of the ocean, Channel Islands, and surrounding Santa Monica Mountains. It triggered memories from when I attended

UC Santa Barbara and was embarking on my own journey to manhood.

Deon seemed equally impressed with the surroundings. We had arrived early and groups of men were busy setting things up for the soon-to-be-arriving participants. One group of guys asked if we wanted to help build the sweat lodge which would be used later in the retreat for a healing ceremony. I was tired from the drive, but Deon volunteered right away and went off with the guys to help. I was surprised he jumped right in. He's a quiet, reserved, boy and I knew he had never experienced a sweat lodge and probably didn't know what it was. But off he went to help.

It turned out that the sweat lodge became one of the cornerstone experiences for Deon in the weekend. Our group participated the next day. We listened to Inipi Sweat Lodge Ceremony leader Thomas Alvarez describe the way in which the sweat lodge was used by Native peoples throughout the world to cleanse, pray, and ask for guidance. As we sat listening, Deon seemed to hang on every word and looked proudly at the structure that he had helped construct the previous day.

One of the young men who had participated in a number of previous retreats encouraged our group of adults and young men prior to go into the lodge. "This may be a new experience for many of you and it's not the kind of thing most of us have done where we come from," he told us. "But it can be a very powerful way of asking for guidance and getting support. It will be hot and dark and your natural tendency may be to get away as fast as you can, but hang in there if you can and you'll get something important."

He also told us that sometimes we sweat for others who are carrying a lot of pain and difficulty in their lives but can't be there. He told the group that he was doing the sweat lodge for himself and also for his twin brother who was in prison. I thought of my daughter Angela and her family and wanted to help carry some of the burden of the pain she lived with every day as she dealt with the stresses of her family life.

There were "four rounds" to the experience. Thomas guided our prayers and sang to the spirits. It got very, very hot, but Deon and most of the others hung in there. By the end we all felt cleansed, had been forced to deal with our fears, and felt stronger for having gone through the experience together. After dinner that evening, we met in small "tribal" groups with ten to fifteen adult mentors and kids.

We went around the circle and talked a bit about why we were here. Deon opened up immediately and told the group, "I'm lost in my life and I need guidance." Young and old knew what he meant, and many opened up to their own feelings of being lost. For the first time, I had a deep experience of the violence that so many of these kids live with every day. One boy talked about killings he had seen in his neighborhood and Deon also talked about people he knew who had been killed not far from the apartment where he lived. Another young boy said that he didn't want a lot in life, just to know that he would survive another day. Tears ran down my cheeks thinking that this was the world my grandson and his family lived in. Just staying alive was a task they faced every day, something I had never experienced growing up, or now.

Steve Branker, one of the Men's Center organizers, said, "The pressures that these young men face in everyday life are astounding. Instead of primarily dealing with such things as schoolwork and girlfriends, they are dealing with whether or not they will come back alive after they walk out of their homes each day."

I thought to myself, "God, they're so small and what they are dealing with is so big." I felt the terrible loss and pain that so many experience, but also the courage they had to break free of the life of violence and to reach for something better. I felt deeply blessed to be able to share this experience with my grandson and the other mentors who were committed to helping these kids survive their childhood and grow into adults who had something they could look forward to in life.

As we gathered for our final goodbyes Stephen reminded us about why we were here and what we still had to accomplish. "Our boys, young men, and our mature men are calling on us to explore with clarity what the role of fathers, grandfathers, and mentors should be. If we do not provide a sacred role for our boys as they grow, they are more likely to join a gang, abuse their lovers, abandon their wives and children, subsist in emotional isolation, and become addicted, hyper-materialistic, lonely, and unhappy.

"A boy needs a structure and discipline in which to learn who he is," Stephen continued. "He needs to live a journey that has clear responsibilities and goals. He needs a role in life. Without these, without the role training that accompanies these, he does not know his sacred and important objectives in life."

Deon leaned over and whispered to me, "Can I come back next year?"

"If you want to come back, we'll make it happen," I told him. "And maybe we'll get your Dad and younger brother to be come as well. What do you think?" He just smiled and nodded his head.

Elder Initiation: From Adulthood to Super Adulthood

Throughout most of human history, we married at an early age, had children, raised them, and then by age forty we were dead. There was no need for any focus on becoming elders or the stage of "super adulthood" as I describe it. But now when we are able to live well into our eighties, nineties, and beyond, we have an opportunity to live long enough to pass on our wisdom to the young who follow us.

I just turned seventy-five this year. In 2010 I was invited to be the keynote speaker at one of the ManKind Project's elders gathering. The gathering focused on a simple, yet profound question. "How can we as elders choose to *Occupy Paradise* within ourselves and to manifest this in the world?" The theme was **"Dancing with the paradox of a world on the brink of ruin…or Renaissance."**

I shared my own experiences over the las seventy years and for the first time stepped forward with other men who had reached a stage of their life when they were ready to declare they were now elders.

Within the Mankind Project are a group of men who offer their vision, strength, and wisdom to the community. Terry Jones describes the MKP Path of the Elder this way:

"There is a stage of life beyond adulthood. The older men of MKP call it elderhood. Before the Industrial Era, older people who were still on the land, accessible to the family and the community, often acted as sources of wisdom, celebrants, and mentors. They resided at the center of the village until they died, ready to support the young in their Hero's Journey. These elders taught about the mystery of our oneness with the universe. They fostered an oral tradition and offered what their long-life experience taught them."

Bottom Line: Males Need Meaningful Rites of Passage

The Rites of Passage I have experienced personally have been transformative. I've also seen it change the lives of my children and grandchildren. We now have organizations that provide the ritual support that has been missing in our modern society. I'm enjoying the stage that I call *Super Adulthood* as I grow into my role of elder.

Rule #8:

Celebrate Your True Warrior Spirit and Learn Why Males Duel and Females Duet

"Warriorship here does not refer to making war on others. Aggression is the source of our problems, not the solution. Here the world 'warrior' is taken from the Tibetan pawo, which literally means 'one who is brave.' Warriorship in this context is the tradition of human bravery, or the tradition of fearlessness . . . warriorship is not being afraid of who you are."

~Chögyam Trungpa, *Shambhala: The Sacred Path of the Warrior*

From the time I was six years old, I wanted to be a warrior. I watched *The Last of the Mohicans* and was attracted to Chingachgook and his son Uncas who were the last two members of the tribe. They were resourceful, loyal, and knew how to survive in the woods. As a city kid who grew up without a father, I longed for the support and wisdom that I imagined was transmitted from a native father to his son.

I had been practicing Aikido in Mill Valley, California with instructors George Leonard, Wendy Palmer, and Richard Strozzi-Heckler. Richard had written a book, *In Search of the Warrior Spirit,* and I attended a class that explored warrior ideals. I recorded my experiences in my journal:

It is almost 6:00 p.m. and the sun sets low over the beautiful waters of the Pacific Ocean. Esalen, the legendary center for the exploration of consciousness, is bathed in pink light. I am participating in a weekend workshop called *The Discipline of Harmony: Warrior Virtues Without War.* We have been practicing Aikido and other energy awareness techniques for the entire day. The work has been exhilarating, but within the range of our experience. It is clear from Richard's instructions that something very different will take place after dinner.

"When you return at 8:00 tonight," Richard says, his voice calm but serious, "you will be engaged in an experience in which most of you will die. It is a simulation, but can feel very real to those who engage wholeheartedly. If you choose to play you will learn a great deal about life and death and about what it means to be a warrior."

Richard proceeded to give us the outline of what was to be a life-transforming experience for me. We would "become" Samurai in fifteenth-century Japan and join one of two armies, each led by a Daimyō or warlord. If killed, the warrior would immediately fall and would later be carried to the burial ground to await the end of the war. Richard would play the part of the War God who directed the battle by giving instructions to each Daimyō. He represented the uncontrollable forces of the universe and could act capriciously. Looking in the eyes of the War God was cause for instant death. It was implied that there were other ways we might die, not all ones we could anticipate.

"Go now and prepare yourselves," Richard said. "In two hours we will meet again here and the battle will begin. Do whatever is right for you in preparing over these next few hours, knowing that they may be the last ones you will have on this earth." It was already beginning to feel real.

I walked out of the hall just as the sun was setting over the ocean. I began to feel what it would be like if this was my last sunset. The colors seemed particularly vivid, the sounds of the birds clear and full. I sat on a rock overlooking the cliffs and thought back on my life. I was surprised at how good I felt. I thought of my accomplishments, but they seemed to pale as my thoughts were drawn to my family. Tears washed down my face as I thought of saying goodbye, of things that had not been said during the busyness of our lives.

What would I want to say if my time was short? I began to write to my wife:

"Dear Carlin,

This could be my last night alive and I want you to know that my sadness at not having years to love you and play with you and adventure together is overwhelming."

The tears poured down and I had to wait until I could see again.

"Yet what we have had in our ten years would satisfy many lifetimes. Each moment has been precious, each minute, just one, would make my stay here worthwhile.

"I know we will always be together and who we are and have been will expand through the years. Hold me in your heart as you hold your love of life. Celebrate us.

"With joy overflowing, Jed."

I thought about my children and my men's group and said a prayer to my mother and father. It was getting dark and I was aware that I didn't have much time to say what was in my heart. Damn, I wish I had more time.

To our fifteen-year-old son, Aaron, I wrote, "It doesn't seem right that life should end so suddenly. Perhaps I will have many years ahead but we never know.

> "You have been a special presence in my life since I first met you in Oregon when Carlin came into my life. I remember you sleeping so soundly I marveled at your peacefulness.
> "You are a fine young man and I am very proud of you. I'm privileged to see you grow more into being your own special self. You are sensitive, feeling, strong, enduring.
> "You have already done great things in your young life and you will do more. Know that I love and cherish you. Love, Dad."

With each child I thought about and wrote to, my heart seemed to be breaking wide open and the tears continued to flow.

I hadn't seen my son, Jemal, in six months. He was away at college in St. Louis. I thought of the times I had missed with him growing up apart from me.

> "Jemal, my firstborn, the joy of my life. You've taught me how to love. From the moment I came back into the delivery room even though the doctor told me to leave, I have felt the power of your presence.
> "You are a wise soul and I have learned much from you. You see through illusion and are not afraid to feel the sadness and joy of life.
> "Keep in touch with those feelings. They are the salvation of all that is good in the world.
> "There hasn't been a moment that I haven't loved you. I pass on some of my spirit to you. Just as you have passed some of yours to me.
> "I'll be with you in your silent times, in your poetry, and in your dreams.
> Love, Dad."

The feelings kept pouring out and I felt compelled to go on.

> "Angela, my precious daughter. I've had a special connection with you since I first held you at the adoption agency when you were two-and-a-half months old and you fell asleep in my arms.
> "Your aliveness and joy were wonderful to behold. I'm sorry I wasn't able to honor it as much as I would have wanted.
> "You are a fighter, you have courage and strength and the compassion to love children and animals.
> "You've been a gift in my life. I will love you always, Dad."

Saying goodbye to my wife and children felt devastating, but freeing. When I thought of my men's group, still together after twelve years, I felt a smile come over me. In my wildest dreams I could never conceive a men's group lasting longer than any of my previous marriages. It never occurred to me that at the moment of my death, I might care enough about a man to remember him, more less eight men—John, Tom, Tony, Dick, Denis, Ken, Norman, and Kellie.

"This may be my last night to live and I'm thinking of you all with love and affection, a sly smile, and a deep sense of gratitude for all you have meant to me.

> "You are my brothers, my friends, my teachers, my playmates.
> Think of me with fondness once a year on the anniversary of my passing. Get together, share stories and wine and beer and laughs and tears.
> I honor you and us and our group. I love you."

After finishing the letters, I felt cleansed and peaceful. I walked in the darkness and felt united with all that is and was and will be. As I got ready to return to the lodge, I felt uneasy. The thought struck me that the only person I didn't feel at peace with was my ex-wife, the mother of Jemal and Angela. It had been over ten years since we divorced, but there was still some hurt and anger between us. I decided to write to her as well.

> "Candace, know that I hold you close in my heart. I care about you and honor the time we were together. You were a good friend and companion. Our early times together were joyous. You taught me to frolic and you shared your soul.
> "Our children were a gift to us and I'm glad we are parents together. I hoped we could heal our hurts and fears and anger toward each other. I think of you fondly on this, my last night.
> Jed."

With the possibility of death only hours away, it seemed so easy to let go of my anger, all the ways I had justified our emotional distance. All the hurts seemed trivial. As I walked back into the workshop room, now transformed into an open battlefield, I felt an aliveness I'd never known.

People were sitting along the edge of the rug. Their faces were serious. The room was in semidarkness and Richard's quiet voice told us, "When the sun comes up, it will be the day of the battle." My heart pounded and my mouth was dry. It was feeling very real. We were told to move through the room and allow ourselves to be drawn to one side or the other, either to the army of the North or the army of the South.

I moved North. We were told to select a Daimyō, but could not use words. Any talk or indication that a decision was being made "democratically" would result in death. This was clearly a different world than the one I had left only a few hours ago. Did I want to be the leader and take responsibility for people's lives or be one of the group? As I decided I wanted to lead, someone thrust my arm up in the air. Could I get people to follow me? What if they turned away? I would be disgraced and kill myself. Slowly the group turned to me and one by one bowed as a show of allegiance.

As I spoke to my warriors, I felt a connection to all the true warriors of the past. Their thoughts seemed to flow through me. "There is no need to be afraid," I began, and found that I was actually calm. "We are all connected. Life and death are the same. There are no mistakes and you can't fail. Your job is to be yourself, to be present wholeheartedly. The army of the South is not your enemy; they offer only opportunities for you to confront yourself. Their job is to send us energy and hone us to our true form, like a flintnapper, chipping off bits of superfluous stone, to make us strong and useful. You must be serious on the outside, but joyful on the inside. All that matters is that you move more closely to the center of your being where you will feel connected to all that is. You must honor all life and you must honor death as well, for without death there can be no life. We go into battle in the service of the planet, to nourish and protect it."

But all the philosophy drained away when the War God called each of the Daimyōs to send out a Samurai to face the first confrontation. Now I had to decide who would go into battle, who would face death. My throat got dry. When I pointed to one of the men, I could feel his fear and also his excitement. I was elated when he returned victorious and felt the pain of death as I watched the Samurai of the South fall on the battlefield. Some of the battles were over in an instant, others went on for fifteen or twenty minutes.

Some battles were settled by simple "paper, rock, scissors" confrontations with the loser instantly falling dead as though he or she had been shot. Some were settled by feats of endurance like standing on one foot in a yoga pose. The winner was the one who could stand without falling.

The battles went on for what seemed like hours. Our army of the North won battle after battle until all the South soldiers were defeated. The army of the South had been decimated and the only person left was the surviving Daimyō. Our army still had many soldiers. Somehow we had triumphed. But the War God spoke to me. "You can end the war now and be victorious. You can command that the Daimyō from the South commit seppuku, or ritual suicide. Or you can choose to fight the opposing Daimyō in battle."

In an instant, I chose to fight. I realized I couldn't just send others into battle and I couldn't "win" without going into battle myself. I felt confident that we had won thus far and I would win the final battle. Yet, when we came out for the final battle, I was killed. I instantly fell to the ground and was carried off the battle field and place with the other dead samurai in the burial ground.

I listened, as if I was now in the spirit world as the War God gave one last instruction to the remaining samurai in my army. "You now each have a choice. You can swear allegiance to the new Daimyō and live, or you must commit seppuku and die. The choice is yours."

Life or death, what would I choose? I wondered what those left of my army would choose. I felt a moment of sadness and also pride as each bowed to the Daimyō of the South and ended their own life.

After the conclusion of the Samurai war, all the dead were resurrected and we had a chance to talk about our feelings. We shared insights and understandings long into the night and again the next morning. Most everyone agreed the "game" was very real. Many who died said that they had profound experiences of death and were no longer afraid of dying. That was certainly my experience. On some deep level, I know that death is not the end, that there is a spirit that lives on, and I suspect that we may come back to continue our spiritual growth. I also learned some profound lessons about the warrior spirit.

I felt deeply that the essence of the warrior spirit is love and there are no distinctions between enemy and friend. We really are one. I found though that peace is not the absence of conflict. It isn't some gushy paradise where there are no disagreements and everyone loves everyone. Rather, peace comes through loving confrontation.

Richard said that even combat veterans who had engaged in the Samurai experience felt it was real. Many of them had profound experiences that they had only associated in the past with combat. There may be something important and valuable for men in the experience of battle. But battles need not be destructive. There are many ways to become a warrior.

Understanding the Differences Between Soldiers and Warriors

I've never been a soldier, though there was a time in my first year of college in 1961 when I considered it. The Morrill Land-Grant Acts of 1862 gave federal lands to the states, the sale of which would provide funds to maintain state colleges. It required that courses in mechanics, agriculture, and military tactics be offered. By 1968, the Reserve Officers Training Corps (ROTC) was compulsory at the University of California.

When I was at the university, it was seen as part of college life for all young men. In addition to our other courses, we were required to put on our uniforms, polish our shoes to a "spit shine," and report for duty. We were put in platoons and squads, learned to march in cadence, handle a rife, and to shoot it on the rifle range.

Although I liked playing soldier, hearing the realities of war from men who had actually been soldiers and fought in wars changed my mind. One of the guys in my dorm was older than the rest of us. He had been a Marine and had served for two years fighting covert wars in Vietnam and Cambodia. He gave us a much more realistic view of war and said if he knew then what he knew now, he would never have enlisted.

He said he was drawn to join the Marines by warrior ideals of serving his country, but he said the reality was that he was part of a "military-industrial complex," the term coined by General Dwight D. Eisenhower later in his life after he had become President. "The only warrior values I learned," he told us, "were the values of love and support of the guys you fought with. We were there for the wrong reasons."

Returning Home to Our Warrior Roots

The ideal of a new identity for men which I call *the warrior* is just now beginning to emerge. The essence of this new man is still in the germination phase and is both ancient and modern. In order to get a feel for him, let's listen to what a number of contemporary explorers are saying about the warrior.

"Is now the time," asks Matthew Fox, author of *Creation Spirituality: Liberating Gifts for the Peoples of the Earth,* "when the Earth yearns and humankind yearns for the end of war—to take back the archetype of the spiritual warrior from the Pentagon and bastions of militarism?"

Fox asks who is a warrior today? "A warrior is one who is alert, who concentrates, who contemplates, who centers oneself fully. If the warrior is not well-grounded he or she may die. The warrior is one who faces death. The warrior is also one who is committed to a goal that is larger than the individual ego."

George Leonard, my Aikido instructor and author of many books including *The Ultimate Athlete and Mastery: The Keys to Success and Long-Term Fufillment,* has spent many years developing an understanding of what humans are like when they live fully, with passion and commitment. "The Modern Warrior," says Leonard, "is not one who goes to war but rather one who exhibits integrity in every aspect of living, one who seeks to attain control then act with abandon. For the Modern Warrior, life is vivid, immediate, and joyful. He or she lives each day to the full, and is fulfilled in serving others. To achieve peace in the world and harmony in daily life, it might well be necessary for men and women to re-own the warrior ideal."

Anthropologist Joan Halifax has worked with shamans and healers the world over. She feels strongly that our culture is in need of the warrior's way if we are to survive. "The warrior's way," Halifax tells us, "is to recognize that everything is sacred. All life and death... It is the warrior, the true warrior, who understands the location of the battlefield. The battlefield is not somewhere outside of us, but it's within. The warrior's way leads toward the interior."

So, we see that as "new warriors" we must do battle with our own inner demons. It does not have to do with fighting others. Yet we would be wrong to view the men who are practicing this new ideal as merely self-reflective. Though the battles of the warrior are interior, the work of the warrior involves taking responsibility for all our relations. This sense of social responsibility is exemplified by Danaan Parry, a former physicist with the Atomic Energy Commission who decided the world needed to learn about conflict resolution more than it needed nuclear weapons. Until his untimely death in 1996, he traveled throughout the world to such trouble spots as Northern Ireland to use the warrior ideals to bring about peace between warring groups.

"Our world needs women and men who are willing to walk the Warrior path today," said Parry. In his book, *Warriors of the Heart,* he offers an invitation "for all those who know (maybe not understand, but know) that they have somehow chosen to be a part of something very new, something that could bring our species from the brink of destruction to the doorway of an entirely new concept of human relationships."

The Evolution of the Warrior and the Essence of Being Male

Until recently, exploration of the warrior ideal was the province of psychologists, philosophers, and those with interest in Native American ideals and practices. Now, more social scientists are bringing their expertise to the discussion.

Yuval Noah Harari is the author of *Sapiens: A Brief History of Humankind.* In a chapter on "Terrorism and War," he says, "Terrorists are masters of mind control. They kill very few people but nevertheless manage to terrify billions and rattle huge political structures such as the European Union or the United States. Since September 11, 2001, each year terrorists have killed about fifty people in the European Union, about ten people in the United States, about seven people in China, and up to 25,000 people elsewhere in the globe (mostly in Iraq, Afghanistan, Pakistan, Nigeria, and Syria)."

He contrasts the deaths resulting from terrorism with more common deaths we tend to ignore. "Each year traffic accidents kill about 80,000 Europeans, 40,000 Americans, 270,000 Chinese, and 1.25 million people altogether. Diabetes and high sugar levels kill up to 3.5 million people annually, while air pollution kills about 7 million people per year. So why do we fear terrorism more than sugar, and why do governments lose elections because of sporadic terrorist attacks but not because of chronic air pollution?"

Not only is terrorism a much smaller threat than many people fear, but violence of all kinds is declining, though you wouldn't know it from reading the headlines in the news. In his well-researched and important book, *The Better Angels of Our Nature: Why Violence Has Declined,* Harvard psychology professor Steven Pinker says, "This book is about what may be the most important thing that has ever happened in human history. Believe it or not—and I know that most people do not—violence has declined over long stretches of time, and today we may be living in the most peaceable era in our species' existence."

Why are we so afraid of the wrong things? Why do we seem to be looking for enemies everywhere, even when we are objectively safer than we've ever been? Joyce Benenson has some helpful answers. Dr. Benenson is a professor of Psychology at Emmanuel College in Boston and an Associate Member of the Human Evolutionary Biology department at Harvard University.

In her groundbreaking book, *Warriors and Worriers: The Survival of the Sexes,* she offers new insights about men and women and offers important information based on evolutionary science. She says, "For thousands of years, human females and males have faced different sorts of major problems and found different types of solutions. Women have taken primary responsibility for the long-term survival of vulnerable children. In contrast, around the world, men have taken primary responsibility for fighting wars."

As a result of these different evolutionary challenges, she concludes the following:

At essence, men are warriors and at essence women are worriers. I'm aware that a few lines of summary can trigger a negative reaction in people. Yet, I find Benenson's research findings compelling. This does not mean that all men are violent or that all women worry about the survival of themselves and their children. It does help us better understand our gender-specific tendencies.

Men Like to Fight and Compete in Groups

Although many modern men, including myself, would like to see ourselves as "peaceful warriors," the truth is that males have evolved to fight other males. "What make men unique compared with other species," says Benenson, "is that they like to fight and compete as a group. No example demonstrates this better than war. Unlike most other species, men band together in solidarity to risk their lives to defeat another group. For many thousands of years, human males have engaged in intergroup warfare."

These male behaviors make sense if we think about them in evolutionary terms. "Engaging in physical battle against another group would endanger the lives of everyone in the community," says Benenson. "No one's genes would survive this. The problem can best be solved by delegating fighting the enemy to one specific group: young men. Women can then protect themselves and their children. Older men can supervise from a distance. Young men should fight the enemy in a location as far away as possible from everyone else."

So, for the maximum benefit of all, women and men assume different roles. Women's first job is to take care of themselves. If they die, their children likely die. Then, they must take care of the kids. Hence, it's good if they think of all possible dangers. In other words, they *worry* about everything. Males fight other males in order to protect the women and children. From an early age, males practice being *warriors*.

Benenson concludes, "We are not conscious of being warriors or worriers. Rather, being a warrior or a worrier is like having a special program continually running in the background of your mind." We are not prisoners of our evolutionary past. War is not inevitable, and societies can learn more peaceful ways to solve problems. We can do everything we can to create a society where peaceful warriors can flourish, and at the same time, we can recognize that there are still times when men will be called to battle.

Not only does our evolutionary history create warriors and worriers, it also creates communication patterns where males *duel* and females *duet*.

Males Duel and Females Duet

The different ways men and women have evolved show themselves in the ways we communicate. We all notice that men talk differently than women. Male talk and female talk isn't always obvious since when men talk to women and women talk to men, we have to accommodate each other's natural mode of talking. When I'm with my male friends, I notice that communication is shorter and has an element of friendly put-downs, like when I talk to my friend Lanny about playing racquetball:

Lanny: *Hey, want to play today?*
Me: *Sure, what time?*
Lanny: *Let's do 1:00.*
Me: *Be there. Be prepared to have your butt whupped.*
Lanny: *In your dreams, little man.*
Me: *You've been warned.*
Lanny: *Bye.*
Me: *Bye.*

If I were to write out the dialogue when my wife talks to her women friends about setting a time to meet, it would take three pages. They would talk about feelings. How other friends were doing. The recipe for the lasagna dinner they were planning to make, etc., etc., etc. When I overhear a conversation like that or when I'm listening to my wife, I'm thinking to myself, Jesus, when is she going to get to the point?

John L. Locke is a professor of language science at Lehman College, City University of New York. In his recent book, *Duels and Duets: Why Men and Women Talk So Differently,* he clearly describes the way our evolution-based communication patterns have evolved into the ways men and women talk. He says, **"The more dramatic differences that occur when men talk with men, and women with women, are not the 'gendered' effects of modern culture but the 'sexed' expression of ancient biological dispositions. These dispositions are as different as they are because ancestral men and women competed for the things they need in two fundamentally different ways** (emphasis added)."

Drawing on animal studies, Locke notes that "In birds and mammals, including the other primates, sexually mature males are prone to contend with each other in highly public vocal displays that are aggressive or 'agonistic' in nature. We may think of these engagements as 'duels.' In many primate species, sexually mature females have an equally strong disposition to affiliate with other females, in more private and intimate circumstances, by engaging them in subdued vocal interactions. I refer to these interactions as 'duets'."

Locke summarizes the research on male communication. Males are more likely than females to:

1. Interrupt each other.
2. Issue commands, threats, and boasts.
3. Resist each other's demands.
4. Give information.
5. Heckle.
6. Tell jokes or suspenseful stories.
7. Try to top another's story.
8. Insult or denigrate each other.

By contrast, research indicates that females in same-sex groups are more likely than males to:

1. Agree with other speakers.
2. Yield to other speakers.
3. Acknowledge points made by other speakers.
4. Be polite.
5. Cooperate and collaborate.

Locke concludes by saying, "There is also a rule that applies to female groups: Do what it takes to preserve group harmony. This rule underlies the female tendencies enumerated above. In the case of males, the corresponding rule would be: "Do what is necessary to be seen as *the most wonderful anything*—from strong and knowledgeable to brave and resourceful—whether that means building yourself up or tearing everyone else down."

Our language reflects survival and reproductive needs that were different for males and females throughout our evolutionary history. Why do guys interrupt each other, issue commands, threats, boasts? Why do we tell long, elaborate stories and try to top each other's stories? Why do we playfully insult each other?

I would suggest that we are playing out our Warrior spirits. On the one hand, we are trying to outshine our male competitors so that females who are watching us will choose us, not the other guys. We are also showing the other men present that we are fighters. Given our evolutionary need to protect our tribe, we looked for other guys who we can count on to stand with us if we were being attacked by other men.

In men's groups, I've had guys tell me, "I can't really trust you until we've had a few fights and I know where you stand." Guys can be fighting at one minute, but when there is external danger, they come together as a fighting force. We are always taking the measure of other men and so ritual conflict, including verbal duels, are ways in which we attract women and also serve to help us check out other men to see who we can trust.

The main reason men and women have such difficulty communicating is that we assume we are speaking the same language. Yet, men and women speak two very different languages that are built into our biology. We can learn to communicate in ways that are used by the other sex, but before we can do that, we have to understand why our different languages evolved in the first place.

Behavior and language continually evolve to fit our life circumstances. Yet, it's likely that male and female differences will persist and rather than seeing these differences as fueling the battle of the sexes, accepting our differences can bring us together. "I have come to believe," says Locke, "that biologically supported sex differences in verbal behavior increase the benefits of collaboration in modern life, much as they once conspired, in antiquity, to broaden the foundation for human language."

Bottom Line: Celebrate Your True Warrior Spirit

Although all 12 Rules are helpful, I've found this one on warriorship to be particularly useful. For me, it connected the dots between our evolutionary heritage and our modern lives. From the wisdom of Sitting Bull to today's social scientists, we can recognize that the essence of males is to be warriors. Yet, being a warrior is not the same as being a soldier and though we have built-in tendencies to join with other males to fight those who threaten the peace of our families and communities, we can also work together to change the underlying conditions that cause us to become violent.

Understanding the sex differences between males as warriors and females as worriers has helped me better understand why men and women are the way they are. Learning that males *duel* in our communication while females *duet* helps us all to better accept our male and female essence.

Putting this rule into practice means finding the balance in your own life between different aspects of the warrior. Some people need to practice expressing more of the peaceful, gentle aspect of the warrior ideal. Others need to embrace the stronger, martial aspects. In our communication, some need to get better at dueling, while others need to learn to duet more.

Rule #9

Understand and Heal Your Adverse Childhood Experiences and Male Attachment Disorders

"Freedom is what you do with what's been done to you."

~Jean-Paul Sartre

This is the most difficult chapter for me to write. I've spent most of my life trying to avoid addressing my past wounds and traumas. In fact, until recently I never considered my early life *traumatic*. Sure, my father had a "nervous breakdown," took an overdose of sleeping pills, and was committed to a mental hospital when I was five years old. Yes, my mother left the home to work full-time and I grew up with both an absent father and a death-obsessed mother. And my mother thought that forced enemas were a solution to my constipation. But that was just the way life was. We've all got shit to deal with (no pun intended), I reasoned. And there's no use talking about it or even thinking about it.

In my world, and in the world of most men I know, the past is the past and it's not worth mucking around in it. The Man Box culture tells us that being a man is about forgetting the past, doing what you have to do to succeed. It's about showing your parents, society, and everyone else that we're tough and can take it. It's about fighting to get to the top and looking to the future. Real men don't look back.

It never occurred to me that my lifelong anger and depression and later my two broken marriages had anything to do with my past. All that changed in 1998 when I reached out to a colleague, Dr. Charles Whitfield, because I couldn't seem to heal my depression in spite of the fact that I was receiving good therapy and was taking medications. He told me that the missing piece in my healing might be addressing childhood trauma.

Dr. Whitfield introduced me to the Adverse Childhood Experiences (ACEs) studies developed by Vincent Felitti, MD, former head of Kaiser Permanente's

Department of Internal Medicine in San Diego and Dr. Robert Anda, a medical epidemiologist at the CDC. "The information the studies have provided us is not just helpful," said Whitfield, "it is astounding."

He went on to describe the original studies and what they learned. "Felitti and Anda and their colleagues looked at 9,508 middle-class, middle-aged people in Southern California. All were members of Kaiser's health maintenance organization who were medically evaluated and then each completed a sixty-eight-question survey about seven categories of childhood trauma and subsequent illness. The researchers also had the medical records of each patient with which to verify the findings."

They found that a large percentage of this general medical clinic population reported the following traumatic experiences from their childhoods.

- Physical abuse
- Sexual abuse
- Emotional abuse
- Physical neglect
- Emotional neglect
- Exposure to domestic violence
- Household substance abuse
- Household mental illness
- Parental separation or divorce
- Incarcerated household member

Their findings rocked the world of healthcare. It offered a whole different approach for understanding, treating, and preventing disease—everything from cancer and heart disease to obesity and depression. All these problems, and more, had roots in our childhood experiences of trauma.

They found the following to be true:

- More than half of respondents reported at least one ACE.
- If you have one ACE, you are highly likely to have two or more ACEs.
- The more ACEs you have as a child, the more likely you are to have a whole range of physical and emotional problems as an adult.

I was anxious to see how I would score and answered the following questions developed by the ACE researchers for the general public:

Prior to your 18th birthday:

1. Did a parent or other adult in the household often or very often . . . Swear at you, insult you, put you down, or humiliate you? or Act in a way that made you afraid that you might be physically hurt? No____If Yes, enter 1____

2. Did a parent or other adult in the household often or very often . . . Push, grab, slap, or throw something at you? or Ever hit you so hard that you had marks or were injured?   No_____ If Yes, enter 1_____

3. Did an adult or person at least 5 years older than you ever... Touch or fondle you or have you touch their body in a sexual way? or Attempt or actually have oral, anal, or vaginal intercourse with you?   No_____
If Yes, enter 1_____

4. Did you often or very often feel that . . . No one in your family loved you or thought you were important or special? or Your family didn't look out for each other, feel close to each other, or support each other?   No_____
If Yes, enter 1_____

5. Did you often or very often feel that . . . You didn't have enough to eat, had to wear dirty clothes, and had no one to protect you? or Your parents were too drunk or high to take care of you or take you to the doctor if you needed it?   No_____ If Yes, enter 1_____

6. Were your parents ever separated or divorced?   No_____
If Yes, enter 1_____

7. Was your mother or stepmother:

Often or very often pushed, grabbed, slapped, or had something thrown at her? or Sometimes, often, or very often kicked, bitten, hit with a fist, or hit with something hard? or Ever repeatedly hit over at least a few minutes or threatened with a gun or knife?   No_____ If Yes, enter 1_____

8. Did you live with anyone who was a problem drinker or alcoholic, or who used street drugs?   No_____ If Yes, enter 1_____

9. Was a household member depressed or mentally ill, or did a household member attempt suicide?   No_____ If Yes, enter 1_____

10. Did a household member go to prison?   No_____ If Yes, enter 1_____

Now add up your "Yes" answers: _____ . This is your ACE Score.

I found I had 4 ACEs, which is great if you're playing poker. However, in the game of life four ACEs are very risky. The study found the following increased risk factors for those who had 4 or more ACES compared to those who had none:

- A 4- to 12-fold increase in health risks for alcoholism, drug abuse, depression, and suicide attempt.
- A 2- to 4-fold increase in smoking, poor self-rated health, having more than 50 sexual intercourse partners, and sexually transmitted disease.
- A 1.4- to 1.6-fold increase in physical inactivity and severe obesity.

New Understandings From the ACE Studies

Since the first ACE studies were reported in 1998, there have been hundreds of further studies that have validated the basic findings: Adverse Childhood Experiences (ACEs) can cause later physical and emotional problems in adulthood.

The latest information about current research on ACEs is available on two websites developed by journalist Jane Ellen Stevens: www.AcesTooHigh.com and www.AcesConnection.com. Stevens has been a newspaper and magazine journalist focusing on health, science, and technology for more than 30 years and has been reporting on ACE studies and related research since 2005.

Subsequent to the original ACE Study, other ACE surveys have expanded the types of ACEs so if you have had any of the following experiences add another number to your ACE score.

1. Did you experience racism?   No_____ If Yes, enter 1_____

2. Did you experience gender discrimination?   No_____ If Yes, enter 1_____

3. Did you witness a sibling being abused?   No_____ If Yes, enter 1_____

4. Did you witness violence outside the home?   No_____ If Yes, enter 1_____

5. Did you witness a father being abused by a mother?   No_____
   If Yes, enter 1_____

6. Were you bullied by a peer or adult?   No_____ If Yes, enter 1_____

7. Were you hospitalized, in foster care, or forced to live away from
   your family?   No_____ If Yes, enter 1_____

8. Did you grow up and live in a war zone?   No_____ If Yes, enter 1_____

9. Did you grow up in an unsafe neighborhood?   No_____
   If Yes, enter 1_____

10. Was a family member deported or did you live in fear of deportation?
    No_____ If Yes, enter 1_____

How ACEs Early in Life Can Lead to Problems Later in Life

It took me many years to really understand how events in childhood, even relatively common ones such as having parents who divorced or had mental health problems, could lead to an increased risk for adult depression or heart disease.

The doctors who designed the initial research had some tentative ideas. Now these ideas have been tested and accepted. They are posted on the Centers for Disease Control and Prevention website. The mechanism for our childhood traumas leading to later problems as adults goes like this:

Adverse Childhood Experiences (ACEs) leads to faulty neurodevelopment, which leads to social, emotional, and cognitive impairment, which leads to adoption of risky health behaviors, which leads to disease, disability, and social problems, which leads to a shortened life and early death.

This has helped me understand how ACEs had contributed to the problems I experienced as a child and also later in life. As noted early, I experienced 4 ACEs growing up. I came to understand that the effect of these early traumatic experiences had caused a disruption in how my brain functioned. As a child, I felt different. With my father locked up in a mental hospital and my mother terrified that I would end up like my father, I went on with my life, but I always felt afraid. I worried constantly about whether I would end up like my father. Would I be locked up? Would I feel so depressed I would want to die?

Without knowing it, my brain chemistry, and even the way my genes turned on certain pathways and turned off others, had been affected by the ongoing toxic stress in my life, not just from the life events I experienced, but also from the ways it impacted my social, emotional, and cognitive development. I had a difficult time trusting other people. I lived in a fantasy world with imaginary friends. Not being able to trust the world of adults, I retreated into my own world.

Over the years I engaged in risky behaviors in an attempt to deal with the emotional pain I was experiencing. As a child I climbed trees and wanted to get to the very top. It terrified my mother, but it was my way of trying to escape from my stressful family life. Later in life, I engaged a risky sexual behavior. I experienced manic highs and depressive lows. I became a workaholic trying to stay super busy so I wouldn't have to face my fears and worries.

As an adult, I had a number of physical ailments. I suffered breathing problems all my life, with childhood and adult asthma. My manic-depressive behavior and acting-out sexual behavior strained my relationships, and I was married and divorced twice before I was able to get a handle on my ACEs and get the understanding, counseling, and support I needed.

Male Attachment Disorders: How ACEs Can Undermine a Man's Relationships

Not only are relationships an important part of our lives, but a good relationship can make our lives worthwhile and keep us healthy. In their book, *Loneliness: Human Nature and the Need for Social Connection,* social scientists John Cacioppo and William Patrick report that "When people are asked what pleasures contribute most to happiness, the overwhelming majority rate love, intimacy, and social affiliation above wealth, or fame, even above physical health."

One of the great tragedies of having unhealed ACEs is that they undermine our ability to have healthy, joyful relationships. Looking back, it's clear that my unrecognized ACEs contributed to my two divorces and that healing my ACEs has contributed to the fact that Carlin and I have been happily married for nearly forty years now.

Too many men suffer from what I call *Male Attachment Disorder,* or MAD for short. Our childhood wounds keep us irritable, angry, and undermine our ability to be truly intimate in our love lives. Here are eight aspects of MAD.

1. Agitation and anger.
Our Adverse Childhood Experiences undermine our ability to trust others and to have a healthy sex and love life as an adult. For men, the pain often expresses itself as irritability and anger. I was always agitated like a cat on a hot tin roof and easily triggered. Men's anger causes us to become increasingly cut off from others, which increases our loneliness and makes us even madder.

2. Male-type depression.
Depressed women often turn their sadness inward. Depressed men become more irritable and angry. Male-type depression usually goes unrecognized, and irritable and angry men usually cause others to withdraw from them, which increases their pain and suffering. Feeling misunderstood and cut off from others, they tend to deny their own contribution to the problem and often blame their wives or partners.

3. Impulsiveness and risk-taking.
MAD men are impulsive and take more risks. I was successful in my work, wrote books, and spoke all over the world. Risk-taking can be an asset at work, but at home it kept everything on edge. You never knew what I might do next. Men, in general, take more risks than women, but men who suffer from ACEs take greater risks than

most. One client of mine continued to have unprotected sex with strangers despite knowing that he was putting himself at risk of getting AIDS.

4. Need for control.
When men grow up with unrecognized and unhealed ACEs, their lives become increasingly out of control. Inside, they feel confused and frightened. Yet, they are often unwilling to address their internal fears and so they do everything they can to control others. One of my clients tried to control every aspect of his wife's social life. He wanted her to dress in clothes that he approved of for her, and if she was a minute late in getting ready for an outing, he would go into a rage.

5. Resistance to love and guidance.
Men like this are hungry for guidance and love, but they resist it at every turn. Even caring offers of support or suggestions about taking better care of themselves or going to the doctor for a checkup is met with angry resistance. Carlin often tried to tell me that I needed help, but I refused, vehemently. Since I couldn't trust my caregivers growing up, I had a horrific time trusting those who loved me later.

6. Denial and blame.
Men often deny that they are responsible for any of the problems in their lives. They blame the government, the people at work, and most often the people closest to them. They have huge fights with their kids and often become enraged. They also blame their wives. For years, I refused to recognize and accept that I had a problem. I blamed it on everything else—stress, work, politics, my kids, my wife—anything but my life and what was really causing the problem. When I talk to male clients, I often have to get them to see that it isn't their *wife* that is out of control, but it is their *life*. I help them to stop trying to get their wife to change and begin getting them to change their lives.

7. Addictive personality and behavior.
One of the most common ways men attempt to deal with the pain and discomfort of unhealed ACEs is the increased use of alcohol and other drugs. Often, use begins with a natural desire to relax from the stresses of life, but often becomes habitual as the unhealed wounds from the past make relationship increasingly stressful. Many then drink, use drugs, or find other means of relief and a vicious cycle begins.

8. Confusion and helplessness.
Since men don't often recognize the underlying cause of their problems, their relationships become increasingly frustrating and dysfunctional and they feel increasingly confused and helpless. The men often withdraw even more, may have an affair in an attempt to find the love they so desperately need, but as the title of my book says,

they are *looking for love in all the wrong places.* They are looking outside themselves to deal with feelings. These men need to look inside and deal with the underlying causes.

Fortunately, addressing our ACEs and childhood trauma can help men heal from our male attachment disorders.

Trauma: It's Not What You Think

When most of us think of trauma, we think of extreme situations—soldiers facing extreme stress in battle, children being sexually abused, or an adult being raped. We don't think of trauma as the more subtle and common events that occur in most of our lives as we are growing up. The ACE studies have shown conclusively that events don't need to be extreme in order to have serious, negative consequences later in our lives.

In their book, *Code to Joy: The Four-Step Solution to Unlocking Your Natural State of Happiness,* George Pratt, PhD, Peter Lambrou, PhD, and John David Mann illustrate the way in which we underestimate the effect of common ACEs. They ask you to imagine you are standing just outside your home, surrounded by a dense fog, so thick you can't see the other side of the street in front of you. You look to the left, to the right, but can't see more than fifty feet in any direction. You are surrounded. You feel cut off from everything and you feel frightened and alone.

They ask, how much water does it take to create the blanket of fog that has completely isolated you from your world? The surprising answer is *a few ounces.* The total volume of water in a blanket of fog one acre around and one meter deep would not quite fill an ordinary drinking glass. The fog actually contains 400 billion tiny droplets suspended in the air creating an impenetrable cloak that shuts out light and makes you shiver.

This is what happens when we have painful experiences that we just can't shake. Pratt and Lambrou call it "the fog of distress" and it is this fog that occurs when we experience one or more ACEs. The underlying cause may be as common as a few ounces of water, but the impact can change our lives.

"Typically, this vague sense of unease parks itself in the background," say the authors, "like the annoying hum of a refrigerator or air conditioner we have learned to block out from our conscious awareness." We get on with our lives and forget the ACEs we grew up with. However, as the studies show, they affect our lives nonetheless. "Whether we are aware of it or not, it pervades our existence like an insistent headache, interfering with our ability to have healthy relationships, to perform to our potential at work, or to have lives that are anywhere near as fulfilling as they could be."

Their conclusion is similar to what the researchers found with the ACE studies. "Over the years, that background hum can sabotage our careers, friendships, marriages." It's not surprising that since the wounds occur in our most intimate relationships in our families, their impact is felt in our most intimate adult relationships.

Bessel van der Kolk, MD, is one of the world's leading experts on trauma. In his book, *The Body Keeps the Score: Brain, Mind, and Body in the Healing of Trauma,* he says, "Trauma affects not only those who are directly exposed to it, but also those around them. The wives of men who suffer from PTSD tend to become depressed, and the children of depressed mothers are at risk of growing up insecure and anxious. Long after a traumatic experience is over, it may be reactivated at the slightest hint of danger and mobilize disturbed brain circuits and secrete massive amounts of stress hormones."

The Good News About ACEs and Trauma is That They Can Be Healed

Before I learned about ACEs, it never occurred to me that childhood trauma had anything to do with my adult problems. I just thought my anxiety, depression, asthma, breathing problems were just things I had to learn to live with. After I learned about ACEs, I felt I understood better why I am the way I am, but I thought there was nothing I could do about it. *You can't change what happened in the past.* But I was wrong. We actually can change the past and we can do that by literally changing our minds.

I first learned about this from Bruce Lipton, PhD, an internationally recognized authority in bridging science and spirit and a leading voice in new biology. In his book, *The Biology of Belief: Unleashing the Power of Consciousness, Matter & Miracles,* he introduced research that shows that we can actually change the way our genes operate by changing the environment, including the way we think about what has happened to us in the past. He shows that genes and DNA do not control our biology, but instead, DNA is controlled by signals from outside, including the energetic messages emanating from our positive and negative thoughts.

I learned that I was not stuck with the problems that resulted from my ACEs or even from my genetic vulnerability to depression and bipolar disorder that I inherited from my father. I could change the program by changing my environment—what I ate, how I slept, the kind of exercise I did, how I connected with friends and family, and most importantly, how I thought.

In her book, *Mind Over Medicine: Scientific Proof That You Can Heal Yourself,* Lissa Rankin, MD shares her own story of how she healed herself and how we can too. "We've been led to believe that when we get sick, it's our genetics," she says, "or it's just bad lack and doctors alone hold the keys to optimal health." Through her research, she discovered that the health care she had been taught to practice was missing something crucial: a recognition of the body's innate ability to self-repair and an appreciation for how we can control these self-healing mechanisms with the power of the mind.

A new film, *Is Your Story Making You Sick,* features experts in the field and offers a new approach for healing past trauma. Learn more about these issues in the resource section at the end of the book.

ACE Science in Action: Getting the Help We Need

ACE science has revolutionized our view of health and illness. When someone went to a doctor or counselor with complaints, we looked at the person through the lens of a *disease model*. We looked for the underlying causes of the disease and asked *what's wrong with this person?* A trauma-informed model changes the paradigm. Instead of seeing the person as "sick," we see them as having responded to early trauma in a way that helped them survive in the past, but may be problematic now.

Rather than wondering what's wrong with you, we want to know *what happened to you*. We recognize the creative ways the person survived past trauma and help them see that they're not to blame for their problems, but they are responsible for seeking the truth of what happened to them and get the help they need to heal.

Here are the steps I have found helpful in getting the help you need.

• Become curious about your past and how it may have impacted your later life.

When I first read the ACE studies twenty years ago, my first reaction was, Wow, could this be true? I wanted to learn about my own ACEs.

• Answer the ACE questions and get your score.

Getting our score gives us power. We can't change something we're not aware is causing a problem.

• Recognize that there is a connection between our wounds from the past and our adult physical and emotional problems.

We have to begin to connect the dots of our lives, to see how the adverse childhood experiences from our past are connected to our present anxiety, depression, anger, heart disease, diabetes, etc.

• Understand the way in which the events of the past cause us to develop certain beliefs about ourselves including the following: I'm not loveable. I am worthless. I am powerless. I am not safe. I cannot trust anyone. I am bad. I am alone.

• Get your resilience score.

When I first got my ACE score, I was excited to finally understand a lot more about my childhood and its connection to my adult issues, but it also felt overwhelming. I wondered if I was doomed to live with the chronic problems resulting from ACEs. The good news is that healing can happen no matter what our ACE score may be.

I found that, in fact, it was already happening. Even while I was experiencing ACEs as a child, I also had experiences that were making me stronger. Over time, the ACE researchers came to recognize our human resilience allows us to moderate the potential impact of ACEs. Here are some of the potential positive beliefs and experiences that many of us carry. Which ones are true for you?

1. I believe that my mother loved me when I was little.

2. I believe that my father loved me when I was little.

3. When I was little, other people helped my mother and father take care of me and they seemed to love me.

4. I've heard that when I was an infant someone in my family enjoyed playing with me, and I enjoyed it, too.

5. When I was a child, there were relatives in my family who made me feel better if I was sad or worried.

6. When I was a child, neighbors or my friends' parents seemed to like me.

7. When I was a child, teachers, coaches, youth leaders, or ministers were there to help me.

8. Someone in my family cared about how I was doing in school.

9. My family, neighbors, and friends talked often about making my life better.

10. We had rules in our house and were expected to keep them.

11. When I felt really bad, I could almost always find someone I trusted to talk to.

12. As a youth, people noticed that I was capable and could get things done.

13. I was independent and a go-getter.

14. I believed that life is what you make it.

How many of these 14 protective factors did you have as a child and youth? Of these, how many are still true for you? _____

It was heartening to remember that in addition to the traumatic experiences, there were many experiences where I felt care for, loved, and supported, not only by my parents but also by others.

• Work with a trauma-informed counselor or therapist.

Fortunately, there are many people who have been trained to help us address these issues. The AcesTooHigh website brings together the latest information on how ACEs science is being used here in the US and throughout the world. I often read and reread the section on their site that is called "ACES Science 101."

I also recommend you check out the companion site, ACEsConnection.com. Jane Ellen Stevens says, "If you're working to lower ACE scores in your personal, work, play, faith-based or community life—and this includes any endeavor, from art to politics—please consider joining ACEs Connection. It's the companion social network to ACEsTooHigh.com. ACEsConnection.com is for people who are implementing—or thinking about implementing—trauma-informed and resilience-building practices based on ACEs research. As of February, 2019 there were 27,000 members in the community."

Bottom Line: Understand and Heal Your Adverse Childhood Experiences

The research on ACEs demonstrates clearly that our childhood experiences can impact our adult physical and emotional health, as well as our adult love lives. Although unrecognized and untreated ACEs can increase our risk of developing everything from heart disease to troubled marriages, we are not prisoners of our past or doomed to a life of pain and suffering.

In order to heal, we have to be willing to look honestly and our past trauma. For men, this can be difficult. Our Man Box culture tells us that we're tough and can handle anything that happens to us without needing help. Yet, the new rules of manhood enable us to reach out for support.

Rule #10

Heal Your Father Wound and Become the Father You Were Meant to Be

"A psychiatrist once said to me, 'You will begin to forgive the world when you forgive your father.'"

~"The Man in the Overstuffed Chair," Tennessee Williams,
Antæus magazine, No. 45/46 (Spring/Summer 1982)

We all have a father somewhere in our lives. Some fathers have been a loving presence in our lives since the moment we were conceived. Most of us have grown up in families where our father was absent physically or emotionally and we didn't get the fathering we needed. We know from the ACE studies discussed in Chapter 9 that growing up without a loving, supportive, and emotionally engaged father is one of the Adverse Childhood Experiences that can cause later problems in our love lives, in our work lives, and in how we see ourselves as men. In fact, what I call *the family father wound* is the most common and least recognized ACE many of us will experience in our lives.

The history with my father has evolved over the years. For most of my life I told a simple story:

My father left when I was five years old. I was an only child, raised by a single mom. We got along fine without him and though my mother often had difficulty making ends meet, we got by okay. My life growing up was pretty great. Since my mother worked full-time, I had a lot of freedom and had many great adventures taking the bus into Hollywood, going to plays, and watching movies. I got to be an adult by the time I was eight years old.

The truth was, I blocked out a lot of early memories of trauma and only later came to fill in the blanks and tell a more complete story beginning when my uncle Harry drove me to the mental hospital.

"Why do I have to go?" I asked Uncle Harry.

He looked at me with his round face and kind eyes. "Your father needs you."

"What's the matter with him?" I was beginning to cry and I clamped my throat tight to stop the tears.

He turned away and looked back at the road. In our family, we didn't talk about difficult issues. I knew that my father was in a hospital and it was my duty to visit him. It never occurred to me to ask why my mother didn't come to visit. I just knew I was being her "brave little man" by going to visit my father at the hospital, two hours north of our home in Los Angeles.

I shivered thinking about my father's angry outbursts and cold silences and wondered how he would be when I saw him in the hospital.

What I saw at Camarillo State Mental Hospital in 1949 chilled me to my bones. As we walked on cleanly polished floors, I gazed up at the plain off-white walls. I peeked into a big room that had rows of identical, white metal beds that nearly touched each other. Women in some of the beds were moaning and others were sitting in chairs rocking. I tried to pull away and turn around, but my uncle held my hand and led us to the visitor's room.

People were everywhere and they were all in motion. A man in a white hospital gown walked around in circles, mumbling to himself as he made strange gestures with his fingers. A woman ran into the room yelling, "Don't let them take me. Jesus, save me." Two orderlies grabbed her by the arms and took her out of the room. A group of men walked back and forth, talking, but not to each other. A woman with gray hair dressed in a long dress that had once been blue, but was now faded nearly to white, twirled in circles and sang a sweet, sad song.

"Uncle Harry, please let's go home." This place wasn't like anything I'd ever experienced in my life and I was terrified.

"It's going to be okay," Uncle Harry told me. But he looked scared himself.

Along the sides of the room men and women sat in wooden chairs, their bodies rocking in a strange way. They looked like little toy ducks that bob up and down sipping water. I thought of men I'd seen in the synagogue who prayed as they rocked up and down, bending from the waist.

I noticed my father at the back of the room. He jumped to his feet when he saw us. I wanted to go to him, but I held back. He looked strange. His hair was messed up. His clothes hung on him, and he had a wild look in his eyes I had never seen before.

I visited my father for an entire year. He clearly was getting worse, not better, and eventually he didn't even know who I was. I felt traumatized by his leaving and even more traumatized by our visits. Years later, I learned that the movie *The Snake Pit* starring Olivia de Havilland was filmed there, and I resonated with the horrors depicted in the film.

In this telling of the story, I had to deal with my father's mental illness, and the suicide attempt that precipitated his commitment to the mental hospital. I had to delve deeply into my own depression and bipolar disorder and what I may have inherited from my father. I got a better understanding of what caused the despair that let to my father's time in Camarillo when I found his journals where he recounted his feelings and experiences during this difficult time of his life.

September 2, 1948:
"The heaping up of many failures unbalances a man's worth and I often lose complete faith in myself. The feelings of inferiority are overwhelming. I must constantly be reminded of my accomplishments, no matter how small, to keep my self-respect and belief in my intrinsic worth."

September 14, 1948:
"How much can my wife stand? When in this world will I ever have a piece of bread that isn't encrusted with fear and doubt, with all those moldy devils turning my blood to water and my stomach to mush. I feel like a gutless zero."

October 10, 1948:
"Oh, Christ, if I could only give my son a decent education—a college degree with a love for books, a love for people, good, solid knowledge. No guidance was given to me. I slogged and slobbered and blundered through two-thirds of my life. I can't make a decent living and it's killing me."

December 8, 1948:
"Your flesh crawls, your scalp wrinkles when you look around and see good writers, established writers, writers with credits a block long, unable to sell, unable to find work, Yes, it's enough to make anyone blanch, turn pale and sicken."

January 24, 1949:
"Faster, faster, faster, I walk. I plug away looking for work, anything to support my family. I try, try, try, try, try. I always try and never stop."

June 8, 1949:
"A hundred failures, an endless number of failures, until now, my confidence, my hope, my belief in myself, has run completely out. Middle aged, I stand and gaze ahead, numb, confused, and desperately worried. All around me I see the young in spirit, the young in heart, with ten times my confidence, twice my youth, ten times my fervor, twice my education. I see them all, a whole army of them, battering at the same doors I'm battering, trying in the same field I'm trying. Today I feel my hope and my life stream are both running desperately low, so low, so stagnant, that I hold my breath in fear, believing that the dark, blank curtain is about to descend."

Two weeks after this last entry, my father took an overdose of sleeping pills. Like millions of men, then and now, he felt like he couldn't support his family and as a result he was consumed with shame. He felt hopeless and didn't see a way out. He blamed himself for his inability to find work and didn't see the invisible constraints that society places on men. He believed it was his own fault if he couldn't find work. In his mind it meant he had let his family down and was a failure in the eyes of his wife, his son, and himself.

But luckily, his life didn't end. I still get tears in my eyes reading his journal entries as he struggled to make a living and wrote his poetic lament, "When in this world will I ever have a piece of bread that isn't encrusted with fear and doubt, with all those moldy devils turning my blood to water and my stomach to mush. I feel like a gutless zero."

The Rest of the Story on the Way to Healing the Father Wound

To understand the full story of healing the father wound, you have to understand the excitement of a young man leaving his home in Jacksonville, Florida to come to New York. It was May 17, 1929 and my twenty-two-year-old father had a dream. Here's how he described it in his journal:

"From as far back as I can remember, I wanted to be an actor. With the plaudits of my Little Theatre devotees ringing in my ears, I left my hometown. For the privilege of driving a *poultry farmerette* and her family to New York, I received free transportation. After an arduous thousand-mile journey, we arrived. The farmerette and her children went one way. I checked into the Grand Hotel. One day was all I could afford.

"A squib in the *Morning Telegraph* hit me between the teeth. The famed actress, producer, and director Eva Le Gallienne was auditioning people for her repertory company. That was my cue to head to 14th Street. The stairs were rickety but the smell was just right. My nostrils were dilating like those of a full-grown rabbit. This was the theatre."

He described the initial interview with Miss Le Gallienne's assistant, who he impressed enough to be granted an audition the next day with Miss L herself.

"The rickety stairs again. I took them slowly. It was stage fright all right. Everything chattered, from my teeth down. There was a cathedral-like hush about the place. This was nice, and no organ music. That made it perfect. Would Miss L be...? But I didn't have a chance to finish the thought. At the top of the stairs, behind a screen, the young producer-director sat, serene and friendly. Young too. Reddish, blond bob. Earrings, blue satin blouse and skirt.

"She didn't waste a second. 'What's your name and what will you do?' A scene from 'The Man Who Came Back.' They liked that at home. I lit a cigarette, and emoted to an imaginary woman on the floor. After my dramatic moment, Miss L gave me a scene to read. That was the audition, no more. She nodded her approval.

'Rehearsals start in two weeks...' Accepted! Accepted! I didn't believe in pinching myself. I bruise easily, but I did have to hold on to a chair to keep from floating up with the frescoes. The seal of approval from Miss L. Just an apprentice, but in a real professional company. Maybe a chance for small parts. Maybe a chance for stardom.

"Two days ago—nobody. Now look at me. One interview, one audition, one acceptance. Batting average . . . . perfect."

My father was on the top of the world.

He spent a full season with Eva Le Gallienne's company. Le Gallienne was a British-born American stage actress, producer, director, translator, and author. She was a Broadway star by age twenty-one, but by the time she was twenty-six she ended her work on Broadway to devote herself to founding the Civic Repertory Theater, in which she was both director, producer, and lead actress. Among the company's apprentices were such hopeful novices as Burgess Meredith, John Garfield, J. Edward Bromberg and Howard Da Silva, who later became famous in theater and films.

But my father had bad luck coming to New York just before the stock market crash in 1929 which brought on the Great Depression. He was even more unlucky when he came to Hollywood following his work in New York at a time during the "Red Scare" when left-wing and progressive writer, actors, and playwrights were blacklisted. My father became increasingly depressed at not being able to make a living and ended up in the mental hospital.

That might have been the end of the story, but my father escaped from the mental hospital and became a street puppeteer in Los Angeles and later in San Francisco. In this final telling of his story, he became a great success, was able to be the man he was meant to be and brought joy to men, women, and children throughout the world, including me and my children. When he died in 1996, there was an article in the *San Francisco Chronicle* titled *Requiem for S.F. Puppet Man:*

The Tenderloin said goodbye to Tommy Roberts [The name my father used after he escaped from the mental hospital], with tears in its eyes and cookies in its mouth. The crowd jammed every seat and spilled out into the hallway. They snatched up free copies of Roberts' poems. "Because of you," said one, "old madness has become new meaning. Because of you, my tongue is no longer lead." Sculptor Ruth Asawa, who made puppets for Roberts, cradled one of them in her arms. Reverend Glenda Hope, who preaches on the streets of the Tenderloin, delivered the eulogy in a wildly colorful flower tunic.

"The black jacket didn't seem appropriate today.

"He and his puppets last appeared at the opening of the New Main Library in San Francisco last month. It took Roberts about two hours to walk the half mile to the library on his son's arm.

"Einstein once said that one should not strive to be a man of success, but a man of value," his son, Jed, said."

Paper cups of bright red punch were raised all around.

"Him and me, we got along good," said the guy from down the hall. "He was the puppet man."

I know there are millions of men like my father who feel the pain of trying to live up to the demands that society imposes on men. Like many children of such fathers, I, too, had to deal with the trauma of growing up in a family where my father was absent, first emotionally and later after he was gone physically.

The Family Father Wound is Pervasive and Its Effects Ripple Through Society

According to the National Center for Fathering, "More than 20 million children live in a home without the physical presence of a father. Millions more have dads who are physically present, but emotionally absent. If it were classified as a disease, fatherlessness would be an epidemic worthy of attention as a national emergency."

The family father wound impacts four critical areas of our lives:

- Our physical health
- Our emotional health
- Our relationship health
- Our social and political health

The effects of growing up without a loving, engaged father ripple through the generations and contribute to many of the most serious problems we face in our society today including:

- Drug and alcohol abuse
- Depression and suicide
- Teen pregnancy
- Sexual dysfunction, harassment, and addiction
- Poverty
- Unhappy marriages
- Crime, conflict, and violence
- Fear and aggression between groups

In their book, *The Boy Crisis: Why Our Boys Are Struggling and What We Can Do About It,* Warren Farrell and John Gray cite the following statistics about the negative impact of the absent fathers on their children, particularly on our boys.

- Children with father loss have, by the age of nine, a 14% reduction in chromosome telomere length—the most reliable predictors of life expectancy. In addition, the telomere loss is 40% greater for boys than for girls.

- Living in a home without a dad has a greater correlation with suicide among teenagers than any other factor.
- Every 1% increase in fatherlessness in a neighborhood predicts a 3% increase in adolescent violence.
- Among youths in prisons, 85% grew up in a fatherless home. Prisons are basically centers for dad-deprived young men.
- Dad deprivation increases the likelihood of teenage motherhood.
- Dad-deprived boys search for structure and respect in gangs.
- A study of ISIS fighters concluded that almost all male and female fighters had in common "some type of an 'absent father' syndrome."

Fatherlessness has become so pervasive in society that it has come to be accepted as normal. Yet, it is anything but normal. Fatherlessness perpetuates the cycle of fathers producing children who are wounded, who themselves grow up to become, or to marry, a wounded man.

In working with men for more fifty years now, I'd venture to say that all of us have father issues to work on, even those of us who had fathers who were a positive presence in our lives. Here are the things I've learned that I think are most helpful.

Understanding the Father Wound

When our fathers are distant either through divorce, death, or disengagement, we are left with a deep wound, which we most often fail to recognize. The psychologist, James Hollis, says, "When men feel the wound they cannot heal, they either bury themselves in a woman's arms and ask her for healing, which she cannot provide, or they hide themselves in macho pride and enforced loneliness."

Until I was forced to address my father wound at mid-life when the relationship with my wife was deteriorating, I had tried both options Hollis describes. I was forever trying to get the women in my life to give me the love I mistakenly believed they were withholding. When that didn't work, I would become angry and demanding, and then I'd withdraw into hurtful silence.

"All men, whether they know it or not, hunger for their father and grieve over his loss," says Hollis. "They long for his body, his strength, his wisdom." I believe this is true for women as well. But it's a different kind of wound for men. Women can identify with their mothers, and though they will feel wounded if a father is gone, they don't feel as lost as men feel when we grow up without an emotionally engaged father.

I know I missed my father's body, strength, and wisdom and never felt fully embodied as a man until I worked through my father wound issues. No matter what I did, how many women I'd slept with, or how successful I was at work, I never felt like a grownup man.

"A father may be physically present, but absent in spirit," says Hollis. "His absence may be literal through death, divorce, or dysfunction, but more often it is a symbolic absence through silence and the inability to transmit what he also may not have acquired." Most of us suffer from growing up with a distant, absent, or dysfunctional father, who himself grew up in a family where he was wounded by a distant, absent, or dysfunctional father.

It's no wonder that rates of depression and suicide are on the rise, particularly among older, white males. Further, more and more people are suffering from chronic pain and are overdosing on pain medications.

Do You Suffer From a Family Father Wound?

According to Roland Warren, former head of the National Fatherhood Initiative, "Kids have a hole in their soul in the shape of their dad. And if a father is unwilling or unable to fill that hole, it can leave a wound that is not easily healed."

For millions of men and women, the father wound influences our health and well-being, but we are not aware that it exists.

Here's **The Father-Wound Quiz** I use in my counseling practice to help people assess whether they may have been impacted by an absent father. Please check off each statement that is true for you.

- ❑ My father died when I was still a child.
- ❑ My parents divorced or were separated when I was young.
- ❑ My father was physically present, but emotionally distant.
- ❑ Growing up, my father worked a lot and he didn't have enough time to be with me.
- ❑ My father was very critical of me.
- ❑ I never felt I could please my father.
- ❑ My father rarely said, "I love you, I'm proud of you, I believe in you".
- ❑ One or both of my parents had mental health problems.
- ❑ One or both of my parents had drinking or drug problems.
- ❑ I sought out father-figures to help compensate for my father's absence.
- ❑ During adolescence I was angry a lot and sometimes got into fights.
- ❑ During adolescence I was eager to fall in love or had early sexual experiences.
- ❑ Having a best friend was extremely important to me.
- ❑ I felt lonely and depressed growing up, even though I may have covered it well.
- ❑ As an adult I have had difficulty finding and keeping a healthy relationship.
- ❑ I've been married and divorced at least once.
- ❑ I have difficulty committing to a relationship.
- ❑ I sometimes pick partners who aren't good for me in the long run.
- ❑ "Looking for love in all the wrong places" may have been written for me.

- ❑ With my own children, I worry about whether I'm being a good parent.
- ❑ I've vowed to be a different kind of father than my father was for me.
- ❑ I have been very successful at work, but less than successful in my love life.
- ❑ With my spouse or partner I often feel like a critical parent or a demanding child.
- ❑ I haven't made as much money as I'm worth or become as successful as I want.

Even those with healthy, involved fathers will check off a few of these statements. However, if you checked six or more, you may be suffering from the effects of an absent father. The more items you checked, the deeper the wound is likely to be.

Women Also Suffer From Father Wounds

One of the things I came to realize in my own life is that growing up with a distant, absent, or dysfunctional father means that we also grew up with a distant, absent, or dysfunctional mother. Before my father left when I was five, my mother worked at home and my dad had a number of short-lived jobs outside the home. After he left, my mother was forced to go out to work and I was left in various childcare arrangements.

It took me a long time to recognize that my mother experienced her own father wound. I knew my mother's father died when she was five years old, but she never talked about him. She seemed to have the attitude that losing her father was a fact of life and you just have to push your feelings down and get on with things. Growing up, I adopted the same attitude she had. It wasn't until I began writing my book, *My Distant Dad,* that I learned about my mother's father, John Kohn, and how his loss impacted my mother and was passed on to me.

In recent years, Mark Wolynn's book, *It Didn't Start with You: How Inherited Family Trauma Shapes Who We Are and How to End the Cycle,* helped me see that trauma and its impact on our lives didn't begin and end with what happened in my own childhood. It could ripple through the generations. Could the death of my mother's father be part of my own father wound? As William Faulkner reminds us, "The past is never dead. It's not even past."

One of the key language exercises Wolynn describes is to find our "core sentence," which captures our worst fear. Mine was *I'm alone and abandoned and those I love the most will die.* I always thought the origins of these fears were from growing up with a depressed father who tried to commit suicide and a mother who was obsessed with her own death. I had come to understand the father wound resulting from my lost father. But now I wanted to understand how the death of John Kohn, my mother's father, had impacted my life as well.

After my mother died, I asked my Aunt Florence, my mother's younger sister, about their father and what she remembered about who he was and how his death affected their lives. She didn't reply. My mother's silence about her father also seemed to extend to her sister, who was two years younger than my mom. I did receive a letter from her husband, my Uncle Bert. "I've been delegated to answer your letter about your grandfather," he wrote. "I don't know much. All Florence would say is that he died when she was a few years old." That was it, the full extent of the family history of John Kohn.

They did send a picture. But there was nothing written on the back. There was no name, no date, and no indication of where the picture was taken. I didn't even know for sure if it was my grandfather. It was frustrating knowing so little about him.

The picture shows a good-looking young man with dark hair, maybe in his late twenties, sitting on a chair with a book in his lap. He's looking straight at the camera. He's wearing a stylish porkpie hat. There's a bicycle behind him and two or three chairs stacked beside him. Over his left shoulder, you can make out part of the window of the building behind him. I took the picture to one of the meetings of my men's group with the hope that they might see things in the picture that would help me know if he was really my grandfather and what they might intuit about him, since I knew nothing.

"He looks like you," Tom said. "Same nose, the dark hair you had when you were younger."

"In most photos of that period the men posed formally, unsmiling," said Denis. "He's got a devilish little smile that reminds me of you."

It felt wonderful to me to have people see me in the picture of my grandfather. Maybe this really was the long-lost John Kohn.

"And look at how he's dressed," Tom continued. "Starting with the hat on his head, white shirt and tie, dark vest with pens in the pocket and a watch chain. He's holding a book that looks well read and he's wearing sleeve garters to keep the cuffs on his shirt from becoming soiled. This could have been you if you had been living at the time."

"Wow, that's amazing," I joined in. "That's the problem I always have with shirts. If they fit around my chest, the sleeves are too long."

"And look at his shoes and the cuffs on his pants," Dick pointed out. "The cuffs are about two inches long and his shoes have large heels. Looks to me, like he's a short guy like you, getting the most out what he's got."

Everyone laughed at that. They also noticed a painting of a good-looking woman in the shop window over his shoulder. "Got to be related to you," Tom said. "He's got an eye for good-looking women."

I noticed a cigarette on the sidewalk. I guessed he put it down just before the picture was taken and I thought of my mother who was a life-long smoker, which likely contributed to her death and likely contributed to John Kohn's early death at age thirty. As I came to see the full extent of the father wound in my life, it was like the puzzle pieces of my own life finally fell into place. I had a deep sense of peace and a feeling of wonder and the impact of our childhood wounding and how important it is for us to understand how fathers who are distant, absent, rejecting, or dysfunctional can impact our lives.

The Family Father Wound Makes Healthy Love Relationships Difficult

Like most people I was interested in sex from an early age. When I was seven years old, I was playing sexual games with little girl down the street. We explored each other's genitals and pretended to "play doctor." When we got caught by our parents, we weren't allowed to play together for a month. My mother wasn't too upset. I heard her talking to one of her neighbor friends and commenting, "Yeah, all kids play sex games and experiment. It's no big deal."

It is true that all children experiment and want to learn about our bodies and what they are capable of doing. Yet, early sexual experimentation and preoccupation can be indicators of childhood trauma and loss.

Numerous studies show that adverse childhood experiences, including a father's absence, can cause males and females to have early sexual experiences in adolescence or even earlier. Young women often report that they went along with sexual overtures because they wanted to feel wanted and desired. Only later did many realize that they were hungering for the love and affection of a father.

Young men who have grown up without the love and support of a father often become hyper-masculine, trying to cover their insecurities by showing they are a "real man." Often this involves becoming sexually flirtatious or aggressive.

Later, we often have difficulty finding a partner to settle down with. Or, we may find a partner, but our relationships are a roller coaster of ups and downs. We have trouble developing and maintaining real intimacy.

Attachment Wounds from Lost Fathers Can Be Healed

If you want great sex and love that lasts forever and never gets boring, there are some things you need to know that most of us have never learned. Forget about learning how to argue better. Forget about experimenting with new sexual positions or finding new sex toys.

Instead, get to the emotional underpinnings of your relationship by recognizing that you are emotionally attached to and dependent on your partner in much the same way that a child is on a parent for nurturing, soothing, and protection.

Many people recognize the importance of loving care and physical contact with infants and children for their emotional growth and development. But we think that once we grow up, we no longer need that kind of care. We believe that we must be more independent, stand on our own two feet, and take care of many of these emotional needs on our own. Men, in particular, are socialized to believe that it isn't manly to cry, to ask to be held when we are afraid, or to be talked to with quiet words of kindness and love.

This is a case where our evolutionary roots may not serve our own happiness. Women may be drawn to strong men, but they'll have a much better love life with a man who is emotionally responsive. Men may be drawn to multiple partners, but they'll have a much better sex life with a woman who they commit to now and forever.

Dr. Sue Johnson is a clinical psychologist, the developer of Emotionally Focused Couple Therapy, and a recognized leader in the new science of healthy relationships. She's written a number of important and helpful books and I consider her one of the most important guides for men and women who want a successful sex and love life.

In her books, *Hold Me Tight: Seven Conversations for a Lifetime of Love* and *Love Sense: The Revolutionary New Science of Romantic Relationships,* she offers simple, but scientifically tested guidance for having the sex and love lives all of us desire.

Much of modern psychotherapy has told people that there is something childish or emotionally immature about being attached to an adult lover. We have used terms like codependent, needy, and wimpy to describe people who express those needs. But that is beginning to change.

In Dr. Johnson's program she says that the key to a lifetime of good sex and love was "emotional responsiveness."

How A.R.E. You Really? Dr. Johnson asks rhetorically and uses A R E to summarize her simple guidance.

A is for Accessibility: Can I reach you?

This means staying open to your partner even when you have doubts and feel insecure. It often means being willing to struggle to make sense of your emotions so these emotions are not so overwhelming. You can then step back from your irritability, anger, and fear and can tune in to your lover's needs for connection and attachment.

R is for Responsiveness: Can I rely on you to respond to me emotionally?

This means tuning in to your partner and showing that his or her emotions, especially attachment needs and fears, have an impact on you. It means accepting and placing a priority on the emotional signals your partner conveys and sending clear signals of comfort and caring when your partner needs them. Sensitive responsiveness always touches us emotionally and calms us on a physical level.

E is for Engagement: Do I know you will value me and stay close?

The dictionary defines "engaged" as being absorbed, attracted, pulled, captivated, pledged, involved. Emotional engagement here means the very special kind of attention that we give only to a loved one. We gaze at them longer, touch them more. Partners often talk of this as being emotionally present. This kind of emotional bonding is what is present when we are having the best sex and love we could imagine.

The One Thing That Men Want More Than Sex

How many times have we heard the phrase, "All men want is sex?" When I was 17 years old, I was sure it was true. When I was 37 years old, I suspected it might not be true. And now that I'm 75 years old, I know it's not true. Now, don't get me wrong, sex can be wonderful at any age, but there's something that is more important than sex, but it's something that men have difficulty admitting and women have difficulty giving.

I call this something *a safe harbor.* The world of boys and men is a world of competition. By the time we become adults, we've already been battered and bruised by the world of competition and rejection. We long for that safe harbor where we don't have to pretend to be someone we're not in order to be chosen. We long for someone who sees us for who we are and wants us anyway, who can hold us and touch, not just our body, but our hearts and souls.

In other words, we want the feeling of being nurtured that most of us didn't get enough of when we were children. But admitting these needs makes us feel like little boys, not big strong men. Better to be manly with our sexual desire and then once we're inside her body, we can relax, be ourselves, and be infused with love. That's the hidden desire we have when we have sex.

Just as it's difficult for men to ask to be held, nurtured, and touched, it's often difficult for women to give that kind of intimacy. There are three main reasons, which are often subconscious:

First, women have their own conditioning about men being men. If he doesn't want sex, they worry that they may not be attractive enough.

Second, a man wanting to be held and nurtured triggers feelings that they are dealing with a boy, not a man. We all have to remember that we carry a little child inside us and adults need the same kind of loving attention and embrace that infants want and need.

Third, women fear men who don't feel manly. They know that the most violent men are men who feel weak and powerless. They've often had experiences with men allowing themselves to be gentle and vulnerable, only to have them respond with anger and rage later. It takes a lot of time and maturity for men to admit to themselves that they need a safe harbor where they can be nurtured and embraced by a woman. It takes a lot of courage to let his woman know he may want sex, but more important is his need for security, love, and nurture. **It requires a level of wisdom to know that allowing ourselves to be as vulnerable as a child may be the manliest thing we will ever do.**

For a woman, she must also go beyond her own conditioning and be open to a man who is making himself vulnerable in new ways. She must have a great deal of self-love and self-confidence to accept being a safe harbor. She must also have the strength to protect herself, when his shame at being vulnerable turns to anxiety, anger, or depression. It isn't easy for men and women to take these kinds of risks, but the payoff is a lifetime of deepening love and intimacy.

This is what Dr. Sue Johnson and others have found in their research. In order to have a great sex and love life, we need to feel safe and welcomed. When our partner holds us close and allows entry into her body, we feel we've finally come home.

Bottom Line: Heal Your Father Wound

This rule may be your most important one. So many of us have grown up without the support of a loving, engaged father, we forget how much we need him. We also fail to realize how his absence impacts our adult relationships. When we heal our father wounds, we not only heal ourselves, but we also heal our relationship with our wives and children. We can then truly become the fathers we were meant to be.

Rule #11

Treat the Irritable Male Syndrome and Male-Type Depression

When women are depressed, they eat or go shopping. Men invade another country. It's a whole different way of thinking.

~Comedian Elayne Boosler

Irritability and anger seem to be dominating our personal, professional, and political lives these days. A cover story in a recent issue of *The Atlantic* was titled "The Real Roots of American Rage." Written by Pulitzer Prize-winning writer Charles Duhigg, the article gives us "The untold story of how anger became the dominant emotion in our politics and personal lives—and what we can do about it."

Duhigg notes that anger can be positive. It energizes people to solve problems and can bring about positive political change by uniting people to address social ills such as sexism and racism. But anger can also be divisive and destructive. What the article doesn't address, though it is clear from the examples given, is that irritability and anger are problems that are much more common in men than in women.

We've all known a grumpy old man or two. Maybe he was the guy down the street who chased you off his lawn when you were a kid. Hollywood turned grumpy old men into comic icons in movies starring Jack Lemmon and Walter Matthau. While we sometimes laugh off the chronic crabbiness of a friend, we're just as likely to dismiss it as an unfortunate but inevitable part of being a man. But as we will see, there is more to this kind of behavior than what we see on the surface and it is no joking matter for those who are experiencing it or those who must live with a chronically irritable man.

For some, this kind of irritability has come on slowly over a period of months and years. For others, it seems like someone has flipped a switch and Mr. Nice has turned into Mr. Mean. "God, it's like he's hormonal," one woman told me. When I explained that she wasn't too far from the truth, she snapped back, "I knew it."

When I was conducting research for my book, *The Irritable Male Syndrome,* I conducted a survey in partnership with *Men's Health* magazine. The response was overwhelming. Nearly 6,000 men filled out the Irritable Male Syndrome Questionnaire. The respondents ranged in age from 10 to 75. The results were surprising and gave an initial look into the world of men:

Stress is a significant issue for men.

Only 8% said they are almost never stressed.
46% said they are often or almost always stressed.

Sex is a major concern.

46% of the men said they are almost never sexually satisfied.

Depression and irritability are related.

21% of men said they are depressed often or almost always. Only 9% said they are almost never irritable; 40% are irritable often or almost always.

Emotions related to depression are significant.

Only 7% said they almost never have a desire to *get away from it all,* but 62% said they often or almost always desire to do so.
Only 11% said they almost never have a strong fear of failure, but 55% said they often or almost always have a strong fear of failure.
Only 12% said they almost never feel burned out, compared to 44% who said they feel burned out often or almost always.
12% said they almost never feel empty inside, while 48% said they feel empty often or almost always.

What is The Irritable Male Syndrome?

In working with irritable, angry, and depressed men and their families for more than fifty years now, I've come to see irritable male syndrome (or IMS for short) as a multidimensional problem that affects and is affected by hormonal, physical, psychological, emotional, interpersonal, economic, social, sexual, and spiritual changes. One of the reasons it is so difficult to understand and deal with is its complexity.

We would like to see a problem as either physical or psychological; biological or social; personal or interpersonal. The result is we go to one specialist to treat our heart, a different one to take care of our psyches, and still a third to deal with physical pain. No one deals with the whole person, much less the person in the context of his family, community, and social environment. We are learning about the very nature of life, how the genes lay the foundation for who and what we are. But we seem to be losing the larger picture of what it means to be a healthy human being. We are social beings and can't be understood apart from our mates, our parents, our children, our friends, our communities, the world we live in, and our view of the spiritual world beyond.

I've devoted my professional life to addressing these issues that are complex and cut across traditional disciplines. I've learned how to see and understand the whole man in all his complexities and to understand and treat the most significant, difficult, and challenging problems men face.

So, what exactly is IMS?

In trying to describe something that is new, it is difficult to come up with a short, accurate, and useful definition. But here's a definition that has helped me work with men and their families and help them deal with these confusing and complex issues.

The Irritable Male Syndrome (IMS) is a state of hypersensitivity, anxiety, frustration, and anger that occurs in males and is associated with biochemical changes, hormonal fluctuations, increasing stress, loss of male identity, and worries about the future of humankind.

The 4 Core Symptoms of IMS

For the original study that led to the book, I developed a questionnaire that has now been taken by more than 60,000 men and 25,000 women. It helps men and women see whether IMS is a problem for a man. You can take the quiz, get your score, and learn more about how IMS impacts your own life here: http://menalive.com/irritable-male-syndrome-ims-quiz/.

Let me share with you what went into this particular definition. Working with males (and those who live with them) who are experiencing IMS, I have found there are four core symptoms that underlie many others.

The first is **hypersensitivity.** The women who live these men say things like:

- I feel like I have to walk on eggshells when I'm around him.
- I never know when I'm going to say something that will set him off.
- He's like time bomb ready to explode but I never know when.
- Nothing I do pleases him.
- When I try to do nice things, he pushes me away.
- He'll change in an eye-blink. One minute he's warm and friendly. The next he's cold and mean.

The men don't often recognize their own hypersensitivity. Rather, their perception is that they are fine but everyone else is going out of their way to irritate them. The guys say things like:

- Quit bothering me.
- You know I don't like that. Why do you keep doing it?
- Leave me alone.
- No, nothing's wrong. I'm fine. Quit asking me questions.
- The kids always . . . (it's always negative). The kids never . . . (do the right things).
- Why don't you ever . . . (Fill in the blank: want sex, do what I want to do, do something with your life, think before you open your mouth, do things the right way).
- You damn . . . (Fill in the blank: fool, bitch, etc.). As IMS progresses, the words get more hurtful.
- They don't say anything. They increasingly withdraw into a numbed silence.

One concept I have found helpful is the notion that many of us are "emotionally sunburned," but others don't know it. We might think of a man who is extremely sunburned and gets a loving hug from his wife. He cries out in anger and pain. He assumes she knows he's sunburned, so if she "grabs" him she must be trying to hurt him. She has no idea he is sunburned and can't understand why he reacts angrily to her loving touch. You can see how this can lead a couple down a road of escalating confusion.

The second core emotion is **anxiety.**

Anxiety is a state of apprehension, uncertainty, and fear resulting from the anticipation of a realistic or fantasized threatening event or situation. As you will see, as you delve more deeply into IMS, men live in constant worry and fear.

These kind of worries usually take the form of "what ifs." What if I lose my job? What if I can't find a job? What if she leaves me? What if I can't find someone to love me? What if I have to go to war? What if something happens to my wife or children? What if my parents die? What if I get sick and can't take care of things? The list goes on and on.

The third core emotion is **frustration.**

Princeton University's WordNet offers two definitions that can help us understand this aspect of IMS.

1: the feeling that accompanies an experience of being thwarted in attaining your goals. Synonym is "defeat."
2: a feeling of annoyance at being hindered or criticized. The dictionary offers an enlightening example to illustrate the use of the word: "her constant complaints were the main source of his frustration."

IMS men feel blocked in attaining what they want and need in life. They often don't even know what they need. When they do know, they often feel there's no way they can get their needs met. They often feel defeated in the things they try to do to improve their lives. The men feel frustrated in their relationships with family, friends, and on the job. The world is changing and they don't know where, how, or if they fit in.

Author Susan Faludi captures this frustration in her book *Stiffed: The Betrayal of the American Man.* The frustration is expressed in the question that is at the center of her study of American males. "If, as men are so often told, they are the dominant sex, why do so many of them feel dominated and done in by the world?" The frustration that is often hidden and unrecognized is a key element of IMS.

The fourth core emotion is **anger.**

Anger can be simply defined as a strong feeling of displeasure or hostility. Yet anger is a complex emotion. Outwardly expressed, it can lead to aggression and violence. When it is turned inward, it can lead to depression and suicide. Anger can be direct and obvious or it can be subtle and covert. Anger can be loud or quiet. It can be expressed as hateful words, hurtful actions, or in stony silence.

For many men, anger is the only emotion they have learned to express. Growing up male, we are taught to avoid anything that is seen as the least bit feminine. We are taught that men "do" while women "feel." As a result, men are taught to keep all emotions under wraps.

When we are brought up to believe that expressing emotions is *unmanly,* we cannot show we are hurt, afraid, worried, or panicked. When men begin going through IMS, it is often anger that is the primary emotion and the only one they were taught it was *manly* to express.

Whereas feelings like anger, anxiety, and frustration can occur quickly and end quickly, irritability can develop into a mood state that can last over a long period of time and can trigger these feelings over and over again. It can have a major impact on our whole lives. "When we're in a mood it biases and restricts how we think," says Paul Ekman, who is professor emeritus of psychology and former director of the Human Interaction Laboratory at UC San Francisco, and head of PaulEkmanGroup. Dr. Ekman is one of the world's experts on emotional expression.

In describing these kinds of negative moods, Ekman continues, "It makes us vulnerable in ways that we are normally not. So, the negative moods create a lot of problems for us, because they change how we think. *If I wake up in an irritable mood, I'm looking for a chance to be angry* [emphasis mine]. Things that ordinarily would not frustrate me, do. The danger of a mood is not only that it biases thinking but that it increases emotions. When I'm in an irritable mood, my anger lasts longer, and is harder to control than usual. It's a terrible state, one I would be glad never to have."

I've described the four core symptoms: Hypersensitivity, anxiety, frustration, and anger. Now let's examine the five core causes: Biochemical changes, hormonal fluctuations, stress, loss of male identity, and worries about the state of the world.

The 5 Core Causes of IMS

The first core cause: **Biochemical changes.**

Most people have heard of the brain neurotransmitter serotonin. When we have enough flowing through our brains, we feel good. When there isn't enough, we feel bad. Siegfried Meryn, MD, one of the authors of *Men's Health & The Hormone Revolution* calls serotonin "the male hormone of bliss." Women have the same hormone in their brains and it has an equally positive effect on them. "The more serotonin the body produces," says Dr. Meryn, "the happier, more positive and more euphoric we are. Low serotonin can contribute to a man's irritability and aggression."

One of the most common causes of low serotonin levels is our eating and drinking habits. For instance, research has shown that protein, if consumed in excessive quantity, suppresses central nervous system serotonin levels. Many men were taught to believe that eating lots of meat would make them manly. Not only are there hormones injected in meat to make the animals fatter, but the protein contained in the meat can be harmful as well.

Judith Wurtman, PhD and her colleagues at the Massachusetts Institute of Technology found that a high-protein, low-carbohydrate diet can cause increased irritability in men. They found that men often mistake their cravings for healthy carbohydrates, such as those found in vegetables like potatoes, rice, corn, squash, etc., with cravings for protein found in meat. "Eating protein when we need carbohydrates," says Wurtman, "will make us grumpy, irritable, or restless."

Wurtman's team also found that alcohol consumption increases serotonin levels initially. However, chronic use dramatically lowers serotonin, resulting in depression, carbohydrate cravings, sleep disturbances, and proneness to argumentativeness and irritability. It may be that the male propensity to eat too much meat and drink too much alcohol is contributing to lower serotonin levels in brain chemistry, which leads to symptoms of IMS.

The second core cause: **Hormonal fluctuations.**

In order to understand the way in which hormonal fluctuations cause IMS in men, we need to know something about testosterone. Theresa L. Crenshaw, MD, author of *The Alchemy of Love and Lust,* describes testosterone this way: "Testosterone is the young Marlon Brando—sexual, sensual, alluring, dark, with a dangerous undertone."

She goes on to say that "It is also our 'warmone,' triggering aggression, competitiveness, and even violence. *Testy* is a fitting term." We know that men with testosterone levels that are *too high* can become angry and aggressive. But recent research shows that most hormonal problems in men are caused by testosterone levels that are *too low*.

Dr. Gerald Lincoln, who coined the term "Irritable Male Syndrome," found that lowering levels of testosterone in his research animals caused them to become more irritable, biting their cages as well as the researchers who were testing them.

Testosterone levels go down as we age, which may be one of the reasons that male irritability and anger are increasingly common as men get older. Testosterone levels also go down when we experience loss, feel threatened, become depressed, or stressed. All of which are increasingly common in men's lives today.

The third core cause: **Being stressed out.**

We all know the feeling. Someone is always making more demands, and no matter how hard we try to stay on top of things, we seem to be getting farther and farther behind. If we have a job, we're often working more hours for less money. The economy is in turmoil. Our savings are dwindling, and our hopes for retirement seem to be fading away. We all recognize the feeling of being *stressed out*. But what exactly is stress and why is stress reduction so important?

In my experience as a psychotherapist, I have found that stress underlies most of the psychological, social, and medical problems that people face in contemporary society, including IMS. For most of us, stress is synonymous with worry. If it is something that makes us worry, then it is stressful.

We can't avoid stress, nor would we want to. Life is change and change is life. The problem arises when there is too much change in too short a time. We might think of the problem that leads to the Irritable Male Syndrome as "dis-stress" or "overstress." Distress and overstress can cause untold difficulties if not understood and prevented.

So, what can we do to relieve the buildup of stress? There's actually a very simple answer. If you think about the kinds of stresses our bodies are designed to meet, they all involve physical activity. When a wild animal came into the camp of our hunter-gatherer ancestors, we either fought or ran away. In either case, we utilized a lot of physical energy. It's physical activity that allows the body to attend to the stress and then to return to normal.

In our modern world, we usually don't have wild animals bursting into our living rooms. The stresses are more psychological than physical. Yet the reaction is the same. Our bodies release stress hormones that can be dissipated only through physical activity. So, if you build up stress every day, you must do something physical every day. Walk, run, take an aerobics class. As the saying goes, "just do it." You'll feel better and it's a sure-fire way to treat IMS.

The fourth core cause: **Loss of male role identity.**

For most of human history, the male role was clear. Our main job was to "bring home the bacon." We hunted for our food and shared what we killed with family and tribe. Everyone had a role to play. Some were good at tracking animals. Others excelled at making bows and arrows or spears. Some men were strong and could shoot an arrow with enough force to kill a buffalo. Others were skilled at singing songs and doing dances that invoked the spirit of the animal and made the hunt more effective.

But now many of us work at jobs that we hate, producing goods or services that have no real value to the community. We've gotten farther and farther away from the basics of bringing home food we've hunted or grown ourselves. The money we receive is small compensation for doing work that is meaningless. And the men with some kind of job, no matter how bad, are the lucky ones. More and more men are losing their jobs and can't easily find new ones.

In her book, *Stiffed,* Susan Faludi concludes that male stress, shame, depression, and violence are not just a problem of individual men, but a product of the social betrayal that men feel as a result of the changing economic situation we all face. One of the men Faludi talked to at length, Don Motta, could be speaking for millions of men in this country who have lost their jobs.

"There is no way you can feel like a man," says Motta. "You can't. It's the fact that I'm not capable of supporting my family... I'll be very frank with you," he said slowly, placing every word down as if each were an increasingly heavy weight. "I . . . Feel . . . I've . . . Been . . . Castrated."

As Faludi interviewed men all across the country, she uncovered a fact that most men and women know all too well. Men put a lot of their identity and sense of self-worth into their jobs. If we aren't working or can't support our family, we feel that we're not really men. Even men who choose to retire often feel lost and inadequate. We need to help men know that there is more to who they are than a paycheck. But we also have to develop societies that create meaningful work that can provide a decent living.

The fifth core cause: **Worries about the state of the world.**

Most of us are so busy just trying to deal with what is in front of us—paying the bills, dealing with the kids, helping with aging parents, trying to stay healthy—that we don't have time to think about the big issues that determine our future. But these issues are real, and they impact how we feel and act, even when they are out of our conscious awareness.

One of the world's leading futurists, Richard Heinberg, sums up the realities that we face. In his book, *The Party's Over: Oil, War, and the Fate of Industrial Societies,* he says, "The world is changing before our eyes—dramatically, inevitably, and irreversibly. The change we are seeing is affecting more people, and more profoundly, than any that human beings have ever witnessed. I am not referring to a war or terrorist incident, a stock market crash, or global warming, but to a more fundamental reality that is driving terrorism, war, economic swings, climate change, and more: the discovery and exhaustion of fossil energy resources."

Whether we want to address these issues or attempt to push them out of our awareness, they are real and one of the core reasons that men are irritable, angry, and depressed. We are clearly living in a world out of balance. We appear to be heading over a cliff and many are afraid that there's no way to avoid it.

All five core causes are related. Any one of the five mentioned above could have a major impact on a man and contribute to IMS. But what makes it even more difficult is that they interact with each other. When a man doesn't feel he has meaningful work, for instance, his stress levels go up and his testosterone levels go down. When men are stressed, they often drink too much, which lowers their testosterone as well as their serotonin levels.

The good news is that by changing any one of the core causes, we can impact all of them. Here are a few things a man can do now:

- Have your hormone levels checked. Find out if your testosterone is low.
- Eat healthy food with a balance of carbohydrates, fats, and proteins.
- Exercise every day.
- Look for work that is meaningful.
- Support a united effort to address our use of fossil fuels and deal with global climate change.
- Resist the temptation to run away from the global realities we face or to displace our fears and anger onto others.
- Be patient and kind when dealing with people who have different views than our own.

Men and Women Speak Out About IMS and How it Impacts Their Lives

One of the reasons I wrote *The Irritable Male Syndrome* was to help the many men and women who are suffering through a problem they don't understand. As a therapist, it makes me sad to see so many couples splitting up at the very time of life that they could be enjoying each other the most. I'm often frustrated seeing the tension that builds between young men and their families, tensions that can tear a family apart and can lead to alcohol or drug abuse, aggression, violence. It makes me angry to see so many of our young men, good, caring guys, who are ending up involved with the criminal justice system.

The other reason is a lot more personal and closer to home. After many years of being in a wonderful marriage, something seemed to be eating at the very roots of our joy and commitment. Carlin and I had both been married before and had merged our families when we got together. She had three sons and I had a son and a daughter. We raised her youngest son and my daughter together. The stresses of life and family accumulated without our being aware of them, until IMS moved into our home with us.

I became more irritable and angry, but didn't notice it at the time. When I did, I tended to blame it on something she had said or done. At first my irritability and anger were indirect. I wouldn't be overtly aggressive, but passive aggressive. I would forget to put things away after I had used them. I would spill things on the floor and not quite get them cleaned up completely. Something would break and I would pretend that I didn't notice.

Later, the feelings began to blow up. I became more argumentative, demanding, and uptight. I started becoming more critical of Carlin, though I would have insisted I wasn't criticizing, I was just pointing out ways she could improve things. Carlin tried to point out the changes she was seeing in me, but I would immediately become angry and defensive.

I finally found a therapist who helped me understand what was going on and how to address all five of the underlying causes. I changed my diet, began exercising more, went to weekly sessions with the therapist, and dealt with the stresses in my relationship. I learned to meditate and found ways to stay calm, even when I had to interact with "difficult people." By the time the book was published, I was in a position to help others. Here are a few of the initial concerns that brought people into my counseling practice.

"Last month a man came home from work with my husband's face but he did not act at all like the man I married. I've known this man for 30 years, married 22 of them and have never met this guy before. Angry, nasty, and cruel are just a few words to describe him. He used to be the most upbeat, happy person I knew. Now he's gone from Mr. Nice to Mr. Mean. In spite of how he treats me I still love my husband and want to save our marriage. Please, can you help me? MK"

For about a year now (it could be even longer, it's hard to know exactly), I have gradually felt my husband of 22 years pulling away for me and our family. He has become more sullen, angry, and moody. His general life energy is down and his sex drive has really dropped off.

Recently he has begun venting to anyone who will listen about how horrible we all are. He is particularly hard on our 19-year-old son, Mark. It's so surprising because our son has always been super industrious and competent.

The thing that bothers me the most is how unaffectionate he has become. I don't even get the hugs and affection like I did in the past and when he does touch me, I feel grabbed rather than caressed. My husband used to be the most positive, upbeat, funny person I knew. Now it's like living with an angry brick! I'm totally confused. What's going on? Can you help us? Thank you, LT.

Some of the women felt the changes came on gradually. For others, things seemed to go quickly from day to night, from Dr. Jekyll to Mr. Hyde. All were confused about what to do. Often the women got involved first, but the men knew there was a problem and soon the men were reaching out for help.

I also counseled men who were well aware of the problem and were reaching out for help. Rick is a 52-year-old married man, with children ages 22 and 26.

I think my irritability is related to the time of life I am in and to the stresses that seem to be mounting both at work and at home. I'm an electrical engineer and work for a large company in the Midwest. There has been a great deal of "consolidation" over the last few years and many people have been let go or forced into early retirement. Even though I have been here a long time and don't think I am vulnerable to losing my job, I still worry.

There is always so much to do and there never seems to be enough time to do it all. I have trouble staying on top of it all. I don't have much physical or mental energy these days. All of this is affecting my sleep. My wife keeps asking me what's wrong. I don't know what to tell her. I usually answer that nothing is wrong. When she persists I often snap at her.

Although I love my wife, I feel we have grown apart over the years. We used to be very close, but now we often seem like strangers at times and that creates its own kind of stress. I often feel unappreciated, unheard, uncared about. She expresses the same feelings. Even though we are aware of it, we don't seem to be able to do anything about it. It's very discouraging and depressing. Please, can you help us?

I was able to help Rick and his family. Many men feel ashamed that they need help, but more men are recognizing the problem and are reaching out before the problems get worse and undermine their health and the health of their relationship.

Liz Langley, former columnist for the *Orlando Weekly* newspaper, offered the follow comments after learning about Irritable Male Syndrome. "Just as men have had to concede that there's a real, scientific reason for our moody silences and sharp behavior, and it's PMS, not RBS (raving bitch syndrome), we might be able to take comfort in the fact that they have to confront this crap, too. It might just be IMS rather than IBS (insensitive butt-hole syndrome) that makes them as dumbfounding as they can be."

Irritable Male Syndrome and Male-Type Depression

Sometimes one person or event can change your life for the better. This happened for me when I met Kay Redfield Jamison. I knew that Dr. Jamison was one of the experts in the mental health field, is Dalio Professor of Mood Disorders and Psychiatry at Johns Hopkins University School of Medicine, and is co-author of the standard medical text, *Manic-Depressive Illness: Bipolar Disorders and Recurrent Depression.* I greatly admired her academic and clinical experience treating people suffering from mental illness.

I was surprised to learn that five years after her text on the subject was published, she "came out" and acknowledged that she also suffered from the illness. She wrote about her personal experiences in her book *An Unquiet Mind: A Memoir of Moods and Madness.* I still remember picking up the book at my local bookstore and reading the book cover. "For even while she was pursuing her career in academic medicine, Jamison found herself succumbing to the same exhilarating highs and catastrophic depressions that afflicted many of her patients, as her disorder launched her into ruinous spending sprees, episodes of violence, and an attempted suicide."

I immediately bought the book and realized two things as I devoured the book in one sitting. First, she was telling my story as well as her own. Second, if she could be open about sharing her own challenges with depression, maybe I could as well.

Although we talk about "mental illness" as being an illness just like a physical illness, there is still stigma associated with it. As a professional who treated other people's problems, I had trouble recognizing that I suffered from the same issues that confronted my patients and worried that I would be shunned by my colleagues and lose my livelihood if I acknowledged my own problems.

But as I read her courageous book, it gave me hope. Two sentences totally nailed me. This was exactly how I felt.

> *"You're irritable and paranoid and humorless and lifeless and critical and demanding, and no reassurance is ever enough. You're frightened, and you're frightening, and 'you're not at all like yourself but will be soon,' but you know you won't."*

I still remember breaking into sobs when I read these words. I recalled things my wife, Carlin, had told me which I kept denying. Here they were and I knew they were true. I had become *irritable, paranoid, humorless, lifeless, critical,* and *demanding.* She was right on in saying that "no reassurance is ever enough." No matter what Carlin tried to do to reassure and support me, I always wanted more—more understanding, more touch, more support, more, more, more.

I was both *frightened* and *frightening.* Carlin said I would get that "beady-eyed" look in my eyes. She said it chilled her to the bone and made her want to pull away from me. I may have looked frightening to her, but inside I felt terrified. I knew I was pushing her away, just when I needed her the most, but I couldn't control my emotions. I knew I needed help and I was finally ready to get it.

I began seeing a psychiatrist who felt that medications would help, but also believed that therapy was essential, as well as monitoring my moods and symptoms. I learned that depression often runs in families, and it helped me to look at my father's history of depression.

Males and Females Often Experience Depression Differently

J. Douglas Bremner, MD, is Professor of Psychiatry and Radiology and Director of the Clinical Neuroscience Research Unit at Emory University School of Medicine where he conducts research on stress-related illnesses. In a very interesting experiment, he gathered a group of former depression patients. With their permission, he gave them a beverage that was spiked with an amino acid that blocks the brain's ability to absorb serotonin, the neurotransmitter that is associated with happiness. The most popular antidepressants, such as Prozac, Celexa, and Paxil are among a class of medications called *selective serotonin reuptake inhibitors* or SSRIs. By blocking the brain from absorbing serotonin, Bremner was creating an instant chemical depression.

What I found fascinating were the gender-specific differences in the way men and women reacted to the potion that blocked the effects of serotonin. Typical of the males was John, a middle-aged businessman who had fully recovered from a bout of depression, thanks to a combination of psychotherapy and Prozac. Within minutes of drinking the brew, however, "He wanted to escape to a bar across the street," recalls Bremner. "He didn't express sadness ... he didn't really express anything. He just wanted to go to Larry's Lounge."

Contrast John's response with that of female subjects like Sue, a mother of two in her mid-thirties. After taking the cocktail, "She began to cry and express her sadness over the loss of her father two years ago," recalls Bremner. "She was overwhelmed by her emotions."

One of the most consistent findings in the social epidemiology of mental health is the gender gap in depression. Many studies indicate that depression is approximately twice as prevalent among women as it is among men.

Depressed Men Get Irritable and Angry

Ron Kessler, PhD, a professor of health care policy at Harvard Medical School, describes depression in men this way. "When you study depression among children, they don't talk about being sad, they talk about being angry and irritable," he said. "Children don't have the cognitive capacity to make sense of all their feelings. There's a great similarity between children and men. Men get irritable; women get sad."

That was certainly my own experience dealing with depression, which became clear to me when my wife and I attended a family program for one of our sons who was having trouble with drugs. One of the things they did for families was to give us all a test for depression. They found many families who had kids with drug problems also had problems with depression.

As it turned out, my wife scored high on the depression test they gave us, and I scored low. The counselor we saw there recommended that my wife see a doctor when we returned from the weekend. She did, was diagnosed as suffering from depression, and received medications and therapy. Her life improved dramatically.

But, we still had a lot of problems in our relationship. I would still fly off the handle and become angry, and at times enraged. Carlin suggested that maybe I might have problems with depression myself. I kindly pointed out that she was the one that had scored high on the depression scale and that I had a low score.

"I still think you're depressed," she said. "You're sure not happy. You're irritable, angry, and hypersensitive. The least little thing can set you off." After screaming back, "God damn it, I'm not angry and who wouldn't be irritable when they have to put up with all the things I have to put up with."

Luckily, having dealt with her own depression, she was tolerant of my outbursts, backed off, but continued to encourage me to see a doctor.

I finally agreed to see someone and after numerous interviews and discussions, the doctor diagnosed me as suffering from depression. She put me on medications and engaged me in therapy. It was the best decision of my life, and I have my wife to thank for hanging in there with me.

It was amazing how our lives began to improve when both of us had gotten to the roots of our depression and found ways to help ourselves and each other. When both people recognize there is a problem, they can work together toward a solution. One of the main things we began to see as things improved was our sense of humor came back. While we were depressed, we were always very serious, worried, and on edge. Now we've learned to laugh and play again.

The experience with me and my wife, as well as what I saw with clients, convinced me that men and women often experience depression differently.

I have developed a chart to describe the main differences in the ways males and females experience depression.

I want to emphasize that this is a short-hand summary of thousands of people I have seen. Most depressed people will find they identify with some things on both sides of the chart. Some men will find themselves predominantly on the female side and some women will find themselves predominantly on the male side. But generally speaking, these differences hold true for depressed females and males. What I describe in the following chart is based on my clinical experience working with men and women. I felt it was so important to understand gender differences that I conducted a research study that was titled, *Male vs. Female Depression.*

Depressed Females	Depressed Males
Blame themselves for problems	Blame others for problems
Feel sad and tearful	Feel irritable and unforgiving
Sleep more than usual	Have trouble sleeping or staying asleep
Vulnerable and easily hurt	Suspicious and guarded
Try to be nice	Overtly or covertly hostile
Withdraw when feeling hurt	Attack when feeling hurt
Often suffer in silence	Over-react, often sorry later
Feel they were set up to fail	Feel the world is set up to fail them
Slowed down and nervous	Restless and agitated
Maintain control of anger/ May have anxiety attacks	Lose control of anger/May have sudden attacks of rage
Overwhelmed by feelings	Feelings blunted, often numb
Let others violate bounderies	Rigid boundaries; push others away
Feel guilty for what they do	Feel ashamed for who they are
Uncomfortable receiving praise	Frustrated if not praised enough
Accept weaknesses and doubts	Deny weaknesses and doubts
Strong fear of success	Strong fear of failure
Need to "blend in" to feel safe	Need to be "top dog" to feel safe
Use food, friends, and "love" to self-medicate	Use alcohol, TV, sports, and "sex" to self-medicate
Believe their problems could be solved if only they could be a better . . . (spouse, co-worker, parent, friend)	Believe their problems could be solved if only their . . .)spouse, co-worker, parent, friend) would treat them better
Wonder, "Am I loveable enough?"	Wonder, "Am I being loved enought?"

Bottom Line: Treating Irritable Male Syndrome and Male-Type Depression.

Dealing with Irritable Male Syndrome (IMS) and male-type depression can help millions of men find healing and hope for the future. It can also help millions of women who are living with and loving these men. Together we can move ahead to find and our mission in life and have the clarity, strength, and vision to carry it out.

Rule #12

Find Your Mission in Life
and Do Your Part to Save Humanity

"Don't ask yourself what the world needs. Ask yourself what
makes you come alive, and then go do that. Because what the
world needs are people who have come alive."

~Howard Thurman

I've come to believe that we all have a mission in life, a calling that can emerge early in life but most definitely draws our attention as we reach midlife. We may resist the calling or embrace it early in life, but, like a bottle of good wine, it gets better with age. No one describes this process better than the psychologist James Hillman.

I first encountered Hillman at workshops with Robert Bly and Michael Meade. Individually, they each offered a unique contribution to the process of becoming your own man. Bly offered his poetry, accompanying himself on an old stringed bouzouki. Mythologist Michael Meade told stories and shared ancient myths while playing a mesmerizing conga drum. James Hillman was much less flamboyant but equally powerful as he shared his unique perspective on psychology and the essence of who we are. Together, the threesome took us into the underworld and none of came back unchanged.

Hillman put me in touch, for the first time, with the idea of "the soul's code." By the time I met Hillman, I had already done considerable men's work. I had embraced my life mission "to awaken the masculine soul." But Hillman, Bly, and Meade helped me understand my mission from multiple perspectives and to recognize how to put it into practice.

In his book *The Soul's Code: In Search of Character and Calling,* Hillman introduces his unique concept this way:

"There is more in human life than our theories of it allow. Sooner or later something seems to call us onto a particular path. You may remember this 'something' as a signal moment in childhood when an urge out of nowhere, a fascination, a peculiar turn of events struck like an annunciation: This is what I must do, this is what I've got to have. This is who I am."

We can all reflect on Hillman's words and think about these moments in our lives when something shifted in us unexpectedly.

I had just gone to the print shop to pick up my new business cards. The card proudly proclaims, "Jed Diamond, Ph.D., *Helping men and the women who love them since 1969.* I suddenly realized that I had actually been doing this since I was five years old, beginning when I made the drive with my uncle to visit my father in the mental hospital.

James Hillman wouldn't have been surprised by my realization. Hillman offers numerous examples of men and women who became famous for their calling, but who began as small children afraid to answer it. One of his examples is of the world famous bull fighter Manolete. Hillman says, "As a child, Manolete did not seem in any way to be a prospective bullfighter. The man who changed old styles and renewed the ideals of the corrida was a timid and fearful boy."

Hillman describes the young Manolete's early life. "Delicate and sickly, having almost died of pneumonia when he was two, little Manuel was interested only in painting and reading." This all changed when he was about eleven and saw a bullfight. After that, nothing else mattered much except the bulls.

I was also small and sickly as a kid, lost in my own world of fantasy. When I was thrown into the mental hospital to "help my father," I felt lost and overwhelmed. Hillman says that's not uncommon. Our early experiences are overwhelming because some inner knowing is pulling us toward our calling long before we are old enough to fully embrace it.

How do we explain this inner knowing that calls us to our mission in life? Hillman calls it the *acorn theory*. Just as the tiny acorn carries within it the blueprint for becoming a giant oak tree, so do each of us carry within us the code that will eventually bring us into the full flowering of our calling in life.

The acorn theory expresses that unique something that we carry into the world, that is unique to us, which is connected to what Hillman calls our "daimon." I loved the word when I first read it. It seems so mysterious and I liked the resonance with my own name, "Diamond."

Hillman notes that *daimon* is what the Greeks called this inner guidance system. The Romans called it your *genius.* Christians referred to it as our *guardian angel.* Eskimos and others who follow shamanic practices say it is your *spirit* or your *animal soul.* In more recent times the Romantics, like Keats, said the call came from the *heart.*

Hillman helped me understand a lot about my childhood and later life. "I want us to envision that what children go through has to do with finding a place in the world for their specific calling," says Hillman. "They are trying to live two lives at once, the one they were born with and the one of the place and people they were born into. The image of destiny is packed into a tiny acorn, the seed of a huge oak on small shoulders."

That's why it's so important that we look closely at our Adverse Childhood Experiences. As we come to understand our mission in life, we see these early traumas in a new light. Rather than seen as simply wounds from which we must recover, we can also see them as providing the experiences we needed in order to become the men we were meant to be.

Exploring Our Family History and Accepting Our Unique, Authentic Self

Finding our mission begins with these early inklings of desire that pull or push us in a direction that later turns out to presage our calling in life. But they also come by exploring our life story. The idea of the acorn theory tells us that we enter the world with a calling, key things we need to do, and core values that make up who we are.

In my Jewish tradition, there's a story that before we enter the world at birth, we are brought before God and given us the story of our lives and all the details about our life journey and calling. But just before we are sent into the world, the Angel Lailah (the personification of night) snaps her finger against our upper lip and we forget everything. The little indentation or philtrum in our upper lip is the reminder that our life story is given to us at birth and it is our job to re-remember it.

Hillman says that the *daimon* even selects the egg and the sperm, who our parents are to be, and the other happenings in our lives to support us in bringing the world our unique contribution. He emphasizes that this isn't a scientific theory. "We have to make it clear that this is a myth, not a truth. It doesn't have to be believed, and it's not a theory that has to be proven. It's a worldwide myth, and it's a way of thinking or reflecting about life. It's something you entertain to see what the story does for you."

For me, it has allowed me to see my whole life experience, the bad and the good, as contributing to who I am as a man and what my mission in life will be. Believing in the acorn theory has allowed me to see clues along the way and to trust that all the trials and tribulations of life are a positive part of the journey.

Male Menopause: The Most Passionate, Powerful, Productive, and Purposeful Time of a Man's Life.

Often, we come to embrace our life calling as we go through "the change of life," which is called menopause in women, andropause in men, or what I call "male menopause," because I found the changes to be similar in both sexes.

In the introduction to my book, *Male Menopause,* I offer the following definition:

"Male menopause, also called andropause, begins with hormonal, physiological, and chemical changes that occur in all men generally between the ages of forty and fifty-five. These changes affect all aspects of a man's life. Male menopause is, thus, a physical condition with psychological, interpersonal, social, and spiritual dimensions."

I went on to describe the underlying purpose of this transition stage this way:

"The purpose of male menopause is to signal the end of the first part of a man's life and prepare him for the second half. Male menopause is not the beginning of the end, as many fear, but the end of the beginning. It is the passage to the most passionate, powerful, productive, and purposeful time of a man's life."

I can still remember the day it hit me. I was three days shy of my forty-fourth birthday when my mother died. She was seventy-nine years old. As I dealt with the funeral arrangements, I thought to myself, *I'm in the second half now. Every day I live, I'll be getting closer to death.* At first the thoughts were disturbing. I felt lost and alone without my mother. My father was still alive at the time and would live until he was eighty-nine, but I could feel the reality of mortality. Gradually, the recognition of death in my future energized me to get more serious about what I wanted to do with my life and what legacy I would want to leave for my children, grandchildren, and for future generations.

For some, the second half of life is a time to slow down, begin to spend less time in the world of work, and to have more leisure time. For those of us who get in touch with our calling or life purpose, this is a time to expand and offer our gifts to the world. Many of us don't fit into the mold of the current world of big business and we become entrepreneurs.

I first met Steve Dailey when he signed up to take my year-long training program for practitioners who were interesting in making a great living doing men's work. For years I had been asked if I knew other people in different parts of the US and throughout the world who specialized in working with men. I always had to say I didn't, but finally decided to train some myself. Steve was one of the most experienced students in the class.

Recently he started the Entrepreneur Excellence Alliance to support men in the second half of life. He speaks to many men I know, including myself. Most of us who are drawn to being entrepreneurs and running our own business recognize that things change in the second half of life. We want more balance between work and life, greater ease, more time to do the things we want. And we know that time is running short. We also know that we have more responsibilities in the second half of life. Like me, many have grown children and grandchildren. We want a better world for them and we recognize that we don't have a lot of time to waste.

Another colleague of mine, Zachariah Reitano, has started a new health company, simply called Ro, a digital health clinic. Ro focuses on the needs of mid-life men and women and will likely help everyone improve their health throughout their lives. He says, "The future of healthcare is one in which providers are not replaced but empowered by technology, unburdened from administrative paperwork, and liberated to practice medicine in concert with their patients where and when they need it most."

He goes on to say, "Men's health, and more precisely, the relationship men have with their health, is broken: how we diagnose it, how we talk about it, how we feel about it, how we communicate it, how we suffer with it, how we ignore it, and how we deal with it." Ro is a new concept in health care for all.

The Time of Our Lives and The Challenges We Face

We can't separate our mission in life from the time in which we live. I was born in 1943 and have flashes of memory from World War II. I came of age during the Vietnam era and became a war resister when it was clear to me that wars would never solve our problems. I first became fully aware of the state of the world and its implications when I sat in a sweat lodge ceremony at men's gathering in 1993 and had a vision of the ship of civilization sinking and the emergence of lifeboats to a more sustainable future. I described the vision in Chapter 4.

That same year, 1993, I attended an event with the mythologist Michael Meade and author Clarissa Pinkola Estés, PhD, author of *Women Who Run With the Wolves: Myths and Stories of the Wild Woman Archetype*. Toward the end of the day, Clarissa offered a poem, which seemed to surprise Michael as well as the audience, since no one seemed to know she wrote poetry. When I first heard her share the title, the hair on the back of my neck stood up. "I have a poem I'd like to share," she said in a voice that was quiet and a bit tentative. "It's called Father Earth."

Father Earth!

There's a two-million-year-old man no one knows.
They cut into his rivers,
They peeled wide pieces of hide from his legs,
They left scorch marks on his buttocks.
He did not cry out.
No matter what they did to him, He did not cry out.
He held firm.
Now he raises his stabbed hands and whispers that we can heal him yet.
We begin the bandages, the rolls of gauze, the gut, the needle, the grafts.
Slowly, carefully, we turn his body face up,
and under him, his lifelong lover, the old woman,
is perfect and unmarked.
He has laid upon his two-million-year-old lover
all this time, protecting her with his old back, with his old scarred back.
And the soil beneath her is fertile and black with their tears.

I've recited the poem many times over the years and it never ceases to move me. One man in the audience whispered, with tears running down his cheeks, "Finally, a woman understands men."

The poem reminds me how empowered women became when they changed their view of the deity from "God the Father" to "Goddess the Mother." I think, in the same way, men are empowered when we truly recognize our connection to the Earth. Embracing Father Earth is a powerful shift in consciousness for men.

The psychologist and author Sam Keen who wrote *Fire in the Belly: On Being a Man* calls on us all to align our mission and life-calling with the times we live in. At this time in human history, we are facing the reality that we are out of balance with the Earth and in order to survive and thrive, we must reconnect in a healthy way. Sam Keen offers this simple call to action:

"The radical vision of the future rests on the belief that the logic that determines either our survival or our destruction is simple:

1. The new human vocation is to heal the earth.
2. We can only heal what we love.
3. We can only love what we know.
4. We can only know what we touch."

I believe that Keen is calling on us to heal our relationship to the Earth. We can no longer treat Earth is simply a commodity to exploit for human benefit. The Earth, in truth is a living being, Gaia. Just as the organs in our bodies must function together in support of the whole, all of life on Earth must be in balance with the other parts.

Yet, we are living at a time when it is becoming increasingly difficult to solve our problems. In her book, *The Watchman's Rattle: A Radical New Theory of Collapse,* sociobiologist Rebecca Costa says that we have reached a "cognitive threshold" where humans can no longer "think" their way out of their problems.

"Think of *the cognitive threshold* in this way," she says. "The rate at which the human brain can evolve new faculties is millions of years slower than the rate at which humans generate change and produce new information. So, from a strictly biological standpoint, the human brain can't help but fall behind. There is simply no way an organ that requires millions of years to adapt can keep up with change that now occurs in picoseconds."

Costa believes that there are two early signs that a society is approaching collapse: (1) gridlock: when societies are unable to comprehend or resolve large, complex problems; and (2) when people substitute beliefs for knowledge and fact. In order to avoid collapse, we must take a different approach to solving problems.

Our Mission Must Include Healing Our Inner World as Well as the Outer World

Terry Patten has focused his work on this new approach to problem solving. In his book, *A New Republic of the Heart: An Ethos For Revolutionaries*, he says, "Even as we are verging on world-changing breakthroughs in science, technology, consciousness, cooperation, and leadership, we're also verging on catastrophic breakdowns of our planetary ecology, as well as our cultural cohesion, economic and social order, and, of course, our politics. We are clearly approaching a moment of truth."

He describes four aspects of our work we must do to actualize our life's mission:

1. **Inner work.** We take on daily practices of conscious movement and sitting meditation. We will relate to every moment and aspect of our lives as an opportunity for practice, growth, and transformation.

2. **Interpersonal work.** We create conditions conducive to our quickly becoming an authentic community of practice, deepening our we-space naturally in our dyads, pods, breakout sessions, and service work.

3. **Outer work.** We engage and deepen our functional capacities through practical service to projects dedicated to restoring wholeness to our natural, social, political, and/or cultural worlds.

4. **Co-creating a new pattern.** We "break the mold" by engaging all these practices as expressions of an emerging new republic of the heart, in a loving and fierce spirit. Together we endeavor to establish a new collective field of consciousness, expressing awakening, service and friendship, rooted in radical acceptance and defiantly joyful hope.

Arjuna Ardagh offers helpful guidance in discovering the map that can help us find our mission in life. He also offers specific practices we can build into our life to keep us on track and in touch with our most brilliant ideas. His book, *Radical Brilliance: The Anatomy of How and Why People Have Original Life-Changing Ideas*, is a wonderful resource for men and women at any time of life, but particularly as we move into the second half and address issues of purpose and meaning.

Wisdom @ Work: The Making of the Modern Elder

Although we can find our mission in life at any age, I've found that it most often happens at mid-life and beyond. The eminent psychoanalyst, Carl Jung, recognized the importance of midlife and the change in perspective it offers. "Midlife is the time to let go of an over-dominant ego and to contemplate the deeper significance of human existence," Jung reminds us. "We cannot live the afternoon of life according to the program of life's morning, for what was great in the morning will be little at evening and what in the morning was true, at evening will have become a lie."

As we move into our fifties and sixties, our calling literally calls out to us and demands that we pay attention. We long to make a difference, to leave our mark, to contribute in some small way to the betterment of humankind. This is what happened to Chip Conley.

I first met Chip on a walk in San Francisco. I was looking for a place to hold a workshop I was planning on "Sex, Men, and Relationships." I had heard there was an interesting hotel called Hotel Phoenix that wasn't too expensive and was kind of quirky. When I walked in to check it out, Chip was behind the desk. He was a good-looking guy who exuded hospitality and I immediately felt at home.

He told he had recently purchased the hotel because he was looking for an inexpensive but high quality place for his parents to stay in San Francisco when they visited but couldn't find one. So, he decided to create his own. He showed me around and I was impressed by the beauty of the rooms and the uniqueness of the property.

I hosted a great event at the Phoenix and participants at my event thought the place was fabulous. The rooms each had a unique theme, and the courtyard with swimming pool was a great place to socialize. Chip went to buy other hotels and became a hospitality entrepreneur with the aptly named Joie de Vivre Hospitality (JdV), transforming a run-down inner-city motel into the second largest boutique hotel brand in the country. He eventually sold JdV after running it as CEO for twenty-four years and turned his attention to an earlier passion, writing, and had numerous best-sellers including *The Rebel Rules: Daring to Be Yourself in Business.*

With all his business success, you might think he would want to retire. But that's not Chip's style. He was 52 years old when he was contacted by the young founders of Airbnb to help them turn what seemed a good idea, to rent out residential living spaces, into a thriving business. He was hired to bring his expertise as a hotelier and businessman, but soon realized he had as much to learn about the new world of technology as he had to teach about providing a great place for people to stay.

He describes his experiences in his latest book, *Wisdom@Work: The Making of a Modern Elder.* In describing the book, which was published in 2018, he says, "I experienced a profound 'aha' during my time at Airbnb, understanding the value in being a 'mentern' who's both mentor and intern. This book might have the greatest effect on the workplace and maybe society since I believe elder wisdom is about to make a comeback."

Conley recently launched the Modern Elder Academy, the world's first midlife wisdom school. The school helps midlife workers "reset, restore, and repurpose" their lives through one- or two-week programs in Baja, California. "I'm doubling down on Elder," Conley says. "At the Academy, workers needing to reboot their resumes and their lives learn to evolve out of past knowledge and past experience and to become a vital, relevant part of the modern economy."

Conley's experience with Airbnb taught him that elders are vital to life in our modern times, but we have to be life-long learners. We can't just sit back and pontificate to the younger generation about what they should be doing. "It's a new kind of elder emerging in the workplace, not the elder of the past treated with reverence, but valued for their relevance," Conley explained. As the world of work becomes more challenging and diverse, Conley's new mission is to make sure that older employees are included in that diversity drive, too, bringing the emotional intelligence and wisdom that comes with age.

Certainly, we live at a time when the world needs all the help it can get. We are called upon to step forward to become the wisdom keepers and wisdom seekers that can help us stay afloat and to survive and thrive the great changes going on in the world. In an article she wrote in 2008, "Do Not Lose Heart, We Were Made for These Times," Clarissa Pinkola Estés offered encouragement to us all:

"My friends, do not lose heart. We were made for these times. I have heard from so many recently who are deeply and properly bewildered. They are concerned about the state of affairs in our world now. Ours is a time of almost daily astonishment and often righteous rage over the latest degradations of what matters most to civilized, visionary people.

"One of the most calming and powerful actions you can do to intervene in a stormy world is to stand up and show your soul. Soul on deck shines like gold in dark times. The light of the soul throws sparks, can send up flares, builds signal fires, causes proper matters to catch fire. To display the lantern of soul in shadowy times like these—to be fierce and to show mercy toward others; both are acts of immense bravery and greatest necessity."

Bottom Line: Find Your Mission in Life and Do Your Part to Save Humanity

These are amazing times to be living and we can feel overwhelmed. Yet, as Clarissa reminds us, "we were made for these times." We don't have to do everything, just the part that our *daimon* calls us to put into action. One of the reasons I'm writing this book is to offer opportunities to bring us together. We don't have to be lone rangers. Working together, we can change the world. I hope you'll join me.

I want to create a tribe of kindred spirits who are committed to putting these twelve rules into practice. If my experiences and mission resonate with you, I hope you'll reach out and connect.

I look forward to hearing from you. Come visit me at www.MenAlive.com

Resources for Further Exploration

Rule #1: Join a Men's Group

Joseph Culp. Film "Welcome to the Men's Group." http://www.themensgroupmovie.com/.

Jed Diamond. *Inside Out: Becoming My Own Man.* San Rafael, Ca: Fifth Wave Press, 1983.

Evryman. https://evryman.com/

Betty Friedan. *The Feminine Mystique.* New York: Dell, 1963.

Herb Goldberg. *The Hazards of Being Male: Surviving the Myth of Masculine Privilege.* New York: Nash Publishing, 1976.

Bill Kauth. *A Circle of Men: The Original Manual for Men's Support Groups.* New York: St. Martin Press, 1992.

New Warrior Training Adventure. Mankind Project, https://mankindproject.org/new-warrior-training-adventure/.

Sallie Tisdale. *Advice for Future Corpses (and Those Who Love Them): A Practical Perspective on Death and Dying.* New York: Touchstone, 2018.

Rule #2: Break Free From the Man Box

Cameron Conaway, *Man Box.* Pontiac, Ill: Lasting Impact Press, 2018.

Laura Dabney. https://lauradabney.com/.

James DeMeo. *Saharasia: The 4000 BC Origins of Child Abuse, Sex-Repression, Warfare and Social Violence in the Deserts of the Old World.* Greensprings, Or: Orgone Biophysical Research, 1998.

Chellis Glendenning. *My Name is Chellis & I'm in Recovery from Western Civilization*. Boston: Shambhala Publications, 1994.

Mark Greene. *The Little #MeToo Book for Men*. New York: ThinkPlay Partners, 2018.

Paul Kivel. *Men's Work: How to Stop the Violence That Tears Our Lives Apart*. Center City, Minn: Hazelton, 1992.

Ann Neitlich. *Building Bridges: Women's & Men's Liberation*. Cambridge, MA: Building Bridges, 1985.

Tony Porter. http://www.acalltomen.org/.
    TED talk, https://www.ted.com/talks/tony_porter_a_call_to_men
    Breaking Out of the Man Box: The Next Generation of Manhood. New York: Skyhorse, 2016.

Promundo, https://promundoglobal.org/.
    The Man Box: A Study of Being a Young Man in the US, UK, and Mexico.
    https://promundoglobal.org/resources/man-box-study-young-man-us-uk-mexico/

Silvers, Ann. https://annsilvers.com/.
    Abuse of Men by Women: It Happens, It Hurts, and It's Time to Get Real About It. Gig Harbor, Washington: Silver Springs Publishing, 2014.

Leonard Szymczak and Rick Broniec, www.wakeupandshowup.com/.
    Wake Up, Grow Up, and Show Up: Calling Men into the 21st Century

Rule #3: Accept the Gift of Maleness

Simon Baron-Cohen.
    https://www.autismresearchcentre.com/people_Baron-Cohen
    The Essential Difference: The Truth About the Male & Female Brain. London: Penguin, 2007.

Roy F. Baumeister. *Is There Anything Good About Men: How Cultures Flourish by Exploiting Men*. New York: Oxford University Press, 2010.

Robert Bly, James Hillman, and Michael Meade, Editors. *The Rag and Bone Shop of the Heart: Poems for Men.* New York: HarperCollins, 1992.

Louann Brizendine. http://www.drlouannbrizendine.com/
The Female Brain. New York: Morgan Road Books, 2006.
The Male Brain. New York: Broadway Books, 2010.

Theresa L. Crenshaw. *The Alchemy of Love and Lust.* New York: G.P. Putnam's Sons, 1996.

James M. Dabbs. *Heroes, Rogues and Lovers: Testosterone and Behavior.* New York: McGraw-Hill, 2000.

Hector A. Garcia. *Sex, Power, and Partisanship: How Evolutionary Science Makes Sense of Our Political Divide.* New York: Prometheus Books, 2019.

John Gray and Arjuna Ardagh. *Conscious Men.* Nevada City, California: Self X Press, 2016.

Michael Gurian. https://www.michaelgurian.com/
What Could He Be Thinking? How a Man's Mind Really Works. New York: St. Martin's Press, 2003.
How Can I Help Him? A Practitioner's Guide to Working with Boys and Men in Therapeutic Settings. Spokane, WA: Gurian Institute, 2011.

Yuval Noah Harari. https://www.ynharari.com/
Sapiens: A Brief History of Humankind. New York: HarperCollins, 2015.
21 Lessons for the 21ˢᵗ Century. New York: Spiegel & Grau, 2018.

Harville Hendrix and Helen LaKelly Hunt. https://harvilleandhelen.com/
Making Marriage Simple: 10 Relationship-Saving Truths. New York: Harmony Books, 2013.

Marianne J. Legato. The Foundation for Gender-Specific Medicine, https://gendermed.org/
Eve's Rib: The New Science of Gender-Specific Medicine and How It Can Save Your Life. New York: Harmony Books, 2002.
Why Men Never Remember and Women Never Forget. Emmaus, PA: Rodale, 2005.

Carista Luminare and Lion Goodman. www.ConfusedaboutLove.com.

David C. Page. Professor of biology at the Massachusetts Institute of Technology (MIT).
Video, "Why Sex Really Matters."
https://www.youtube.com/watch?v=nQcgD5DpVlQ

Kenneth R. Pelletier. *Change Your Genes, Change Your Life: Creating Optimal Health With the New Science of Epigenetics.* San Rafael, Ca: Origin Press, 2019

Rule #4: Embrace Your Billion Year History of Maleness

Jared Diamond. http://www.jareddiamond.org/
The Third Chimpanzee: The Evolution and Future of the Human Animal. New York: HarperCollins, 1991.

Jed Diamond. *The Warrior's Journey Home: Healing Men, Healing the Planet.* Oakland, CA: New Harbinger, 1994.

Riane Eisler. *The Chalice and the Blade: Our History, Our Future.* New York: HarperCollins, 1988.

Matthew Fox. *The Hidden Spirituality of Men: Ten Metaphors to Awaken the Sacred Masculine.* Novato, Calif: New World Library, 2008.

Jaak Panksepp and Lucy Biven. *The Archaeology of Mind: Neuroevolutionary Origins of Human Emotions.* New York: W.W. Norton, 2012.

Daniel Quinn. http://ishmael.org/
Ishmael. New Yor k: Bantam, 2009.
Beyond Civilization: Humanity's Next Great Adventure. New York: Harmony Books, 1999.

Adam Rutherford. *A Brief History of Everyone Who Ever Lived: The Human Story Retold Through Our Genes.* New York: The Experiment Publishing, 2017.

Chris Stringer. *Lone Survivors: How We Came to Be the Only Humans on Earth.* New York: Times Books, 2012.

Brian Swimme & Thomas Berry. *The Universe Story: From the Primordial Flaring Forth to the Ecozoic Era.* San Francisco: Harper San Francisco, 1992.

Rule #5: Recognize Your Anger and Fear Toward Women

David D. Gilmore.
  Manhood in the Making: Cultural Concepts of Masculinity. New Haven: Yale University Press, 1990.
  Misogyny: The Male Malady. Philadelphia. University of Pennsylvania Press, 2001.

Sam Keen. *Fire in the Belly: On Being a Man.* New York: Bantam Books, 1991

Sam Keen and Gifford Keen. *Prodigal Father, Wayward Son: A Roadmap to Reconciliation.* Studio City, Ca: Divine Arts, 2015.

National Association of Baby Boomer Women. https://nabbw.com/.

Gary Wilson. *https://www.yourbrainonporn.com/.*
  The Great Porn Experiment. https://www.youtube.com/watch?v=wSF82AwSDiU
  Your Brain on Porn: Internet Pornography and the Emerging Science of Addiction. United Kingdom: Commonwealth Publishing, 2017.

Rule #6: Learn the Secrets of Real Lasting Love

Angeles Arrien. http://www.angelesarrien.com/
  Four-Fold Way: Walking the Paths of the Warrior, Teacher, Healer and Visionary. San Francisco: HarperSanFrancisco, 1993.

  Second Half of Life: Opening the Eight Gates of Wisdom. Boulder, CO: Sounds True, 2007.

Jed Diamond. www.MenAlive.com
  The Enlightened Marriage: The 5 Transformative Stages of Relationships and Why the Best is Still to Come. Wayne, New Jersey: Career Press, 2016.

Helen Fisher. http://www.helenfisher.com/
  Anatomy of Love: A Natural History of Mating, Marriage, and Why We Stray. New York: W.W. Norton, 2016.
  Why We Love: The Nature and Chemistry of Romantic Love. New York: Henry Holt, 2004.

John Gottman and Nan Silver. *What Makes Love Last? How to Build Trust and Avoid Betrayal.* New York: Simon & Schuster, 2012.

Harville Hendrix and Helen LaKelly Hunt. *Making Marriage Simple: 10 Relationship-Saving Truths.* New York: Harmony Books, 2013.

Anne Holmes, National Association of Baby Boomer Women. https://nabbw.com/.

Sue Johnson. *Love Sense: The Revolutionary New Science of Romantic Relationships.* New York: Little Brown, 2013.

Scot McKay. http://www.deservewhatyouwant.com/.

Paul J. Zak. *The Moral Molecule: The Source of Love and Prosperity.* New York: Dutton, 2012.

Rule #7: Undergo Meaningful Rites of Passage From Youth to Adulthood to Super Adulthood

Robert Bly. http://www.robertbly.com/
Iron John: A Book About Men. New York: Addison-Wesley, 1990.
The Sibling Society. New York: Addison-Wesley, 1996

Evryman. https://evryman.com/

Good Men Project. https://goodmenproject.com/

Gurian Institute. https://gurianinstitute.com/

Stephen Johnson. http://www.drstephenjohnson.com/
The Sacred Path: The Way of the Spiritual Warrior. Woodland Hills, Ca: Sacred Path Press, 2013.

ManKind Project. https://mankindproject.org/

Frederick Marx. https://warriorfilms.org/.

Films:
Rites of Passage. https://warriorfilms.org/rites-of-passage/
Hoop Dreams. https://warriorfilms.org/portfolio/hoop-dreams/

Men's Center Los Angeles. http://www.menscenterlosangeles.com/

Mark Schillinger. Young Men's Ultimate Weekend and Challenging Teen-Age Sons. http://www.challengingteenagesons.com.

Sterling Institute of Relationship. https://www.sterling-institute.com/

Arnold van Gennep. *The Rites of Passage.* Chicago: University of Chicago Press, 1960.

Rule #8: Celebrate Your True Warrior Spirit and Learn Why Males Duel and Females Duet

Joyce Benenson with Henry Markovits. *Warriors and Worriers: The Survival of the Sexes.* New York: Oxford University Press, 2014.

Terry Dobson and Victor Miller. *Aikido in Everyday Life: Giving in to Get Your Way.* Berkeley, Ca: North Atlantic Books, 1995.

Matthew Fox. *The Hidden Spirituality of Men: Ten Metaphors to Awaken the Sacred Masculine.* Novato, Ca: New World Library, 2008.

Richard Strozzi Heckler. https://strozziinstitute.com/
In Search of the Warrior Spirit. Berkeley, Ca: Blue Snake Books, 2011.
Aikido and the New Warrior: Berkeley, Ca: North Atlantic Books, 1985.

George Leonard. *The Way of Aikido: Life Lessons from an American Sensei.* New York: Plume, 2000.

John L. Locke. *Duels and Duets: Why Men and Women Talks So Differently.* New York: Cambridge University Press, 2011.

Danaan Parry. *Warriors of the Heart: A Handbook for Conflict Resolution.* Sonoma, Ca: Earth Stewards Network, 2009.

Steven Pinker. *The Better Angels of Our Nature: Why Violence Has Declined.* New York: Viking, 2011.

Chögyam Trungpa. *Shambhala: The Sacred Path of the Warior.* Berkeley, Ca: Shambhala Publications, 2015.

Rule #9: Understand and Heal Your Adverse Childhood Experiences and Male Attachment Disorder

ACEs Connection. www.AcesConnection.com

ACEs Too High. www.AcesTooHigh.com

Adverse Childhood Experiences (ACEs), Center for Disease Control and Prevention. https://www.cdc.gov/violenceprevention/childabuseandneglect/acestudy/index.html

John Cacioppo and William Patrick. *Loneliness: Human Nature and the Need for Social Connections.* New York: W.W. Norton, 2008.

Vincent Felitti. Reflections on the Adverse Childhood Experiences (ACE) Study. https://www.youtube.com/watch?v=-ns8ko9-ljU

> The Adverse Childhood Experiences Study—the largest, most important public health study you never heard of—began in an obesity clinic. https://tinyurl.com/hoyz2mf.

Johann Hari. *Lost Connections: Uncovering the Real Causes of Depression—And the Unexpected Solutions.* New York: Bloomsbury, 2018.

Is Your Story Making Your Sick? A film by Frances Causey, https://story.movie/.

Bruce Lipton. *The Biology of Belief: Unleashing the Power of Consciousness, Matter, and Miracles.* Santa Cruz, Ca: Mountain Love Productions, 2015.

Donna Jackson Nakazawa. *Childhood Disrupted: How Your Biography Becomes Your Biology, And How You Can Heal.* New York: Atria Books, 2015.

George Pratt and Peter Lambrough. *Code to Joy: The Four-Step Solution to Unlocking Your Natural State of Happiness.* New York: HarperOne, 2012.

Lissa Rankin. *Mind Over Medicine: Scientific Proof That You Can Heal Yourself.* Carlsbad, Ca: Hay House, 2013.

Bessel Van Der Kolk. *The Body Keeps the Score: Brain, Mind, and Body in the Healing of Trauma.* New York: Viking, 2014.

Charles Whitfield. *The Truth About Depression*. Deerfield Beach, Fl: Health
Communications, 2003.

Mark Wolynn. https://www.markwolynn.com/
*It Didn't Start With You: How Inherited Family Trauma Shapes Who We Are and
How to End the Cycle*. New York: Viking, 2016.

Rule #10: Heal Your Father Wound and
Become the Father You Were Meant to Be

Jed Diamond. *My Distant Dad: Healing the Family Father Wound*. Pontiac, Ill:
Lasting Impact Press, 2018.
*Healing the Family Father Wound: Your Playbook for Personal and Relationship
Success*. Pontiac, Ill: Lasting Impact Press, 2018.

James R. Doty. *Into the Magic Shop: A Neurosurgeon's Quest to Discover the Mysteries
of the Brain and the Secrets of the Heart*. New York: Avery, 2016.

Charles Eisenstein. *The More Beautiful World Our Hearts Know is Possible*. Berkeley,
Ca: North Atlantic Books, 2013.

Warren Farrell and John Gray. *The Boy Crisis: Why Our Boys Are Struggling and
What We Can Do About It*. Dallas, Tx: BenBella, 2018.

James Hollis. *Under Saturn's Shadow: The Wounding and Healing of Men*. Toronto:
Inner City Books, 1994.

Sue Johnson. *Hold Me Tight: Seven Conversations for a Lifetime of Love*. New York:
Little Brown, 2008.

Rule #11: Treat the Irritable Male Syndrome and Male-Type Depression

Lisa Friedman Bloch and Kathy Kirtland Silverman. *Manopause: Your Guide to
Surviving His Change of Life*. Carlsbad, Ca: Hay House, 2012.

Theresa L. Crenshaw. *The Alchemy of Love and Lust: Discovering our Sex Hormones
and How They Determine Who We Love, When We Love, and How Often We
Love*. New York: G.P. Putnam's Sons, 1996.

Jed Diamond. *The Irritable Male Syndrome: Understanding and Managing the 4 Key Causes of Depression and Aggression.* Emmaus, PA: Rodale, 2004.
Mr. Mean: Saving Your Relationship from the Irritable Male Syndrome. San Rafael, CA: Vox Novus, 2010.

Paul Ekman. *Emotions Revealed: Recognizing Faces and Feelings to Improve Communication and Emotional Life.* New York: Times Books, 2003.

Mo Gawdat. https://www.onebillionhappy.org/
Solve for Happy: Engineer Your Path to Joy. New York: North Star Way, 2018.

Richard Heinberg. *The Party's Over: Oil, War, and the Fate of Industrial Societies.* Gabriola Island, Canada: New Society Publishers, 2005.

Kay Redfield Jamison.

An Unquiet Mind: A Memoir of Moods and Madness. New York: Vintage Books, 1995.
Touched With Fire: Manic-Depressive Illness and the Artistic Temperament. New York: Free Press, 1993.

John Lynch and Christopher Kilmartin. *The Pain Behind the Mask: Overcoming Masculine Depression.* New York: Routledge, 2013.

Marianne J. Legato. *Why Men Die First: How to Lengthen Your Lifespan.* New York: Palgrave, 2008.

Andrew Solomon. *The Noonday Demon: An Atlas of Depression.* New York: Scribner, 2001.

Rule #12: Find Your Mission in Life and Do Your Part to Save Humanity

Arjuna Ardagh. https://radicalbrilliance.com/.
Radical Brilliance. Nevada City, CA: SelfXPress, 2018.

Chip Conley. https://chipconley.com/
Wisdom @ Work: The Making of a Modern Elder. New York: Currency, 2018.

Rebecca Costa. http://www.rebeccacosta.com/
   The Watchman's Rattle: A Radical New Theory of Collapse. New York:
      Vanguard Press, 2010.

Steve Dailey, https://www.achievementbridge.com/

Jed Diamond.
   Male Menopause. Naperville, Ill: Sourcebooks, 1998.
   Surviving Male Menopause: A Guide for Women and Men. Naperville, Ill:
      Sourcebooks, 2000.

Clarissa Pinkola Estes. *Women Who Run With the Wolves: Myths and Stories of the
   Wild Woman Archetype*. New York: Ballantine, 1996.

Charles Eisenstein. https://charleseisenstein.org/
   The More Beautiful World Our Hearts Know is Possible. Berkeley, CA: North
      Atlantic Books, 2013.

Mo Gawdat. https://www.solveforhappy.com/
   Solve for Happy: Engineer Your Path to Joy. New York: North Star Way, 2017.

James Hillman.
   The Soul's Code: In Search of Character and Calling. New York: Random House,
      1996.
   The Force of Character and the Lasting Life. New York: Random House, 1999.

Terry Patten. https://www.terrypatten.com/
   A New Republic of the Heart: An Ethos For Revolutionaries. Berkeley, Ca: North
      Atlantic Books, 2018.

Zachariah Reitano. www.getroman.com/learn; https://www.getroman.com/
   our-story/zach/
   At present there are three verticals that are powered by Ro (www.ro.co). Roman
      (www.getroman.com) addresses men's health issues, Rory (www.hellorory.
      com) addresses women's health issues, and Zero (www.quitwithzero.com)
      addresses addiction starting by helping people quit smoking.

John Schinnerer. https://guidetoself.com/.

Stu Zimmerman. https://www.onlythesource.com/.

About the Author

I am a licensed psychotherapist with a PhD in International Health and a Master's degree in Social Work. My passion is to help men do three things:

1. Live a fully authentic life
2. Love deeply and well
3. Make a positive difference in the world

My wife attributes our successful 39-year marriage to the fact that I've been in a men's group for 40 years.

For 50 years, I have been a pioneer in the field of gender medicine and men's health.

You can connect with me here:

On my website: www.MenAlive.com
Twitter: https://twitter.com/menalivenow
Facebook: https://www.facebook.com/Dr.Jed.Diamond

Made in the USA
Lexington, KY
27 September 2019